Human Population Genetic Research in Developing Countries

T0172945

Human population genetic research (HPGR) seeks to identify the diversity and variation of the human genome and how human group and individual genetic diversity has developed. This book asks whether developing countries are well prepared for the ethical and legal conduct of HPGR, with specific regard to vulnerable target group protection. The book highlights particular issues raised by genetic research on populations as a whole, such as the potential harm specific groups may suffer in genetic research, and the capacity for current frameworks of Western developed countries to provide adequate protections for these target populations.

Using the People's Republic of China as a key example, Yue Wang argues that since the target groups of HPGR are almost always from isolated and rural areas of developing countries, the ethical and legal frameworks for human subject protection need to be reconsidered in order to eliminate, or at least reduce, the vulnerability of those groups. While most discussion in this field focuses on the impact of genetic research on individuals, this book breaks new ground in exploring how the interests of target groups are also seriously implicated in genetic work. In evaluating current regulations concerning prevention of harm to vulnerable groups, the book also puts forward an alternative model for group protection in the context of HPGR in developing countries. The book will be of great interest to students and academics of medical law, ethics, and the implications of genetic research.

Yue Wang is a lecturer in Xi'an Jiaotong University, People's Republic of China, Research Staff of Information Security Law Research Centre at Xi'an Jiaotong University.

Biomedical law and ethics library

Series Editor: Sheila A. M. McLean

Scientific and clinical advances, social and political developments and the impact of healthcare on our lives raise profound ethical and legal questions. Medical law and ethics have become central to our understanding of these problems, and are important tools for the analysis and resolution of problems – real or imagined. In this series, scholars at the forefront of biomedical law and ethics contribute to the debates in this area, with accessible, thought-provoking, and sometimes controversial ideas. Each book in the series develops an independent hypothesis and argues cogently for a particular position. One of the major contributions of this series is the extent to which both law and ethics are utilised in the content of the books, and the shape of the series itself.

The books in this series are analytical, with a key target audience of lawyers, doctors, nurses and the intelligent lay public.

Available titles:

About the Series Editor

Professor Sheila McLean is International Bar Association Professor of Law and Ethics in Medicine and Director of the Institute of Law and Ethics in Medicine at the University of Glasgow.

Human Population Genetic Research in Developing Countries

The issue of group protection

Yue Wang

Routledge
Taylor & Francis Group

LONDON AND NEW YORK

First published 2014
by Routledge
2 Park Square, Milton Park, Abingdon, Oxfordshire OX14 4RN

and by Routledge
711 Third Avenue, New York, NY 10017

First issued in paperback 2015

Routledge is an imprint of the Taylor & Francis Group, an informa business

British Library Cataloguing in Publication Data
A catalogue record for this book is available from the British Library

Library of Congress Cataloging-in-Publication Data
A catalog record has been requested for this book

ISBN13: 978-1-138-93750-5 (pbk)
ISBN13: 978-0-415-83539-8 (hbk)

Typeset in Garamond
By Cenveo Publisher Services

Contents

1 Introduction

In the 13th century, the English philosopher Roger Bacon had already pointed out that development in medicine would never be the same as in the natural sciences because scientists could 'multiply their experiments till they get rid of deficiency and errors'. On the other hand, the physician was unable to do this 'because of the nobility of the material in which he works'.[1] This assertion illustrates that issues concerning the ethics of research involving human beings have been raised for centuries.

Nowadays, our society is still facing many complicated and controversial issues related to biomedical science and technology, especially the need to define the boundaries of research on human beings and how to provide adequate protection to human subjects in research involving human subjects. 'Research involving human subjects' is a broad concept including a wide variety of research. Generally, it can be conceptualised in two broad categories: therapeutic research, which includes most clinical trials, can be distinguished from so-called 'non-therapeutic' research in that the former has a possibility of immediate benefit to the subjects, whereas the latter has no such potential.

Medical research involving human subjects and its risks

It is self-evident that, from the standpoint of promoting the development of biomedical science and technology, as well as contributing to human knowledge, there is a need for research involving human subjects. However, the risks of harm that may be caused by medical research also should not be ignored.

A 'risk-benefit assessment' or 'risk-benefit ratio' is a common expression in biomedical research involving human subjects.[2] Risk involves both the

---

1 Rothman, D. J. (1998) 'The Nuremberg Code in Light of Previous Principles and Practice in Human Experimentation' in Ulrich Tröhler and Stella Reiter-Theil in cooperation with Eckhard Herych (eds) *Ethics Codes in Medicine: Foundations and Achievements of Codification Since 1947* (Ashgate: Aldershot) at 50.
2 Weijer, C. (2000) 'The Ethical Analysis of Risk', *Journal of Law, Medicine and Ethics*, vol. 28, pp. 344–61.

probability and the magnitude of harms to human research subjects, and cannot be equated simply with the magnitude of negative outcome, such as serious physical injury or death. Under this approach, a proper analysis of risk requires consideration of the probability of harm occurring, since a one-in-a-million risk of death is likely to be regarded differently to a one-in-ten risk of death. However, magnitude of risk is also significant, so that a risk of death would be viewed differently from a risk of minimal physical harm. Human subjects may be exposed to a wide spectrum of risks as a result of participation in medical research. Weijer divided such risks of harm into four categories: physical, psychological, social and economic.[3] He described each type of risk briefly as follows:

> Physical risks: The research subject may suffer bodily harm – minor or serious, temporary or permanent, immediate or delayed – as a result of his or her participation in the study.
> Psychological risks: Study participation may affect the research subject's perception of self, cause emotional suffering (e.g., anxiety or shame), or may induce aberrations in thought or behaviour.
> Social risks: Research findings, or even study participation itself may expose subjects to the possibility of insurance or employment discrimination, or other forms of social stigmatization.
> Economic risks: Research subjects may directly or indirectly bear financial costs related to research participation.[4]

More than one type of risk may occur in a single biomedical research protocol involving human subjects. An example provided by Weijer can illustrate this clearly. In research into a new drug for people with acutely symptomatic schizophrenia, although there are effective drugs for this disease at present, patients are randomly assigned to take various types of drug: a new antipsychotic drug, a standard drug or a placebo. These human subjects are treated in a hospital for a period of time, where they are assessed with a variety of psychometric scales.[5] In this medical research, since the new drug may have serious adverse effects, some of which may even be irreversible, human subjects who take the new drug may suffer physical harms, such as continuing hallucinations or paranoia, and they may be at increased risk of suicide. Human subjects who are assigned to the placebo will be deprived of needed treatment for a period of time, which may lead to the deterioration of the disease. Meanwhile, although this is rare, participating in this placebo-controlled research may also lead to psychological harm, such as emotional suffering caused by exacerbation of the disease because of the absence of

3 ibid.
4 ibid at 346.
5 ibid at 345.

treatment, since human subjects may sometimes believe that they are taking a placebo, no matter whether they are in fact taking a real medicine. Due to the existence of potential risks of harm caused by randomised trials involving placebos, the Helsinki Declaration (as amended) required that placebos should only be used in very limited circumstances. It noted in Article 32 that:

> The benefits, risks, burdens and effectiveness of a new intervention must be tested against those of the best current proven intervention, except in the following circumstances:
> The use of placebo, or no treatment, is acceptable in studies where no current proven intervention exists; or
> Where for compelling and scientifically sound methodological reasons the use of placebo is necessary to determine the efficacy or safety of an intervention and the patients who receive placebo or no treatment will not be subject to any risk of serious or irreversible harm. Extreme care must be taken to avoid abuse of this option.[6]

Realising the risks of harm for human subjects in biomedical research, all international declarations and conventions, without exception, declare that the welfare of human subjects is the first priority. For example, the Helsinki Declaration emphasises this principle several times in the introduction. Article 3 states that '[I]t is the duty of the physician to promote and safeguard the health of patients, including those who are involved in medical research. The physician's knowledge and conscience are dedicated to the fulfilment of this duty'.[7] The Universal Declaration on Bioethics and Human Rights also declares the welfare of human subjects as the first priority, and set it as a basic principle which has to be respected. In Article 3, it states that '[T]he interests and welfare of the individual should have priority over the sole interest of science or society'.[8] The European Convention on Human

---

6   The WMA Declaration of Helsinki Ethical Principles for Medical Research Involving Human Subjects was adopted by the 18th WMA General Assembly, Helsinki, Finland, June 1964, and amended by the 29th WMA General Assembly, Tokyo, Japan, October 1975, 35th WMA General Assembly, Venice, Italy, October 1983, 41st WMA General Assembly, Hong Kong, September 1989, 48th WMA General Assembly, Somerset West, Republic of South Africa, October 1996 and the 52nd WMA General Assembly, Edinburgh, Scotland, October 2000, 53rd WMA General Assembly, Washington 2002 (Note of Clarification on paragraph 29 added), 55th WMA General Assembly, Tokyo 2004 (Note of Clarification on paragraph 30 added), 59th WMA General Assembly, Seoul, October 2008. The full text of the Helsinki Declaration can be seen on the official website of the World Medical Association (WMA) at http://www.wma.net/en/30publications/10policies/b3/index.html (last visited 4 July 2013).

7   ibid Article 3.

8   The Universal Declaration on Bioethics and Human Rights was adopted by UNESCO's General Conference on 19 October 2005. The full text of the Universal Declaration on Bioethics and Human Rights can be seen on the official website of UNESCO at

Rights and Biomedicine, in Article 2, similarly declares that '[T]he interests and welfare of the human being shall prevail over the sole interest of society or science'.[9]

Although we agree with the necessity of medical research involving human subjects, in the absence of effective ethical and legal regulations on the conduct of biomedical research involving human subjects, the welfare of human subjects could be harmed or ignored. Therefore, all of the existing international declarations, ethical guidelines and national legislation on biomedical research are dedicated to the development and improvement of human subject protection in an effort to avoid or minimise harm to their interests.

In general terms, the fundamental aims of ethics are to achieve two objectives: to tell us how we ought to act in a given situation, and to provide us with strong reasons for doing so.[10] Research ethics is 'basically about means of ensuring that vulnerable people are protected from exploitation and other forms of harm'.[11]

It has been said that the beginning of the ethics of research involving human subjects was Claude Bernard's 1865 book, *An Introduction to the Study of Experimental Medicine*.[12] In this book, he described the power of human experimentation on both the benefit side and the harmful side in detail. Based on this analysis of human experimentation, he concluded that research must always be in the best interests of the subject, as follows:

> Experiments, then, may be performed on man, but within what limits? It is our duty and our right to perform an experiment on man whenever it can save his life, cure him or gain him some benefit. The principle of medical and surgical morality, therefore, consists in never performing on man an experiment which might be harmful to him to any extent, even though the result might be highly advantageous to science, i.e., to the health of others.[13]

It can be seen from this assertion that his research ethical theory insisted on the obligations and responsibilities of physicians and researchers.

---

http://portal.unesco.org/en/ev.php-URL_ID=31058&URL_DO=DO_TOPIC&URL_SECTION=201.html (last visited 27 July 2013).

9 The European Convention for the Protection of Human Rights and Dignity of the Human Being with regard to the Application of Biology and Medicine: Convention on Human Rights and Biomedicine was done at Oviedo, Spain (4 April 1997). The full text can be seen on the official website of the Council of Europe at http://conventions.coe.int/Treaty/en/Treaties/Html/164.htm (last visited 4 July 2010).

10 Schuklenk, U. (2005) 'Module One: Introduction to Research Ethics', *Developing World Bioethics*, vol. 5, no. 1, p. 3.

11 ibid.

12 Bernard, C. (1957) *An Introduction to the Study of Experimental Medicine* (Reprint edn, Dover Publications).

13 ibid.

The contemporary focus on ethics in research came about because of the human experiments on prisoners of war and its own citizens conducted by Nazi Germany and Japan during the Second World War.[14] Thereafter, the Nuremberg Code required that 'the voluntary consent of the human subject is absolutely essential'.[15] The World Medical Association's Declaration of Helsinki noted that clinical research could be conducted only when the 'risks involved have been adequately assessed and can be satisfactorily managed. Physicians must immediately stop a study when the risks are found to outweigh the potential benefits or when there is conclusive proof of positive and beneficial results'.[16] Further, in the US, the Ethical Principles and Guidelines for the Protection of Human Subjects of Research (Belmont Report)[17] articulate guidelines for human subject research. The basic principles, such as respect for persons, beneficence and justice have been established and widely accepted in Western countries.

At a practical level, 'respect for persons' is secured through the requirement for individual informed consent. The most concise definition of informed consent to take part in research is 'a decision to participate in research made by a competent individual who has received the necessary information; has adequately understood the information; and after considering the information, has arrived at a decision without having been subjected to coercion, undue influence, inducement or intimidation'.[18] There are four basic elements of informed consent that have been developed since the Nuremberg trials: (i) capacity to consent; (ii) full disclosure

---

14 *United States of America v Karl Brandt et al*, which is also known as 'the Doctors' Trial', was the first of 12 trials for war crimes that the United States authorities held in their occupation zone in Nuremberg, Germany after the end of the Second World War. The record of this trial can be seen on the official website of the US, available at http://www.archives. gov/research/captured-german-records/microfilm/m889.pdf (last visited on 4 July 2013). Unit 731 was a covert biological and chemical warfare research and development unit of the Imperial Japanese Army that undertook lethal human experimentation during the Second Sino-Japanese War (1937–1945) and the Second World War. However, because of political reasons, Japan Unit 731 avoided a procedure like the Nuremberg 'Doctors' Trial'.

15 *Trials of War Criminals before the Nuremberg Military Tribunals under Control Council Law No. 10*, vol. 2 (Washington, D.C.: US Government Printing Office, 1949) 181–82.

16 See note 6.

17 The Belmont Report is a report created by the former United States Department of Health, Education, and Welfare (which was renamed as Health Human Services) entitled 'Ethical Principles and Guidelines for the Protection of Human Subjects of Research', authored by Dan Harms, and is an important historical document in the field of medical ethics. The report was created on 18 April 1979 and gets its name from the Belmont Conference Center where the document was drafted. The full text of this can be seen on the official website of the Office of Human Subjects Research of the US, available at http:// ohsr.od.nih.gov/guidelines/belmont.html#goc2 (last visited 4 July 2013).

18 Council for International Organisations of Medical Sciences (CIOMS) *International Ethical Guidelines for Biomedical Research Involving Human Subjects*: Commentary 4 available at http://www.cioms.ch/frame_guidelines_nov_2002.htm (last visited 4 July 2013).

of relevant information; (iii) adequate comprehension of the information by the participant; and (iv) a voluntary decision to participate and the right to withdraw from participation at any stage without prejudice to the participant. Participant withdrawal should be accepted and withdrawing participants should not be expected to give any reasons for their decision.[19]

Challenges from genetic research and human population genetic research

With the development of modern biology and medical technology, that research ethical and regulation system is facing new challenges.

On 25 April 1953, the article 'Molecular Structure of Nucleic Acids – A Structure of Deoxyribose Nucleic Acid' was published in the well known British scientific journal *Nature* by two young scientists, James D. Watson and Francis H. C. Crick.[20] It has been said that their names have 'joined Darwin and Copernicus among the immortals',[21] and the new era of biology began. Their discovery of the DNA double helix is thought to be the greatest single scientific achievement of the 20th century and a new milestone of human history.

It has been a dream to explore the secrets of life, to solve the puzzles of death, growing old and sickness; to eradicate disease, to improve living standards and prolong human life. For a long time, people have been seeking to solve these puzzles, but although a great deal of financial and personal effort has been expended, and despite quite significant progress having been made in some areas, until recently no great progress had been made in many others.[22] However, the discovery of the importance of genes and the development of genetic technology has enabled human beings to study the secrets of life at the molecular level, and to see glimpses of hope of making greater progress.

Formerly, the understanding of the constitution of human beings was limited largely to what could be seen. However, when science and technology entered the molecular era, the understanding of the constitution of human beings at the level of DNA opened scientific possibilities while at the same time raising some problematic issues.

19 Andanda, P. (2005) 'Module Two: Informed Consent', *Developing World Bioethics*, vol. 5, no. 1, p. 17.
20 Watson, J. D. and Crick, F. H. C. (1953) 'Molecular Structure of Nucleic Acids – A Structure of Deoxyribose Nucleic Acid', *Nature*, vol. 171, no. 4356, pp. 737–38.
21 Hunt-Grubbe, C. 'The Elementary DNA of Dr Watson' *The Times* (14 October 2007).
22 Although 'Today, global life expectancy at birth is about 67 years; two centuries ago it was 30 years or less' (Riley, J. C. (2001) *Rising Life Expectancy: A Global History* (New York: Cambridge University Press)), we still cannot say that we have mastered all the secrets of human life.

According to John Harris:

> It is [human] genetics that is beginning to create a new generation of
> acute and subtle dilemmas that will in the new millennium transform
> the ways in which we think of ourselves and of society. It is genetics,
> bringing both a new understanding of what we are and almost daily
> developing new ways of enabling us to influence what we are, that is
> creating a revolution in thought, and not least in ethics.[23]

The main thrust of this statement reflects contrasting thinking on the genetic
revolution. On the one hand, there is the possibility of benefits that will arise
from the development of genetic technology. For example, the Guidelines for
Human Biobanks and Genetic Research Databases (HBGRDs)[24] of the
Organisation for Economic Co-operation and Development (OECD) noted
that human genetic research 'analysed in conjunction with personal or health
data is particularly promising and will be critical to improvements in the
prevention, detection, diagnosis, treatment, and cure of disease and for the
development of new products and services'.[25] Another example is the Human
Genome Project (HGP), which is the most influential genetic research project
designed to 'determine the complete sequence of the 3 billion DNA subunits
(bases), identify all human genes, and make them accessible for further
biological study'.[26] The potential benefits of the project have been described
as follows:

> Technology and resources generated by the Human Genome Project and
> other genomics research are already having a major impact on research
> across the life sciences. The potential for commercial development of
> genomics research presents US industry with a wealth of opportunities,
> and sales of DNA-based products and technologies in the biotechnology
> industry are projected to exceed $45 billion by 2009.[27]

---

23 Harris, J. (2001) 'Introduction: the Scope and Importance of Bioethics' in *Bioethics*,
J. Harris, ed. (Oxford University Press) at 20.
24 Guidelines for Human Biobanks and Genetic Research Databases (HBGRDs), available on
official website of the Organisation for Economic Co-operation and Development (OECD)
at http://www.oecd.org/dataoecd/41/47/44054609.pdf (last visited 4 July 2013).
25 ibid.
26 'What is the Human Genome Project?', available on the official website of the Human
Genome Project at http://www.ornl.gov/sci/techresources/Human_Genome/faq/faqs1.
shtml (last visited 4 July 2013).
27 'Potential Benefits of Human Genome Project Research', on official website of the
Human Genome Project at http://www.ornl.gov/sci/techresources/Human_Genome/
project/benefits.shtml (last visited 4 July 2013).

Given these factors, some public media sources asserted that biology has been widely predicted to be the foremost science of the 21st century.[28] Some current and potential applications of genetic research include molecular medicine, energy sources and environmental applications, risk assessment, bioarchaeology, anthropology, evolution and human migration, DNA forensics (identification), agriculture, livestock breeding and bioprocessing.[29] This view of genetics reflects an optimistic and positive view of human genetic research; namely, that it should be promoted and conducted because human genetic research may help to unfold the secrets of many human diseases, discover the cures and therapies for human suffering and enrich our knowledge of human origins and evolution.

On the other hand, there are challenges that may result from human genetic research. Genetic science and technology have invoked significant debate on ethical and legal concerns. Genetic research seems potentially to demand an exception to the common reliance on the sufficiency of individual informed consent, which is the core rule of Western research ethics. For example, McGregor has said:

> These regulations and codes based their ethical principles on respect for persons, beneficence, and justice. The principle of respect for persons translates into respect for individual autonomy (determining one's life plan in terms of one's own values and beliefs), respect for privacy (access to a person's private sphere), and respect for confidentiality (not divulging such privileged knowledge). The principle of respect also protects persons with diminished autonomy due to age, illness, mental disability, or particular circumstances that affect one's autonomy. The most direct implementation of the principle seeks and secures informed consent to conduct research. The principle of beneficence focuses on whether the benefits of the research outweigh the risks. Questions of risks are traditionally directed to risks to the individual research participant and the benefit for humanity generally. And the principle of justice requires at least that the selection of subjects is equitable, and questions, for example, why a certain group or population is being targeted for research. Questions of justice should also include that the benefits of research flow to those who take the risks of research, that is, that there be equitable benefit sharing.[30]

28 Yang, H. 'We Will Start to Research the Characteristics of the National/ethnic Disease Gene' (in Chinese) *Beijing Youth* (28 October 2000).
29 ibid.
30 McGregor, J. L. (2007) 'Population Genomics and Research Ethics with Socially Identifiable Groups', *Journal of Law, Medicine and Ethics*, vol. 35, pp. 356–70 at 360–61.

Genetic information not only discloses information about the human subjects concerned, but also discloses genetic information about their relatives, and even certain groups and their members. Thus, the impact of genetic research is complicated by the fact that genetic information may be shared among members of families, ethnic or racial communities, and other groups with a distinctive genetic inheritance. This not only creates special risks for individuals but also widens the scope of people who may be exposed to risk and who must be considered as involved in the research.

The complication will be more serious in the Human Population Genetic Research Project (HPGR). HPGR seeks to identify the diversity and variation of the human genome and how human group and individual genetic diversity has developed. Since HPGR targets specific groups to discover variation, it also raises many pressing ethical and legal concerns, because HPGR may lead to potential risks of harm to specific groups. It seems reasonable to believe that an individualistic autonomy model, focused on direct risks to the subject of research, is ill-suited to the shared nature of group collective genetic information, which is the research target of HPGR. Instead, it will be suggested that another approach to the understanding of autonomy, the relational autonomy model, is more appropriate. This model highlights the need to recognise that an individual exists in a social context, and his or her choices may thus be affected by concerns other than personal ones. It will be explored in more detail later in the book.

Therefore, it is necessary to go on to consider the extent to which the target groups/communities of HPGR and their members are exposed to risks of harm from participation in this type of research, and the kinds of risk need to be identified. There will also be an evaluation of whether the current Western ethical and legal frameworks on research involving human subjects, which are dominated by individualism, can provide adequate protections for target groups/communities in HPGR.

Challenges from HPGR in developing countries

HPGR, like the Human Genome Diversity Project (HGDP),[31] is interested in sampling populations to study how human groups and individual genetic diversity have grown and aims to identify the diversity of the human genome. Ethnic minorities and isolated groups in rural areas of developing countries would be the ideal target groups in HPGR, for the following reasons: (i) members of these groups are relatively homogeneous with respect to ethnic

31 The Human Genome Diversity Project (HGDP) was started by Stanford University's Morrison Institute and a collaboration of scientists around the world. It is an international project that seeks to understand the diversity and unity of the entire human species. The official website of HDGP is available at http://hsblogs.stanford.edu/morrison/human-genome-diversity-project/ (last visited 4 July 2013).

background, environment and lifestyle; (ii) the groups have existed for several thousands of years with a stable resident population; and (iii) the population is large enough to ensure the availability of a sufficient number of potential research participants.

However, ethnic minorities and isolated rural groups in developing countries also have features which may lead to concerns about protecting their interests in HPGR. For example, on 20 December 2000 *Washington Post* staff writers John Pomfret and Deborah Nelson published an article entitled 'In Rural China, a Genetic Mother Lode'.[32] It was a story that reported that a drug company-supported research programme involving Harvard University researchers and six Chinese medical centres were intending to sample the blood and genes of 200 million Chinese people in rural isolated areas to conduct genetic research; in addition, these resources would be incorporated into foreign products without bringing any benefit to the Chinese people who furnished the genetic resources. Harvard Provost Fineberg said that '[w]e were very mindful of having the same [ethical] standards applied to them as in the US [and] every effort was made to assure that was the case'.[33] However, this example highlights a question increasingly asked by legal professionals and medical ethicists as developed countries' academic and corporate researchers turn to developing countries to find large amounts of human research materials to conduct HPGR: do these standards provide adequate protections for participants and groups in HPGR?

Target groups of HPGR may be vulnerable because of their members' frequently low educational level, lack of economic and social resources, difficulties in correct understanding of the risks of HPGR or the possibility of undue inducement to take part in research. These common characteristics arguably make them more likely to accept risks that are either not understood or appreciated, or that are unjust. Meanwhile, the researchers or research institutions involved in HPGR, who are mostly research institutions or companies from developed countries, have the potential to take unfair advantage of their superior economic and social resources by offering target groups unfair benefits in exchanging for their participation. Furthermore, the absence of effective and adequate legal regulations and ethical guidelines in most developing countries, as well as poor law enforcement, also exacerbate the vulnerability of target groups in HPGR.

Therefore, the vulnerability of target groups in HPGR in developing countries should be addressed in more detail and depth. In particular, it is essential to evaluate whether or not the dominant (Western) underpinnings of the ethics of research are sufficient to eliminate or reasonably reduce the vulnerability of target groups and provide adequate protections for them in HPGR

---

32 Pomfret, J. and Nelson, D. 'In Rural China, A Genetic Mother Lode' *Washington Post* (20 December 2000).

33 ibid.

in developing countries. In addition, some target groups from rural areas of developing countries have their own cultural sensitivities concerning decision-making patterns, which will also be relevant to this evaluation. This too may mandate a reconsideration of the applicability and practice of HPGR projects and processes. The proposed alternative ethical and legal frameworks for biomedical research should be designed to allow the ethical conduct of human population genetic research which does not harm the interests of vulnerable target groups and individual participants, based on the specific bioethical background and cultural sensitivity of a developing country.

In summary, human genetic research has come a long way, but some aspects of it remain controversial. During the past 20 years, alongside the exploration of human genetic information, debates have focused on how to regulate genetic research and use genetic technology.[34] Human population genetic research creates additional dilemmas that are also significant and urgent, especially in developing countries.

Main contents of the book

Target groups of HPGR are almost always ethnic minorities or isolated groups in rural areas of developing countries. These groups have not only objective characteristics which distinguish them from other groups, such as history, geography, ethnicity, economics, language and religion, but may also have inherent values which lead to the group and its members having a self-perception of the group's distinctiveness. Further, individual members of the group may strongly identify themselves with the group, and particularly with its common spiritual tradition, historical narratives or traditional beliefs. They may also have their own well developed cultural traditions, such as group collective decision making. Meanwhile, the researchers in HPGR are almost always from Western developed countries, who are outsiders of target groups. The personal and cultural forces that link members of groups to each other and to their traditions are of great importance to both the individuals and to the group itself. These traditions are worthy of respect and protection, yet risk being overlooked, ignored or disrespected by researchers from a different tradition.

This book intends to examine current ethical and legal frameworks for research involving human subjects in HPGR, particularly HPGR in developing countries. Therefore, it will argue that the interests of groups in this kind of research should be recognised as being worthy of protection and that this is not available using the Western ethical and legal regulations already in existence. It aims to propose a model that will offer additional protections to groups in HPGR.

---

34 Wilkinson, R. (2010) 'The Governance of Genetic Information: Who Decides? (Publication Review)', *Medical Law Review*, vol. 18, no. 2, pp. 267–73 at 267.

This book is concerned with two aspects of ethical and legal regulations on HPGR. The first relates to an explanation as to why current ethical and legal regulations on human subject protection cannot provide adequate protection to target groups and their members in HPGR. The second element is the vulnerability of target groups in HPGR in developing countries and the additional protections they need. This will require consideration of how and why HPGR may pose risks of harm to both target groups and their members. Having examined these issues, the author will then consider how ethical and legal frameworks can be proposed in developing countries in terms of HPGR.

The People's Republic of China (PRC) will be used as an example to analyse these issues, since it is a good model of developing countries on which to base an analysis of whether or not target populations in HPGR are adequately protected by contemporary legal and ethical regulations of human subject research.

The Chinese population comprises one-fifth of the human species. The Chinese Government officially recognises 56 ethnic groups, one of which is the Han majority (1 billion and 100 million people), and the other 55 are ethnic minorities (totalling about 100 million).[35] The PRC contains rich genetic resources in isolated areas which have idiographic cultures. At the same time, the PRC is the only developing country participating in the HGP. Accordingly, a number of developed countries and their research organisations desire to undertake genomics research in the PRC or collaborative research with Chinese research organisations in this area. In 1996, experts warned that the PRC faces the prospect that the genes of hundreds of millions of its people may become the priceless resources of foreign pharmaceutical companies.[36] As mentioned above in the reference to the Harvard case, these researchers will generally be expected to have met the ethical and legal requirements for conducting their research in their country of origin (generally developed countries). However, the PRC has a thoroughly different legal and cultural background from those developed countries, which leads to the need to consider whether or not existing developed world legal and ethical frameworks provide these research participants with adequate levels of protection and are sensitive to cultural concerns. The legal regulation of HPGR in the PRC, such as it is, including 'Interim Measures for the Administration of Human Genetic Resources 1998'[37] and 'Ethical guidelines

35 Cavalli-Sforza, L. (1998) 'The Chinese Human Genome Diversity Project', *The National Academy of Sciences*, vol. 95, p. 11501.

36 Sleeboom, M. (2005) 'The Harvard case of Xu Xiping: exploitation of the people, scientific advance, or genetic theft?', *New Genetics and Society*, vol. 24, no. 1, p. 60.

37 'Ren Lei Yi Chuan Zi Yuan Guan Li Zhan Xing Ban Fa' ['*Interim Measures for the Administration of Human Genetic Resources 1998*'] (in Chinese), available on the official website of the Ministry of Science and Technology of the PRC at http://www.most.gov.cn/fggw/xzfg/200811/t20081106_64877.htm (last visited 4 July 2013).

for human embryonic stem cell research 2003',[38] is – as will be seen – copied almost word for word from Western legal and ethical frameworks, which means that these regulations are neither designed to provide protection to target groups in biomedical research nor consider the particular position and cultural sensitivities of the populations concerned.

The PRC has a unique cultural and historical tradition, which is distinct from the Western one. The PRC is a country with a history as long as the history of human beings themselves, and is also a country with strong cultural traditions. The largest group, the Han, make up over 92 per cent of the PRC's vast population, and the Han civilisation is the dominant culture in the PRC. Meanwhile, the other 55 ethnic minorities maintain their own rich traditions and customs. It has been said that:

> From the dawn of time, China's history is a story of an immense land with several diverse tribes. It is also one of migrations and conflict, and separation and fusion of cultures. The product of the intermingling of many tribes, the Han people were among the first to settle down and develop an agrarian society ... Over a 2,000 year period, a large number of invaders breached the Great Wall and poured into the Chinese heartland. The Huns, the Mongols, and Manchurians all came – and unlike the plunder and destruction characterized by the barbarian invasions of Rome, these peoples admired what they saw, leading them to stay and assimilate.[39]

The fact that the PRC has its own range of cultural and ethical traditions makes it more difficult to adopt Western individualised ethical and legal frameworks in HPGR. For example, in the PRC's traditional culture, the notion of respect for an individual's right to self-determination is not prominent. In fact, the Confucian concept of relational personhood challenges the assumption that the patient alone should be given the diagnosis and prognosis and the opportunity to make his or her own medical decisions. Social and moral meaning rests in interdependence, which overrides self-determination. Consequently, many Chinese people may give the family or community the right to receive and disclose information, to make decisions and to coordinate patient care, even when they themselves are competent.[40] In contrast, privacy

---

38 'Ren Pei Tai Gan Xi Bao Yan Jiu Lun Li Zhi Dao Yuan Ze' ['*Guidelines for the Moral Principles in Human Embryonic Stem Cell Research 2003'*] (in Chinese), available on the official website of the Ministry of Science and Technology of the PRC at http://www.most.gov.cn/fggw/zfwj/zfwj2003/200512/t20051214_54948.htm (last visited 4 July 2013).

39 See 'Ethnic Minorities in China' available at http://eap.einaudi.cornell.edu/node/9611 (last visited 5 July 2013).

40 Fan, R. (2007) 'Confucian Familism and Its Bioethical Implications' in *The Family, Medical Decision-Making, and Biotechnology: Critical Reflections on Asian Moral Perspectives*, S. C. Lee, ed. (Springer) pp. 15–26 at 15–16.

rights and individual autonomy are the starting points of the protection system of Western countries. In an article on Chinese genetics and ethics by Qiu Ren-zong, one of the most well known bioethicists in the PRC, it is claimed that in traditional medicine in general, medicine is taken as the art of humaneness (*yi ben ren shu*). This means that the doctor loves people, cares for people and does well for people. In his view, the essential core relationship between patient and doctor is not the same as in Western countries; rather, it is based on absolute trust. For example, Qiu says:

> Doctors who practice medicine in China have the capacity to decide the life or death of a patient, so they bear a very heavy responsibility. Traditional China is a patriarchal society in which paternalism is very strong in social life. ... In the encounter between physician and patient, medical decisions are made by the physician, and the doctor's opinion is directive. Although there has been a great change in modern China, and the paternalism in medicine has been considerably weakened, it still prevails.[41]

However, most international conventions and ethical guidelines for human subject research are based on the principles of individual autonomy, beneficence and justice. Considering the special situation in the PRC, patients' undoubted trust in doctors and the emphasis on family and group/community over individual interests can cause problems in terms of medical research which may extend to HPGR.

In addition, in the PRC, 25 per cent of the population is illiterate or semiliterate. The majority of these people are distributed in the isolated rural areas which are attractive targets of HPGR.[42] As was reported in the Harvard story, those target people, whose lives were extremely poor and who had scarcely any medical care, were told that if they participated there would be free medical care – so of course most people volunteered to participate.[43] Even had there been an introduction to the aims and anticipated achievements of this research, which 'adhered to the principle of informed consent', this would be of arguable value in such cases since 'many couldn't read, and few could have guessed at the tangle of scientific and business dreams that lay behind the project'.[44]

For these reasons, this book will use the PRC as an example to analyse how to build new legal and ethical frameworks on biomedical research involving human subjects, with special reference to the protection of vulnerable target

41 Qiu, R. (2004) 'China: Views of a Bioethicist' in *Genetic and Ethics in Global Perspective*, D. C. Wertz and J. C. Fletcher, eds (Kluwer Academic Publisher) at 193.
42 See note 36 at 69.
43 ibid.
44 ibid.

groups and consideration of the specific Chinese bioethical background and cultural sensitivities.

This book consists of seven chapters, including an Introduction and a Conclusion. Before moving to the discussion of HPGR, Chapter 2 will provide a context setting on the human gene, genetic information and genetic research. This will be followed by an analysis on concerns raised by genetic research.

In Chapter 3 and Chapter 4, the risks of harm of HPGR will be identified and an analysis of the deficiencies of the current ethical and legal approaches to human subject protection for HPGR will be undertaken. Chapter 3 will address the role and general rules of consent in the medical context, as well as the specific rules of consent to medical research involving human subjects, including ethical and professional guidance and legal principles. It will then address the risk-benefit distinctions between therapeutic research and non-therapeutic research, and introduce the legal regulations and cases on the protection of the wellbeing of human subjects from an international perspective. Subsequently, it will argue that genetic research raises its own concerns in respect of research ethics and explain the uniqueness of the types of harm caused by genetic research.

Chapter 4 will clarify that in HPGR it is not only individuals but also a population/group that may be at risk of harm, such as psychological harms including shame or humiliation; loss of opportunities and other economic setbacks or loss of insurance or insurability (possibly resulting from stereotyping or stigmatising a group as a whole). Further, this chapter will point out that group/community members may suffer harm without the opportunity of knowing the risks of harm in advance and being able to make decisions as to whether or not to accept them. In addition, contemporary Western legal systems and regulations depend on philosophical statements that identify individual rights as the appropriate foundation for the protection of human beings. For instance, in the context of medical law, one prevalent principle is 'respect for persons', which aims to protect an individual's autonomy through practical measures such as the requirement for legally valid consent to treatment.[45] Furthermore, traditional investigators, institutional review boards or research ethics committees ordinarily pay attention to the risks of harm to the individual participant. The ethical basis of this framework is concern for the individual rather than for groups or particular populations.[46] Thus, some scholars suggest that since the current Western legal system is 'rooted in natural rights theories, social contract theories, Kantian

---

45 Title 45 CFR (Code of Federal Regulations) Part 46, can be seen on the official website of US Department of Health & Human Services available at http://www.hhs.gov/ohrp/45CFRpt46faq.html (last visited 4 July 2013).

46 Underkuffler, L. S. (2007) 'Human Genetics Studies: The Case for Group Rights', *Journal of Law, Medicine and Ethics*, vol. 35, pp. 383–95 at 384.

notions of the individual, and other philosophical antecedents, it is generally assumed by liberal democratic governments that legally cognizable human rights are individual rights, which stand against the potential tyranny of government'.[47] Therefore, it will be argued that at least some of the traditional Western approaches to research are unsuited to this specific kind of research and are particularly inadequate in developing countries, such as the PRC, although some essential rules need to be followed, such as the provision of adequate information when seeking consent.

Chapter 5 will make the case for the protection of groups as potentially vulnerable populations in HPGR. Since HPGR aims to identify specific aspects of the diversity of the human genome, target groups are mostly ethnic minorities or isolated groups in rural areas of developing countries. This chapter will suggest that these groups are vulnerable to three types of vulnerability: consent-based, risk-based and justice-based. According to these concerns, target groups in HPGR may be vulnerable by virtue of a low education level, lack of economic and social resources, failure to recognise cultural sensitivities and the absence of effective and adequate legal regulations and ethical guidelines in most developing countries. Although in respect of international law, there has been some discussion of group rights and some attempts to recognise and protect them, such as the Convention on the Prevention and Punishment of the Crime of Genocide,[48] these declarations are usually aimed at civil and political rights. Group/community protection in the area of biomedical research has not been given much attention in general, beyond the protection of such groups as children and mentally incapacitated adults.[49] However, it will be argued that the target group and its members need to be protected by specific legal and ethical regulations. Thereafter, it will analyse current regulations on vulnerable group protection and attempt to provide revised guidelines to protect groups in population genetic research.

Chapter 6 will focus on issues specifically in developing countries, and the PRC will be used as an example. It will explore the implementation of the current legal framework in respect of human subject research protections in HPGR. This is critically reviewed since it is necessary to explain the problems of existing Chinese regulation in this area. It will then explain the current practices of HPGR in developing countries, specifically in the PRC, while also exploring the bioethical background of the PRC and identifying

47 ibid.
48 The Convention on the Prevention and Punishment of the Crime of Genocide was adopted by the United Nations General Assembly in December 1948 as General Assembly Resolution 260. See http://www.hrweb.org/legal/genocide.html (last visited 4 July 2013).
49 Almost all the international declarations and ethical guidelines on research involving human subject have specific regulations on vulnerable population protection, including the Declaration of Helsinki and the International Ethical Guidelines for Biomedical Research Involving Human Subjects (CIOMS Guidelines).

its special characteristics. Finally, this chapter will address the specific situation of ethnic minorities and isolated groups in rural areas in the PRC, including their cultural sensitivities and contemporary legal protections. It will be argued that in order to protect target groups in HPGR in developing countries, neither can Western standards be merely transplanted into developing countries directly, nor are current legal regulations of developing countries adequate. Rather, a new construct which considers both group vulnerability and specific cultural sensitivities is needed.

In the Conclusion, it will be argued that the only way of adequately protecting target groups in HPGR in developing countries is to construct a tailored ethical and legal framework. It will also make an argument on establishing domestic legislation or legal regulation for target group protection in HPGR in developing countries. The proposals that will be put forward for legal regulation of HPGR in developing countries will highlight the issues of group protection, with reference to international ethical guidelines and the legal regulations of other countries, taking into account the specific cultural sensitivities of developing countries. The proposed solution will be helpful in improving the ethical conduct of biomedical research involving human subjects, as well as vulnerable group protection in developing countries. The principal mechanisms offered by this alternative model could also be a valuable guide as to how to provide adequate protections for target groups in HPGR in international ethical guidelines. Recommendations will be made as to how such a construct might be developed. The author will suggest that group protection should be highlighted in ethical and legal frameworks on biomedical research, specifically in terms of HPGR. The main basis for this derive, first, from the need to take group interests and cultural sensitivities into account, by adopting a model of relational autonomy, enhancing researchers' responsibilities and requiring ethical review of group interests and, secondly, from the need to respect the role of developing countries and their own legal and ethical regulations which fit into their specific social, economic and cultural context.

2 Human genes, genetic information and genetic research

Human genes

At the outset, there are some terms which need to be clarified. The official document of the Human Genome Project (HGP) defined these terms as follows:

> Cells are the fundamental working units of every living system. All the instructions needed to direct their activities are contained within the chemical DNA (deoxyribonucleic acid).
>
> DNA from all organisms is made up of the same chemical and physical components. The DNA sequence is the particular side-by-side arrangement of bases along the DNA strand (e.g., ATTCCGGA). This order spells out the exact instructions required to create a particular organism with its own unique traits.
>
> The genome is an organism's complete set of DNA. Genomes vary widely in size: the smallest known genome for a free-living organism (a bacterium) contains about 600,000 DNA base pairs, while human and mouse genomes have some 3 billion. Except for mature red blood cells, all human cells contain a complete genome.[1]

As *Nature* magazine's reporter Helen Pearson said:

> In classical genetics, a gene was an abstract concept — a unit of inheritance that ferried a characteristic from parent to child. As biochemistry came into its own, those characteristics were associated with enzymes or proteins, one for each gene. And with the advent of molecular biology, genes became real, physical things — sequences of DNA which when converted into strands of so-called messenger RNA could be used as the basis for building their associated protein piece by piece.[2]

---

1 See 'Genomics and Its Impact on Science and Society', full text can be seen on the official website of HGP, available at http://www.ornl.gov/sci/techresources/Human_Genome/publicat/primer2001/primer11.pdf (last visited 4 July 2013).
2 Pearson, H. (2006) 'What is a Gene?', *Nature*, vol. 441, pp. 399–401 at 399.

Every cell in a human body containing DNA has the full set of instructions necessary to create that particular individual.[3] These instructions are encoded in 23 pairs of individual DNA strands which are called chromosomes.[4] These chromosomes carry over 30,000 encoded genes.[5] Each gene performs a specific function, some may perform several, but the functions of only a small amount of genes are currently understood.[6]

In general terms, a gene is unit of heredity, 'a union of genomic sequences encoding a coherent set of potentially overlapping functional products'.[7] There are three basic features of a gene:

(a) It is a relatively independent unit of heredity. As an information unit, a gene can refresh combinations of the genetic make-up of both parents by transferring them to offspring. What is more, a gene can instruct, influence and even decide creatures' traits, such as body structure and living habits.

(b) At a molecular level, a gene is a segment of a DNA molecule, the sequences of nucleotides (or bases) in genes represent the heredity of human beings and other creatures. The information in a gene is encoded in the sequence of base groups of DNA.

(c) Genes are specific sequences of bases that encode instructions on how to make proteins.[8] Gene sequences of DNA, when transferred into strands of messenger RNA, could be used as the basis for building their related protein piece by piece. The gene could not only transmit all of this information through replication, but also could dominate the organism's character by controlling the process of synthesizing protein, which is called 'gene expression'. In other words, a gene exerts its physical function through directing the production of proteins and RNA molecules.

3 Mehlman, M. J. and Botkin, J. R. (1998) *Access to the Genome: The Challenge to Equality* (Georgetown University Press, Washington, D.C.).
4 ibid.
5 The International Human Genome Sequencing Consortium has estimated, based on the rough draft of the genome published in February 2001, that there are approximately 30,000 human genes. However, this number may be incorrect, as complex cellular processing of genes and gene products may result in several possible products from a single gene sequence. See International Human Genome Sequencing Consortium (2001) 'Initial Sequencing and Analysis of the Human Genome', *Nature*, vol. 409, no. 6822, pp. 860–921.
6 See 'Online Mendelian Inheritance in Man', the full text can be seen on the official website of the National Center for Biotechnology Information of the US, available at http://www.ncbi.nlm.nih.gov/ (last visited 4 July 2013).
7 Gerstein, M. B., Bruce, C., Rozowsky, J. S., Zheng, D., Du, J., Korbel, J. O., Emanuelsson, O., Zhang, Z. D., Weissman, S. and Snyder, M. (2007) 'What Is a Gene, Post-ENCODE? History and Updated Definition', *Genome Research*, vol. 17, no. 6, pp. 669–81.
8 See note 1.

Genetic information

What is genetic information

According to Article 2(i) of the UNESCO International Declaration on Human Genetic Data, human genetic data is 'the information about heritable characteristics of individuals obtained by analysis of nucleic acids or by other scientific analysis'.[9] Although the intention of this definition is merely to set out the relationship between human genetic information and scientific research, it suggests that the real value of the gene is not its physical substance but the information carried in it.

In general, genetic information is the information for making all of the proteins required by all organisms. These proteins determine, among other things, how the organism looks, how well its body metabolises food or fights infection, and sometimes even how it behaves.[10]

Genetic information, as Laurie summarised, has the following features and functions, and it:

> ... relates to families and not just individuals; can offer a degree of certainty in determining which of those persons is likely to be affected by genetic disease; can provide a measure of predictability in the assessment of likelihood of ill health in particular individuals from an affected group; can reveal secrets about future ill health, even in those who are currently well; can help to determine future risks in future person.[11]

In fact, genetic information is the real research target of all genetic research, while the gene is the material carrier of genetic information. Hence, genes and genetic information have a close relationship with each other. Since most human cells contain two sets of chromosomes[12] which come from both father and mother and each chromosome contains an integrated human genome,[13] in theory, almost every human cell is able to express all human genetic information (one example of an exception to the general rule is that of mature red blood cells).

---

9   *The International Declaration on Human Genetic Data* which was adopted unanimously and by acclamation at UNESCO's 32nd General Conference on 16 October 2003.

10 'About the Human Genome Project' can be seen on the official website of Human Genome Project, available at http://www.ornl.gov/sci/techresources/Human_Genome/ project/about.shtml (last visited 4 July 2013).

11 Laurie, G. (2002) *Genetic Privacy: A Challenge to Medico-Legal Norms* (Cambridge University Press) at 104.

12 Chromosomes are long strands of DNA containing many genes and are packaged in structures. There are approximately 25,000 genes in the human genome.

13 A genome is the entire DNA contained in one cell. The hereditary material in nearly all living organisms is deoxyribonucleic acid or DNA. DNA is held in a cellular structure called the nucleus.

It has been argued that a gene is 'a packet of information encoded within the DNA molecule'.[14] However, this argument confuses the gene and genetic information. The relationship between genes and genetic information is similar to that of a book and the knowledge it contains. The book is the material carrier of its knowledge. Therefore, while a gene contains genetic information, this does not mean that genetic information is the same thing as the gene itself; the gene is matter, but genetic information is intangible. Matter and information are different concepts, and this is the fundamental difference between these two terms.

The genetic exceptionalism debate

With the development of genetic science and technology, research on the human genetic information is the new 'hotspot' of biomedical research. However, it also leads to ethical and legal concerns. In order to understand whether or not there are the particular concerns raised by genetic research, we need to deliberate on the genetic exceptionalism debate and its application to the alleged uniqueness of genetic research.

In 1995, Annas, Glantz and Roche published the article 'Drafting the Genetic Privacy Act: Science, Policy and Practical Considerations'.[15] This article generated a huge debate on what has been described as genetic exceptionalism. Murray, amongst others, has used this term, borrowing from the earlier term 'HIV exceptionalism'.[16] In this debate, the target topic is whether genetic information is different in kind from other medical information and, if so, whether this means that genetic information deserves special legal protection.

Proponents of the special nature of genetic information provide several arguments to illustrate it. In an article on genetic privacy, for example, Gostin indicated that the analysis of genetic information can identify the most sensitive and personal attributes of an individual's life.[17] Annas, Glantz and Roche maintained that genetic information is unique, and concluded that '[t]o the extent that we accord special status to our genes and what they reveal, genetic information is uniquely powerful and uniquely personal, and

---

14 Silver, L. M. (1999) 'Meaning of Genes and "Genetic Rights"', *Jurimetrics*, vol. 40, pp. 9–20 at 11–12.

15 Annas, G. J., Glantz, L. H. and Roche, P. A. (1995) 'Drafting the Genetic Privacy Act: Science, Policy, and Practical Considerations', *Journal of Law, Medicine and Ethics*, vol. 23, no. 4, pp. 360–66.

16 Murray, T. H. (1997) 'Genetic Exceptionalism and "Future Diaries": Is Genetic Information Different from Other Medical Information?' in *Genetic Secrets: Protecting Privacy and Confidentiality in the Genetic Era*, M. A. Rothstein, ed. (Yale University Press) pp. 60–73. HIV exceptionalism is the term used to describe the specific ethical consideration on the research and treatment of HIV.

17 Gostin, L. O. (1995) 'Genetic Privacy', *Journal of Law, Medicine and Ethics*, vol. 23, p. 320.

thus merits unique privacy protection'.[18] They provided three reasons why genetic information is 'uniquely private or personal information'.

First, human genetic information can be seen as the 'future diary' of human beings.[19] This means that genetic information can predict a human being's probable health future. In addition, they argued that genetic information describes an important proportion of an individual's future and may even affect the individual's view on the possibility of having a future. Moreover, genetic information is written in 'code' and in most situations it remains stable and can be stored for a long period of time. As molecular biological technology advances, more of the code can be uncovered. As a result, sensitive information concerning future health probabilities may be learned from gene fragments and genetic information that were stored in the past, without the permission of the individual who is, or was, its originator. In addition, it has been argued that genetic information not only can predict future disease, but also human behaviour. There is, for example, an existing area of research concerning behavioural genetics which seeks to understand both the genetic and environmental contributions to individual variations in human behaviours.[20] According to this research, genes may influence the personality and behavioural characteristics of human beings. This may suggest that genetic information is different from other medical information.

Secondly, genetic information 'divulges personal information about one's parents, siblings and children'.[21] An individual inherits half of his or her genes from each of his or her biological parents, and passes half of these genes to each of his/her biological children. This means that genetic information provides information about others in addition to the individual from whom samples were taken. This does not stop at the door of the family but extends to those larger groups of peoples, such as indigenous people, minority people, or people in isolated areas, who share a specific genetic heritage. Thus, they argued that the 'key feature about genetic information is that it is typically information about a family, or even ... about a larger community not just about an individual patient'.[22] Besides, unlike the use of physical material, information can be used at the same time by a great many people for various purposes without any loss or wastage. The comparison of knowledge contained in a book and genetic information contained in a gene was made previously and is relevant here also. For example, if I send a book to a friend as a gift, I no longer own the book or have any rights to control it again; however, if

18 See note 15 at 366.
19 Annas, G. J. (1993) 'Privacy Rules for DNA Databanks: Protecting Coded "Future Diaries"', *The Journal of American Medical Association*, vol. 270, no. 19, pp. 2346–50.
20 Views from HGP official website, available at http://www.ornl.gov/sci/techresources/ Human_Genome/elsi/behavior.shtml#where (last visited 4 July 2013).
21 See note 15 at 360.
22 Brock, D. W. (2001) 'Genetics and Confidentiality', *The American Journal of Bioethics*, vol. 1, no. 3, pp. 34–35 at 34.

I have read this book, I can still make use of the knowledge gained from information within it. In addition, my use of this knowledge does not prevent the use of this information by my friend who now owns this book.

Thirdly, genetic information could be a new basis for discrimination: '... genetic information and misinformation has been used by governments ... to discriminate viciously against those perceived as genetically unfit to restrict their reproductive decisions'.[23] Genetic discrimination has been defined as 'discrimination against an individual or against members of that individual's family solely because of real or perceived differences from the "normal" genome in the genetic constitution of that individual'.[24] It has been argued that individuals and their family members might encounter genetic discrimination during any interaction with another social institution that provides a benefit or a service, especially in two areas: employment and insurance.[25] From the discovery of DNA's double-helix structure in 1951 to the completion of the HGP in 2003, the development of genetic science and technology has been given wide publicity, and the potentially powerful effects of genetic science and technology have also been predicted, sometimes even overstated. For example, Francis Collins, director of the US National Institutes of Health (NIH) Genome Project, called the HGP the 'Book of Life'.[26] This kind of expression could lead to fears that scientists involved in this area are 'playing God', with all the negative connotations of that phrase.[27] Resulting from the influence of this terminology and media commentary, the public may be concerned that genetic testing will certainly predict a person's future diseases, even future behaviours, such as criminal behaviour. This may lead to or aggravate the potential risks of harms caused by genetic research, such as discrimination and stigmatisation.

From the arguments above, we can summarise that the supporters of genetic exceptionalism rely on two main considerations. First, the ability of genetic information to predict a person's future health status is presumed to be more precise than other forms of health information. Secondly, genetic information is unique when compared with other health information, in the sense that certain types of genetic information can be obtained from any individual, but may reveal the collective information of a certain family, even a group/community. Furthermore, the inappropriate disclosure or misuse of an individual's genetic information could violate the interests of his/her family members or group/community members.

23 See note 15 at 360.
24 Natowicz, M. R., Alper, J. K. and Alper, J. S. (1992) 'Genetic Discrimination and the Law', *American Journal of Human Genetics*, vol. 50, pp. 465–75 at 466.
25 ibid at 466–67.
26 See Collin's statement: 'Fiscal Year 2001 President's Budget Request for the National Human Genome Research Institute', available at http://www.genome.gov/10002083 (last visited 4 July 2013).
27 Chadwick, R. (1989) 'Playing God', *Cogito*, vol. 3, pp. 186–93.

Despite this, the opponents of the uniqueness of genetic information argue that this is an over-dramatic view of the significance of genes and genetic information in human life. They suggest that although there is something to be said for each of the above arguments, on reflection they are unpersuasive.

First, they argue, genetic information is 'neither unique nor distinctive in its ability to offer probabilistic peeks into human's future health'.[28] They have explained that some other medical information or family history also could be used to predict the current and future health status of an individual and even his or her kin. For example, Murray argued as follows:

> Many other things afford equally interesting predictions ... examples include asymptomatic hepatitis B infections, early HIV infection, and even one's cholesterol level. These have implications for future health that are every bit as cogent and sensitive as genetic predispositions.[29]

Secondly, Ross has argued that there being a difference between genetic and other medical information should be 'rejected on the grounds that other types of health information also have significant implications for family members'.[30] For example, the fact that a family member or another person with very intimate relationships is HIV+ is certainly relevant to other family members, some of whom are possibly open to infection, as may be those who come into intimate contact with the infected individual.

Thirdly, Ross concludes that 'threats of discrimination and stigmatization will exist as long as there are differences and that these differences need not have a genetic basis, as current international conflicts illustrate'.[31] In addition, Murray argues that the genetic discrimination argument is not a convincing one, because:

> Institutions and individuals can and have used all sorts of information, both visible and occult, as the basis for discrimination ... But it is difficult to make the argument that it is fair to discriminate on non-genetic factors but unfair to discriminate on genetic ones.[32]

Three types of human genetic information

Both side on the debate above seemed to have their own reasonable points, in favour and against doing so. On closer inspection, however, this debate

---

28 ibid at 64.
29 See note 16 at 64.
30 Ross, R. F. (2001) 'Genetic Exceptionalism vs. Paradigm Shift: Lessons From HIV', *Journal of Law, Medicine and Ethics*, vol. 29, pp. 141–46.
31 ibid at 143.
32 See note 16 at 65.

results from the fact that human genetic information collected from an individual has abundant applications. Different applications would influence the interests of different parties, such as individual participants, certain groups or communities, even all human beings. Therefore, I wish to argue that the human genetic information carried by an individual can be divided into three different types: non-differential human genetic information, individual human genetic information and community/group collective human genetic information. Each of these three types of human genetic information has its own attributes and merits distinctive treatment.

Non-differential human genetic information

Non-differential human genetic information describes the genetic information shared by each human being. It has been shown that nearly 60 per cent of human genes are isogenies with the fruit fly.[33] In addition, the chimpanzee genome is 95 per cent identical to the human genome. On average, a typical human protein-coding gene differs from its chimpanzee ortholog[34] by only two amino acid substitutions; nearly one-third of human genes have exactly the same protein translation as their chimpanzee orthologs. A major difference between the two genomes is human chromosome 2, which is equivalent to a fusion product of chimpanzee chromosomes 12 and 13.[35] The working draft of the IIGP, which was released in 2000 and the complete version published in 2003 reveal that these non-differential genes are present in each human individual. In this sense, non-differential human genetic information could be viewed as a new type of common heritage of mankind.

The view that a resource can be the common heritage of mankind originated from the United Nations Convention on the Law of the Sea and was one of its fundamental principles.[36] The tenet was established in Articles 136 and 137:

33 'Fruit Fly Gene Success' can be seen on BBC News website, available at http://news.bbc. co.uk/1/hi/sci/tech/647139.stm (last visited 4 July 2013).
34 Orthology describes genes in different species that derive from a common ancestor.
35 The Chimpanzee Sequencing and Analysis Consortium (2005) 'Human chromosome 2 resulted from a fusion of two ancestral chromosomes that remained separate in the chimpanzee lineage'; 'Initial sequence of the chimpanzee genome and comparison with the human genome', *Nature*, vol. 437, no. 7055, pp. 69–87.
36 The United Nations Convention on the Law of the Sea (UNCLOS), also called the Law of the Sea Convention or the Law of the Sea Treaty, is the international agreement that resulted from the third United Nations Conference on the Law of the Sea (UNCLOS III), which took place from 1973 through 1982. UNCLOS defines the rights and responsibilities of nations in their use of the world's oceans, establishing guidelines for businesses, the environment and the management of marine natural resources. The Convention concluded in 1982 replaced four 1958 treaties. UNCLOS came into force in 1994, a year after Guyana became the 60th state to sign the treaty. To date, 157 countries and the European Community have joined in the Convention. However, it is now regarded as a codification of the customary international law on the issue.

Article136 Common heritage of mankind: The Area and its resources are the common heritage of mankind.

Article137 Legal status of the Area and its resources:

1. No State shall claim or exercise sovereignty or sovereign rights over any part of the Area or its resources, nor shall any State or natural or juridical person appropriate any part thereof. No such claim or exercise of sovereignty or sovereign rights nor such appropriation shall be recognized.

2. All rights in the resources of the Area are vested in mankind as a whole, on whose behalf the Authority shall act. These resources are not subject to alienation. The minerals recovered from the Area, however, may only be alienated in accordance with this Part and the rules, regulations and procedures of the Authority.

3. No State or natural or juridical person shall claim, acquire or exercise rights with respect to the minerals recovered from the Area except in accordance with this Part. Otherwise, no such claim, acquisition or exercise of such rights shall be recognized.[37]

At present, the scope of this principle has gone beyond the ocean and extended to particular areas and related natural resources, such as outer space and the Antarctic.[38]

Each human being has only one genome which contains about 25,000 genes, and 99.8 per cent of human genetic information is entirely uniform. It has been selected and evolved for thousands of years; hence, it is a gift from nature, like the natural resources of particular areas, such as outer space and the Antarctic. Thus, it is suggested that non-differential human genetic information should be a new type of common heritage of mankind. Neither states nor individuals could claim a proprietary right or sovereignty over non-differential human genetic information. Although enormous sums of human, financial and material resources have been spent on attempting to understand the 99.8 per cent of non-differential human genetic information, and this research is potentially of great medical and commercial value, all mankind has a right to use it in peace and share the benefit from its use.

Individual human genetic information

A tiny amount (0.2 per cent) of human genetic information dominates the diversity of approximately 6 billion human beings, such as height, weight,

---

37 The United Nations Convention on the Law of the Sea can be seen on the official website of the United Nations, available at http://www.un.org/Depts/los/convention_agreements/texts/unclos/unclos_e.pdf, Articles136 and 137 (last visited 4 July 2013).

38 Porras, D. A. (2006) 'The "Common Heritage" of Outer Space: Equal Benefits for Most of Mankind', *California Western International Law Journal*, vol. 37, no. 1, pp. 143–76.

colour of eyes, hair and skin, appearance, character and even the possibility of suffering from certain diseases. This kind of information is individual in nature. It can be used in forensic databases, relationship testing and genetic research on certain diseases.[39] Some biobanks, for example those established in Estonia (Estonian Genome Project),[40] Iceland (Iceland Health Centre Database)[41] and the UK (UK Biobank)[42] aim to collect this kind of genetic information.

Individual human genetic information which contains high specificity has one to one correspondence to a specific human being, except identical siblings. Accordingly, except for such siblings, individual human genetic information directly decides each individual's unique existence in the world. Although individual human genetic information has huge economic and social value, since it can be used in genetic diagnosis and therapy as well as to identify individuals, it is a type of crucial personal information. In some countries, such as the US, personal information is undoubtedly the subject of the right of privacy.[43] Accordingly, the subject has the right to access, collect and obtain the information, keep the information strictly confidential, as well as decide on the use of the information. Identification of individual human genetic information may lead to violations of privacy, especially in the context of the possibility of suffering from certain diseases. For example, if susceptibility becomes known to employers or insurance companies, it may lead to discrimination.[44] Thus, the effective protection of individual human genetic information has become a new challenge in the regulation of privacy.

If individual human genetic information is regarded as being subject to the right of privacy, individual human genetic information 'belongs' to the individual who is the source of the information and, as a result, access to it should be controlled by that individual.

39 Richards, M. (2001) 'How Distinctive is Genetic Information?', *Studies in History and Philosophy of Science Part C: Biological and Biomedical Sciences*, vol. 32, no. 4, pp. 663–87 at 674–77.
40 Tzortzis, A., 'Estonia Looks to Make Mark with DNA Data', *Boston Globe* (19 August 2003) at E1.
41 Adalsteinsson, R. (2004) 'Human Genetic Databases and Liberty', *The Juridical Review*, no. 1, pp. 65–74.
42 Winikoff, D. (2007) 'Partnership in U.K. Biobank: A Third Way For Genomic Property?' *Journal of Law, Medicine and Ethics* vol. 35, no. 3, pp. 440–56.
43 Annas, G. J. (1999) 'Genetic Privacy: There Ought to be a Law', *Texas Review of Law and Politics*, vol. 4, pp. 7–15.
44 See Spaak, T. (2006) 'Genetic Discrimination', *Minnesota Journal of Law, Science and Technology*, vol. 7, pp. 639–55. Also see Hellman, D. (2003) 'What Makes Genetic Discrimination Exceptional?', *American Journal of Law and Medicine*, vol. 29, pp. 77–116. Also see Jungreis, R. (2007) 'Fearing the Fear Itself: The Proposed Genetic Information Nondiscrimination Act of 2005 and Public Fears about Genetic Information', *Journal of Law and Policy*, vol. 15, pp. 221–47.

a) Community or group/collective human genetic information

Community/group collective human genetic information is a useful research tool to explore variations that could lead to knowledge about genetic disorders and possible cures, as well as the origin and migration patterns of peoples.[45] A group of people who live together for a long period of time in a certain area seem more likely to have a similar genetic make-up, especially in isolated areas, because of a number of factors, such as sharing the same habitat, similar life style and inter-marriage. Moreover, the possibility of recessive traits in such groups would be greater than in other populations. For instance:

> Laken and colleagues ... used anonymized samples from a Tay-Sachs data bank in their search for the frequency in Ashkenazi Jews of a particular mutation in a gene predisposing to colon cancer (I1307K in the APC gene). They found that the mutation was present in 6.1% of the Jews in the sample and none of the non-Jews. The authors noted with understandable excitement that this is the commonest cancer-associated mutation in a specific population yet described.[46]

Community/group collective human genetic information reflects the influence of a long period of history, nature and lifestyle. This kind of genetic information, which is common to certain populations, communities or groups of people and contains information about heritability, can be studied and analysed using a large number of samples from these communities and groups.[47] It can be suggested that in the same way that all human beings have collective interests in non-differential human genetic information, although it is carried by individuals, certain communities or groups also could have collective interests in community or group collective human genetic information.

Genetic research

The uniqueness of genetic information in the context of genetic research

Despite the differing arguments on the genetic exceptionalism debate, there are several facts that are accepted by both sides. First, genetic information not only

45　McGregor, J. L. (2007) 'Population Genomics and Research Ethics with Socially Identifiable Groups', *Journal of Law, Medicine and Ethics*, vol. 35, pp. 356–70.

46　Weijer, C. (1999) 'Protecting Communities in Research: Philosophical and Pragmatic Challenges', *Cambridge Quarterly of Healthcare Ethics*, vol. 8, pp. 501–13 at 502.

47　There was an existing example that Harvard's School of Public Health has selected over 6 million people and brought back 16,400 blood samples of asthma patients in the name of therapy. 'Harvard Gene Study in China is Questioned' can be seen on the website of *Los Angeles Times*, available at http://articles.latimes.com/2002/mar/30/news/mn-35514 (last visited 4 July 20013).

discloses information about a human subject, but also discloses genetic information about her or his relatives, and even certain groups and their members. Secondly, genetic information not only shows the present situation of human subjects, but also, potentially, future information about her or him and her or his relatives, and even group members associated with the individual. Thirdly, this future information may be reasonably predictable, although it discloses possibilities rather than certainties. It could, of course, be argued, as above, that these are not characteristics unique to genetic information, since some types of medical information, such as family histories, also have similar characteristics and potential.[48] In the clinical context, it can be accepted that there is no essential difference between genetic information and some other medical information, such as family history. This is because, in the clinical context, the analysis of both genetic information and other health information, including family history, aims to contribute to an accurate diagnosis for this specific patient. However, in the context of genetic research, the situation is different. In fact, family history, which refers to the recollections of illness/disease by family members, is abstract knowledge, which is not necessarily accompanied by a confirmed medical diagnosis. Thus, it may be lacking in accurate knowledge about why these members have become ill or died in the absence of a true understanding about the pattern of disease in this family.[49] In contrast, genetic research in clinical care is targeted on identifying the origin and causes of certain diseases. Genetic information, which is the object of genetic research, can offer a high degree of specificity in predicting the likelihood of disease in other family members or even certain group/community members.

Therefore, in the context of research, I would contend that genetic information does have a uniqueness which distinguishes it from other forms of heath information, including family history. Under the current individualistic rules of consent, if an individual decides to participate in genetic research, the potential risks of harm, such as discrimination and stigmatisations based on its negative results, may be suffered by participants, their family members or even the fellow group members of the participants. Except for the human subject, the other family members and group/community members have no chance to make a decision about the implications of discoveries about their genetic information, and lack protection for their interests.

The concerns that arise from genetic research

Although expressions such as 'coded probabilistic future diary' and 'likely medical future' can be seen as overstated, some of the views of Annas, Glantz

---

48 ibid.
49 Laurie, G. T. (2001) 'Challenging Medical-Legal Norms: The Role of Autonomy, Confidentiality, and Privacy in Protecting Individual and Familial Group Rights in Genetic Information', *Journal of Legal Medicine*, vol. 22, pp. 1–54 at 3.

and Roche are valuable; for example, when they say that compared with other health information, genetic information may have more significant unwanted consequences for families and population groups. In the context of genetic research, compared with other types of biomedical research involving human subjects, the real risk of harm to the subject of research is the inappropriate disclosure or use of negative genetic information, not the risks of harm to the physical body of the human subject. There are two problems which arise from this distinction.

First, in the past any harm that arose in biomedical research would almost certainly be physical harm to the participant and as such would not directly harm third parties' interests or public interests. The samples taken for genetic research are usually blood samples, which are no different from the blood samples taken in routine medical examinations, so the physical harms of genetic research are slight. However, the potential harms of genetic research appear to be associated with the use of, and access to, information. The risks associated with the information-rich nature of genetic research have long been apparent, such as anxiety, distress and other psychological harms to subjects who learn that they carry genes that may predispose them to serious medical problems.[50] The risks of harm caused by genetic research may also include employment and insurance discrimination, discoveries of misattributed paternity, altered relationships between family members, and changes in self-perception. Thus, since these concerns had not been the main ones in traditional ethical frameworks, beginning in the early 1990s there emerged an important new theme in the ethics of biomedical research: namely, that genetic research posed the threat of genetic discrimination.[51]

In consideration of the risks of harm that may be caused by the discovery and use of genetic information, since the HGP began in 1990 a number of national and international regulations and treaties have emerged aiming to prohibit genetic discrimination. These policy documents highlighted the fact that genetic information is in need of specific strict regulation, given its sensitive and distinctive properties which may lead to a high potential for discrimination. For example, in the Universal Declaration on the Human Genome and Human Rights,[52] UNESCO devised special regulations for the human genome and for research subjects participating in research on it.

---

50 Green, R. M. and Thomas, A. M. (1998) 'DNA: Five Distinguishing Features for Policy Analysis', *Harvard Journal of Law and Technology*, vol. 11, pp. 571–91 at 572.

51 Reilly, P. R. (1998) 'Rethinking Risks to Human Subjects in Genetic Research', *American Journal of Human Genetics*, vol. 63, pp. 682–85 at 683.

52 The Universal Declaration on the Human Genome and Human Rights was adopted unanimously and by acclamation at UNESCO's 29th General Conference on 11 November 1997. The full text of the Universal Declaration on Human Genome and Human Rights can be seen on the official website of UNESCO at http://portal.unesco.org/en/ev.php-URL_ID=13177&URL_DO=DO_TOPIC&URL_SECTION=201.html (last visited 4 July 2013).

In addition, some countries also have enacted legislation prohibiting genetic discrimination in health insurance. Two-thirds of the states in the US have enacted laws prohibiting genetic discrimination in employment, and other states also have legislation to regulate genetic discrimination in insurance, protect genetic privacy and govern genetic testing.[53] In 2008, the federal legislation on prohibiting genetic discrimination in the US, the Genetic Information Nondiscrimination Act of 2008 (GINA),[54] was signed. Its aim is to prohibit genetic discrimination in employment and health insurance. These regulations show that the concerns of legislators have turned to the risks of psychological and social harm in genetic research, in contrast to previous concerns about medical research, which concentrated on the physical harms to human subjects.

Secondly, since the genetic information carried by an individual participant is shared by her or his blood family, and even groups or communities, these potential harms could be suffered by the whole family, group or community of the subject. Any harm is not, therefore, limited to the participating individuals. This means that the other parties' interests and potentially the public interest could be at risk. Traditionally, the control of information is exercised by the person to whom the information belongs, or to whom it relates. It is widely accepted that health care professionals owe an obligation of confidentiality to their patients and that only rarely should disclosure without a patient's consent be made. While exceptions to the duty exist, in practice no breach should be made lightly or without good cause.[55] Similarly, in the context of biomedical research, all of the international declarations and ethical guidelines highlight the significance of maintaining the confidentiality and privacy of human subjects by researchers and research institutions.

53 Rothstein, M. A. (2007) 'Genetic Exceptionalism and Legislative Pragmatism', *Journal of Law, Medicine and Ethics*, vol. 35, pp. 59–65 at 59.
54 US Public Law 110-1. 233, 122 Stat. 881 (2008). It was enacted on 21 May 2008. The Act prohibits group health plans and health insurers from denying coverage to a healthy individual or charging that person higher premiums based solely on a genetic predisposition to developing a disease in the future. The legislation also bars employers from using individuals' genetic information when making hiring, firing, job placement or promotion decisions. The full text of the GINA can be seen on the official website of the US government, available at http://www.gpo.gov/fdsys/pkg/PLAW-110publ233/pdf/PLAW-110publ233.pdf (last visited 4 July 2013).
55 For example, Section 6 of GMC Guideline Confidentiality Core 2009 noted that: 'Confidentiality is central to trust between doctors and patients. Without assurances about confidentiality, patients may be reluctant to seek medical attention or to give doctors the information they need in order to provide good care. But appropriate information sharing is essential to the efficient provision of safe, effective care, both for the individual patient and for the wider community of patients'. Section 8 also highlights that the duty of confidentiality is not absolute and provides examples of situations and procedures to disclose personal medical information. The full text of this document can be seen on the official website of the GMC, available at http://www.gmc-uk.org/static/documents/content/Confidentiality_core_2009.pdf (last visited 4 July 2013).

For example, the Helsinki Declaration noted in its first principle that it is the duty of physicians to protect the privacy and confidentiality of personal information of research subjects.[56] In addition, Guideline 19 of the CIOMS Guidelines is entitled 'Safeguarding Confidentiality'. It notes that:

> The investigator must establish secure safeguards of the confidentiality of subjects' research data. Subjects should be told the limits, legal or other, to the investigators' ability to safeguard confidentiality and the possible consequences of breaches of confidentiality.[57]

Medical records are subject to confidentiality or privacy laws that, save in exceptional circumstances, require permission from the person whose records they are for them to be disseminated.[58] All of these regulations on confidentiality and privacy are rooted in the protection of the informational security of the individual who provides the information, as traditionally this is the person who would be harmed by unauthorised disclosure. However, in the context of genetic information, control of the information is more complicated because genetic information collected from an individual participant is shared by his or her blood relatives, or sometimes members of a particular group. For example, when one family member decides to participate in genetic research and tests positive for a disease-related gene, that person's parents, siblings and children all have a chance of carrying that same version of the gene. In addition, close community members may also carry this disease-related gene. Because of this, if research results are revealed in a manner enabling the participant or a group to be identified, not only the participant him- or herself, but also his or her family members and members of his or her community might suffer negative effects, such as an insurance

56 WMA Declaration of Helsinki Ethical Principles for Medical Research Involving Human Subjects was adopted by the 18th WMA General Assembly, Helsinki, Finland, June 1964, and amended by the 29th WMA General Assembly, Tokyo, Japan, October 1975, 35th WMA General Assembly, Venice, Italy, October 1983, 41st WMA General Assembly, Hong Kong, September 1989, 48th WMA General Assembly, Somerset West, Republic of South Africa, October 1996 and the 52nd WMA General Assembly, Edinburgh, Scotland, October 2000, 53rd WMA General Assembly, Washington 2002 (Note of Clarification on paragraph 29 added), 55th WMA General Assembly, Tokyo 2004 (Note of Clarification on paragraph 30 added), 59th WMA General Assembly, Seoul, October 2008. The full text of Helsinki Declaration can be seen on the official website of the World Medical Association (WMA) at http://www.wma.net/en/30publications/10policies/b3/index.html (last visited 4 July 2013), Article 11.
57 The Universal Declaration on the Bioethics and Human Rights was adopted by UNESCO's General Conference on 19 October 2005. The full text of the Universal Declaration on Bioethics and Human Rights can be seen on the official website of UNESCO at http://unesdoc.unesco.org/images/0014/001461/146180E.pdf (last visited 5 July 2013).
58 Gilbar, R. (2004) 'Medical Confidentiality within the Family: The Doctor's Duty Reconsidered', *International Journal of Law, Policy and the Family*, vol. 18, no. 2, pp. 195–213.

company refusing to underwrite a life insurance policy unless the participant agrees to be tested and is found not to have this disease-related gene. Nevertheless, as I have mentioned above, under current research guidelines on research involving human subjects, although family members and community or group members may be exposed to risks of harm caused by genetic research, they have no opportunity to be given relevant information about it or to decide whether or not to participate, unless the subject volunteers this information. What is more, current guidelines do not clearly require institutional review boards or research ethics committees to provide the risk and potential benefits assessment on the interests of family members and community or group members of participants.

In summary, as distinct from the physical harm-oriented traditional assessments of risks, the main risks of harm in genetic research are primarily related to the disclosure of information and research results that could lead to discrimination, social stigmatisation, familial disruption or psychological distress to the human subject and his or her family members.[59] Other risks of harm that may be caused by genetic research include 'inadvertent disclosure of painful facts about family relationships (such as non-paternity); stigmatization associated with having a genetic abnormality; and intra-familial discord'.[60] Although the possibility of the occurrence of these risks might be quite low, these harms can be devastating for individuals and communities if they occur.

59 Beskow, L. M., Burke, W., Merz, J. F., Barr, P. A., Terry, S., Penchaszadeh, V. B., Gostin, L. O., Gwinn, M. and Khoury, M. J. (2001) 'Informed Consent for Population-Based Research Involving Genetics', *Journal of the American Medical Association*, vol. 286, no. 18, pp. 2315–21 at 2318.
60 See note 50 at 573.

3 Consent and human subject protection

While most discussions about the ethics of biomedical research involving human subjects agree that there is a need for it to take place, they also accept the significance of protection for human subjects to ensure their wellbeing and to avoid abuse and exploitation.[1] The requirements of consent, based on the principle of respect for autonomy, have become central measures for the protection of human subjects in Western bioethics and law. These requirements have been developed in the medical treatment context and subsequently applied to medical research. This chapter will also introduce the concept of relational autonomy as a challenge to a highly individualised concept of autonomy. The significance of this challenge is in its invitation to consider the social context of even individual decision-making. This will become relevant when discussing the potential for collective harm to target groups in Human Population Genetic Research (HPGR), highlighting the need for an enriched understanding of the requirements for individual decision-making when people are asked to participate in such research.

Individual autonomy and relational autonomy

> I wish my life and decisions to depend on myself, not on external forces of whatever kind. I wish to be the instrument of my own, not of other men's acts of will. I wish to be a subject, not an object; to be moved by reasons, by conscious purposes, which are my own, not by causes which affect me, as it were, from outside. I wish to be somebody, not anybody; a doer – deciding not being decided for, self-directed and not acted upon by external nature or by other men ... I wish, above all, to be conscious

1 Widdows, H. (2011) 'Localized Past, Globalized Future: Towards an Effective Bioethical Framework Using Examples from Population Genetics and Medical Tourism', *Bioethics*, vol. 25, no. 2, pp. 83–91.

of myself as a thinking, willing, active being, bearing responsibility for his choices and able to explain them by reference to his own ideas and purposes.[2]

Such statements are at the core of Western moral and ethical history, and emphasise and justify the concepts of free choice, self-determination and individual autonomy. For example, Mill argued that the individuality of human beings should be respected by allowing them to make free choices, unless their actions would cause significant harm to others.[3] Kant highlighted the significance of free choice and personal autonomy by stating that a person should be an end in himself and should never be used solely as a means to an end.[4] Dworkin also emphasised the importance of individual autonomy: 'What makes an individual the particular person he is is his life-plan, his projects. In pursuing his autonomy, one shapes one's life, one constructs its meaning. The autonomous person gives meaning to his life'.[5] Of particular interest to this discussion is that in the context of research on human subjects, he further argued for the importance of individual autonomy: 'one's body is irreplaceable and inescapable ... In addition because my body is me, failure to respect my wishes concerning my body is a particularly insulting denial of autonomy'.[6]

Consequently, in both Western medical and research ethics, there exists a strong moral conviction, grounded on notions of human dignity and respect for individual autonomy, that every individual has a prima facie right to self-determination with respect to his or her body. Thus, in the context of medical ethics, autonomy and consent are central concepts.[7]

The term 'autonomy' stems from the Greek words *autos* (self) and *nomos* (rule), literally meaning self-rule or self-governance.[8] The original use of the concept of autonomy was to describe the self-rule or self-governance of independent city states.[9] Since then its use has been expanded to cover the individual. There are, however, various definitions of personal autonomy, as well as different senses in which autonomy may be used. For example, autonomy can be seen as 'the capacity to think, decide, and act on the basis of such thought and decision freely and independently and without ... let or

---

2 Berlin, I. (1969) *Two Concepts of Liberty* (Oxford: Clarendon Press) at 123.

3 Mill, J. S. (1989) *On Liberty* (S Collini edn, Cambridge University Press) at 13.

4 Sedgwick, S. (2008) *Kant's Groundwork of the Metaphysics of Morals: An Introduction* (Cambridge University Press).

5 Dworkin, G. (1988) *The Theory and Practice of Autonomy* (Cambridge University Press) at 31.

6 ibid at 113.

7 Childress, J. F. and Fletcher, J. C. (1994) 'Respect for Autonomy', *Hastings Centre Report*, vol. 24, no. 3, pp. 33–34.

8 Beauchamp, T. L. and Childress, J. F. (2009) *Principles of Biomedical Ethics* (6th edn, Oxford University Press) at 99.

9 ibid.

hindrance',[10] and be employed to refer to an individual's capacity to 'think, decide and act'.[11] Autonomy may further refer to a way of living one's life, with autonomy being seen as a virtue rather than as a simple ability.[12] Alternatively, according to two of the main proponents of the dominant conception of autonomy in a medical context, Beauchamp and Childress, autonomy is the 'personal rule of the self that is free from both controlling interferences by others and from personal limitations that prevent meaningful choice'.[13] On this view, the subject of autonomy is an individual person who 'freely acts in accordance with a self-chosen plan',[14] and to respect the autonomy of individuals is to 'acknowledge their right to hold views, to make choices, and to take actions based on their personal values and beliefs'.[15] This principle has been seen as the moral and ethical basis of the need for consent to medical treatment and is also widely accepted as the dominant rule to prevent harms to human subjects of research.[16]

However, from the late 1980s onwards, some communitarian philosophers and feminists began to criticise the dominance of an over-individualised concept of autonomy, and especially Beauchamp's and Childress's approach to the principle of respect for personal autonomy in bioethics.

This criticism argues that autonomy described in this way presupposes an individual with no social context. It also overstates the presumption about the way in which the individual makes his or her own decisions, as being uninfluenced by others. For example, communitarian philosophers argued that 'self-determination presupposes the existence of a community from which an individual derives many of his or her values'.[17] They stress that the principle of respect for persons must reflect the fact that the individual is situated within a particular community. Miller summarises this argument as follows:

> First, the socialization process determines, or shapes, the values and preferences of individuals; hence, the idea of autonomously chosen values is factually incorrect. Second, an individual's actions, desires, and objectives

---

10 Gillon, R. (1985) 'Autonomy and the Principle of Respect for Autonomy', *British Medical Journal*, vol. 290, pp. 1806–8 at 1806.

11 ibid.

12 Maclean, A. (2009) *Autonomy, Informed Consent and Medical Law* (Cambridge University Press) at 12.

13 See note 8 at 99.

14 ibid.

15 ibid at 103.

16 For example, Beasley, A. D. and Graber, G. C. (1984) 'The Range of Autonomy: Informed Consent in Medicine', *Theoretical Medicine and Bioethics*, vol. 5, no. 1, pp. 31–41. In this article, the explanation of Beauchamp and Childress has been seen as the working definition of autonomy, as the basis of other research.

17 Weijer, C. (1999) 'Protecting Communities in Research: Philosophical and Pragmatic Challenges', *Cambridge Quarterly of Healthcare Ethics*, vol. 8, pp. 501–13 at 504.

are comprehensible only within the context of social conventions and institutions ... Third, the view that an autonomous individual chooses his or her own values, preferences, and desires presupposes a self that does the choosing. This self will have to have a core of values with which to choose, in which case either there are values not autonomously chosen, or it is inexplicable how individuals come to have a set of values.[18]

In addition, feminist theorists have challenged the concept of individual autonomy because of its lack of attention to human relationships; to the 'relational nature of human life'.[19] There are two major concerns which are raised by feminists: (1) the conception of persons, which is dominant in the theory of autonomy, is typically believed to be false; they assert that the theory over-emphasises people's independence and deference to rationality in decision-making. They argue that people sometimes act contrary to their best interests, which undermines the liberal understanding of an autonomous person;[20] (2) the kind of autonomy espoused by the dominant theory has also been questioned, especially since it relies on an ideal of personhood that feminists generally believe to be 'both unrealistic and pernicious'.[21] They believe that people can be harmed by demands to meet the ideal of independence and the implicit definition of persons in medical practice. For example, Wendell argues that this view of personhood could 'turn against people with disabilities as unrealistic demands that they achieve goals deemed appropriate by others or as excuses for refusing to provide necessary services'.[22]

Beauchamp and Childress have responded to this criticism in their most recent edition of *Principles of Biomedical Ethics* as follows:

> Some feminists have sought to affirm autonomy but to interpret it through relationship. These conceptions of 'relational autonomy' derive from the conviction that persons' identities are shaped though social relationships and complex intersecting social determinants, such as race, class, gender, ethnicity, and authority structures. These accounts see persons as interdependent, but they also caution that 'oppressive socialization and oppressive social relationships' can impair autonomy ... Such a relational conception of autonomy is illuminating and defensible as

---

18 Miller, B. (1995) 'Autonomy' in Reich W. T., ed., *Encyclopedia of Bioethics* (Rev. edn New York: Simon & Schuster MacMillan) at 215–20.

19 Keller, J. (1997) 'Autonomy, Relationality and Feminist Ethics', *Hypatia*, vol. 12, pp. 152–64.

20 Ells, C. (2001) 'Shifting the Autonomy Debate to Theory as Ideology', *Journal of Medicine and Philosophy*, vol. 26, no. 4, pp. 417–30 at 422.

21 ibid at 418.

22 Wendell, S., (1996) *The Rejected Body: Feminist Philosophical Reflections on Disability* (New York: Routledge) at 145.

long as it does not neglect or obscure the main features of autonomy that we analyze in this chapter.[23]

Hence, Beauchamp and Childress believe that feminist writers have misunderstood their theory, but arguably they have failed to appreciate the nature of this criticism. Feminists' real criticism focuses on the foundation of their theoretical position, which is the presupposed definition of a person. Ells explained this as follows:

> B&C's [Beauchamp's and Childress's] feminist critics believe that the liberal view of personhood is unacceptable as an 'ideal' on at least two grounds. First, the factual ground: persons simply are not, and cannot be, the sort of beings that the ideal in the dominant conception of autonomy requires ... Second, the consequentialist ground: the imposition of such an ideal by the dominant conception of autonomy can be harmful.[24]

Thus, the feminists cited believe that persons are always and necessarily socially situated, which means that they are always and necessarily in relationships with others. Their alternative conception of autonomy, which emphasises the limitations of Beauchamp's and Childress's conception, is 'grounded on this relational conception of persons as involving the competent exercising of skills, derived and constrained by social circumstances, that facilitate self-direction'.[25]

Although the feminists' accounts of relational autonomy are varying,[26] these alternative conceptions of autonomy have several advantages. First, they

---

23 See note 8 at 103.
24 See note 20 at 422.
25 ibid at 423.
26 For instance, Virginia Held has elaborated a model based on mother-child relations, because mother-child relations are far closer and tighter than ties among friends, and mothering has historically offered women the opportunity to exercise agency more fully than other relationships available to them. Thus, in this relationship, a mother is responsible for assisting a helpless, dependent individual to transform into an independent, autonomous adult. See Held, V. (1993) *Feminist Morality* (Chicago: University of Chicago Press). Friedman and Raymond elaborate a model patterned after relations among friends, which is a comparatively loose relationship seldom embedded in the kinds of goal-oriented activities and institutionalised expectations that characterise such densely ordered practices as medicine or mothering. Raymond emphasises thoughtfulness, reason and caring, a quality of passion that manifests a thinking heart possessed of a robust sense of self, and a striving for the full use of one's powers. Friedman, however, stresses the importance of diverse friendships that afford the opportunity to participate in overlapping communities, so that one acquires a plurality of standpoints from which critically to assess one's choices, values and character, thereby overcoming the tendency uncritically to accept social norms. See Friedman, M. (1993) *What are Friends For?* (New York: Cornell University Press). Also see Raymond, J. (1986) *A Passion for Friends* (Boston: Beacon Press). Anne Donchin proposed a model based on relations among sisters. As sisters are joined together in a relationship

provide a richer and more socially contextualised conception of persons. In some situations of medical treatment, it is not likely that people can make independent and autonomous decisions. For example, a patient may suffer from a serious disease which influences his or her capability to make decisions independently. Even if the disease is not so serious as to influence his or her capacity to exercise independent decision-making, he or she might also be scared by the disease, and be vulnerable, weak and not in control of the situation. In these situations, individualistic autonomy often leaves the patient in a helpless situation when his or her social relationships are excluded, and as a result, the patient often cannot actually make independent and rational decisions and would be more likely to 'fall prey to the implicit manipulation of medical professionals'.[27] Dodds even argued that individualistic autonomy in medical decisions is inapplicable, since 'many of the important, but by no means unusual, health-care decisions that individuals, friends, and families make are far removed from the cool, reflective, clear-headed decision making that is the paradigm of this view of autonomy'.[28]

Secondly, they extend the responsibility for choices to society, since society contributes to the development of the necessary skills for choice. Autonomy should be understood on the basis of an institutional and cultural background. So an account of autonomy cannot be totally individualistic but should recognise that the individual is situated in a large number of social practices, commitments and relations to other people. In practice, there may be certain cultural norms that make it likely that individuals would wish to seek or rely on family or even community views in their decision-making process. For example, in traditional Chinese society, 'the family is based on an extended or clan structure and plays a central role in an individual's life ... Consequently, many Chinese patients may give the family or community the right to receive and disclose information, to make decisions, and to co-ordinate patient care, even when they themselves are competent'.[29] Under a model of individualistic autonomy, reliance on family or community views may be considered to place a person at the mercy of undue influence, which would hamper the exercise of individual autonomy. Under a model of

of equality, the relationship between sisters is 'structured by a common family history and shared expectations that generate obligations'. See Donchin, A. (2001) 'Understanding Autonomy Relationally: Toward a Reconfiguration of Bioethical Principles', *Journal of Medicine and Philosophy*, vol. 26, no. 4, pp. 365–86.

27 Lee, S. C. (2007) 'On Relational Autonomy: From Feminist Critique to Confucian Model for Clinical Practice' in S. C. Lee, ed., *The Family, Medical Decision-Making, and Biotechnology: Critical Reflections On Asian Moral Perspectives* (Springer) pp. 83–93 at 84.

28 Dodds, S. (2000) 'Choice and Control in Feminist Bioethics' in C. Mackenzie and N. Stoljar, eds., *Relational Autonomy: Feminist Perspectives on Autonomy, Agency, and the Social Self* (New York: Oxford University Press), pp. 213–35 at 217.

29 Bowman, K. W. and Hui, E. C. (2008) 'Chinese Bioethics' in P. A. Singer and A. M. Viens, eds., *The Cambridge Textbook of Bioethics* (Cambridge University Press) pp. 397–402 at 400.

relational autonomy, this seeking or relying on outside opinion is not viewed as undue influence, but as reasonable involvement of relevant parties and also permits consideration of the interests of other people who might be influenced by the decision.

Thirdly, feminists make it clear that a new understanding of respect for autonomy requires 'anticipation by others of what is needed to make the choice in question and facilitating that choice accordingly'.[30] Individualistic autonomy is the result of an abstract universalism that does not take into account the daily reality of human life. However, in daily reality, the individual is always situated in a multiplicity of contexts and life situations where dependency on others is very important. The narrative structure of personal identity and of the experiences of the individual, which are based on relational autonomy, show that decision-making should always be regarded as the result of the interactions of the individual with the social context.

Therefore, the critiques made by communitarian philosophers and feminists of individual autonomy are positive challenges to the dominant interpretation of the principle of respect for individual autonomy. No matter what kind of relationship they suggest as a model, they recognise that the individual is not an entirely independent entity but a person who is grounded in important and close social relationships. It means that, when individuals make decisions, they are not in a vacuum, but are always influenced by interactions between themselves and others, and make decisions not only based on their own interests but also how this decision will affect other people relevant to them. An individual may wish to take into account information on how his or her decision may affect others who are important to him or her. Just as individualistic autonomy cannot account for the interests of other relevant parties, it cannot also adequately take account of context. Indeed, in certain contexts, such as HPGR, simply to ensure that the individual research participant has been able to exercise autonomy based on his or her own interests would fail to take into account the interests of other group members. The shared nature of group collective genetic information means that HPGR on some members of the group potentially affects other members of the group who did not consent to participating in the research, or even the whole target group or community. In addition, in some cultures, when the decision would be relevant to the interests of both the group and the individual, individuals may wish to consider and respect the interests of the group as having priority, rather than making the decision only based on their personal interests. Therefore, the author argues that in the context of HPGR, the relational autonomy model would be more appropriate. Before making a decision to participate, an individual would need to be enabled to take into account information on the potential influence of his or her decision on others relevant to him who might be affected by the decision. The exact concerns raised by

30 See note 21 at 423.

adopting an individualised informed consent model, rather than the proposed relational autonomy model, will be discussed in more detail in following chapters.

The role of autonomy and consent in the western medical context

While there are some challenges to the meaning of the principle of autonomy from the philosophical or ethical perspective, the core concept of respect for individual autonomy is still dominant in the Western medical context. Respect for individual autonomy indicates that an individual who has the capacity to make the decision for him- or herself should be permitted to do so without inappropriate external pressure, and that this decision should be respected. Meanwhile, it also implies that no one has the authority to conduct any intervention upon such people's bodies without their consent. Under this principle, when considered in a medical context, consent can be defined as the 'autonomous authorization of a medical intervention or of participation in research'.[31] Ideally, patients or research participants have the right to make choices about their medical care or research participation and to be provided with all available information relevant to such decisions. A person must do more than express agreement or comply with a proposal. He or she must authorise it through an act of informed and voluntary consent. Consent occurs if and only if a patient or research subject, with substantial understanding, and in the absence of substantial control by others, intentionally authorises a physician or researcher to do something.[32]

The consent discussed above is being described at the ethical level. There is another way of looking at consent – one that refers to the rules of consent that determine legally or institutionally valid consent. A legally valid consent may not be exactly the same as autonomous authorisation within an ethical framework; rather, it is a valid authorisation within the framework of legal regulations. Sometimes, a morally or ethically valid consent is not a legally valid one. For example, different countries have various legal ages of consent to surgery. If the legal age of consent is 20 in a certain country, although an average individual aged 19 is capable of understanding relevant information and making an autonomous choice to agree to it, this choice cannot be seen as a legally valid consent. Nonetheless, it could be argued to be a substantially autonomous authorisation. Thus, a legally valid consent is a sufficiently autonomous authorisation under the operative legal regulations. Current legal rules and ethical guidelines concerning medical treatment and biomedical research are all based on this meaning of consent; that is, a legally valid

31 See note 8 at 119.
32 Faden, R. and Beauchamp, T. L. (1986) *A History and Theory of Informed Consent* (Oxford University Press) at 298.

autonomous authorisation from a patient or a participant to certain medical interventions or research. Consent, when discussed further in this book, refers to legally valid consent.

The principles of autonomy and consent are inherent in the civil and political rights and freedoms protected by international human rights law, such as the European Convention for the Protection of Human Rights and Fundamental Freedoms (ECHR)[33] and the International Covenant on Civil and Political Rights (ICCPR),[34] domestic law, such as the Human Rights Act 1998[35] and pre-existing common law in the UK.

At the level of international human rights law, these principles are expressed in both implicit and explicit ways. The ECHR protects a person's freedom to determine how to live his or her own life through a number of articles including freedom of expression and religion, the right to life and liberty of the person and respect for private life, which all provide for respect for individual autonomy. In addition, although Article 3 of the ECHR, which prohibits 'torture or inhuman or degrading treatment or punishment'[36] does not directly refer to medical treatment, the European Commission of Human Rights pointed out in *X v Denmark* that 'medical treatment of an experimental character and without the consent of the person involved may under certain circumstances be regarded as prohibited by Article 3'.[37] What is more, Article 7 of the ICCPR, which is the equivalent article of Article 3 of

33 The Convention for the Protection of Human Rights and Fundamental Freedoms (ECHR) is an international treaty to protect human rights and fundamental freedoms in Europe. Drafted in 1950 by the then newly formed Council of Europe, the convention entered into force on 3 September 1953. The full text of ECHR can be seen on the official website of the European Court of Human Rights, available at http://www.echr.coe.int/NR/rdonlyres/ D5CC24A7-DC13-4318-B457-5C9014916D7A/0/ENG_CONV.pdf (last visited 4 July 2013).

34 The International Covenant on Civil and Political Rights (ICCPR) is a multilateral treaty adopted by the United Nations General Assembly on 16 December 1966, and in force from 23 March 1976. The ICCPR is part of the International Bill of Human Rights, along with the International Covenant on Economic, Social and Cultural Rights (ICESCR) and the Universal Declaration of Human Rights (UDHR). The full text of ICCPR can be seen on the official website of United Nations, available at http://www2.ohchr.org/english/law/ ccpr.htm (last visited 4 July 2013).

35 The Human Rights Act 1998 is an Act of Parliament of the United Kingdom which received royal assent on 9 November 1998, and mostly came into force on 2 October 2000. The full text of Human Rights Act 1988 can be seen on the official website of UK Government, available at http://www.legislation.gov.uk/ukpga/1998/42 (last visited 4 July 2013).

36 See note 33. Article 3 noted that 'Prohibition of torture: No one shall be subjected to torture or to inhuman or degrading treatment or punishment'.

37 *X v Denmark* (1988) 32 DR 282 at 283.

the ECHR, noted specifically that: 'In particular, no-one shall be subjected without his free consent to medical or scientific experimentation'.[38]

At the level of UK domestic law, common law also explicitly includes the need for consent in the medical context. For example, in the case of *Re T,* all three judges in the Court of Appeal supported patient autonomy. They noted that:

> [Lord Donaldson MR]: An adult patient who, like Miss T., suffers from no mental incapacity has an absolute right to choose whether to consent to medical treatment, to refuse it or to choose one rather than another of the treatments being offered ... This right of choice is not limited to decisions which others might regard as sensible. It exists notwithstanding that the reasons for making the choice are rational, irrational, unknown or even non-existent.[39]
>
> [Butler-Sloss LJ]: A man or woman of full age and sound understanding may choose to reject medical advice and medical or surgical treatment either partially or in its entirety. A decision to refuse medical treatment by a patient capable of making the decision does not have to be sensible, rational or well-considered ...[40]
>
> [Staughton LJ]: An adult whose mental capacity is unimpaired has the right to decide for herself whether she will or will not receive medical or surgical treatment, even in circumstances where she is likely or even certain to die in the absence of treatment. Thus far the law is clear.[41]

Furthermore, in the case of *Airedale NHS Trust v Bland,* the House of Lords affirmed the principles of autonomy and consent as follows:

> ... it is established that the principle of self-determination requires that respect must be given to the wishes of the patient, so that if an adult patient of sound mind refuses, however unreasonably, to consent to treatment or care by which his life would or might be prolonged, the doctors responsible for his care must give effect to his wishes, even though they do not consider it to be in his best interests to do so ...[42]

In the case of *St George's Healthcare NHS Trust v S, R v Collins, ex p S,* the Court of Appeal considered and restated the principle as follows:

38 The ECHR states in Article 3 that 'No-one shall be subjected to torture or to cruel, inhuman or degrading treatment or punishment. In particular, no-one shall be subjected without his free consent to medical or scientific experimentation'.
39 *Re T (adult: refusal of treatment)* [1992] 3 WLR 782 at 102.
40 ibid at 116.
41 ibid at 121.
42 *Airedale NHS Trust v Bland* [1993] 2 WLR 316 at 864.

... how can a forced invasion of a competent adult's body against her will even for the most laudable of motives (the preservation of life) be ordered without irremediably damaging the principle of self-determination? When human life is at stake the pressure to provide an affirmative answer authorising unwanted medical intervention is very powerful. Nevertheless the autonomy of each individual requires continuing protection even, perhaps particularly, when the motive for interfering with it is readily understandable, and indeed to many would appear commendable ...[43]

These statements clearly addressed the significance of individual autonomy in the medical context and illustrated recognition of the need for consent by English courts. Since the rules of consent in relation to medical research are similar to those regulating medical treatment, in the next section, the general rules of legally valid consent to treatment will be addressed in more detail.

General rules of medical consent

Aside from the ethical need for consent, there is also a need to consider the legal purpose of consent. Generally speaking, most forms of medical treatments involve physical interventions on the patient, even if only an initial examination and tests. A legally valid consent relieves healthcare professionals of liability for battery, trespass or assault under the laws of both crime and tort.[44] However, in the criminal setting, victims generally cannot give a legally valid consent to bodily harm. This was made clear in the case of *R v Brown*, in which the court held that the consent of men to sado-masochistic sexual activities was not capable of obviating the criminal liability of the actors.[45] Therefore, if a patient's consent is capable of protecting healthcare professionals from prosecutions for medical interventions involving actual bodily harm, medical interventions must be seen as an exception to the general criminal law. This has been accepted by UK courts. For example, in *R v Brown*, Lord Templeman noted that: '[S]urgery involves intentional violence resulting in actual or sometimes serious bodily harm but surgery is a lawful activity'.[46] In *Airedale NHS Trust v Bland* Lord Mustill said that:

... bodily invasions in the course of proper medical treatment stand completely outside the criminal law. The reason why the consent of the

---

43 *St George's Healthcare NHS Trust v S, R v Collins, ex p S* [1998] 3 WLR 936 at 953.
44 Jackson, E. (2009) *Medical Law: Text, Cases and Materials* (2nd edn, Oxford: Oxford University Press) at 173.
45 *R v Brown* [1994] 1 AC 212.
46 ibid at 231.

patient is so important is not that it furnishes a defence in itself, but because it is usually essential to the propriety of medical treatment.[47]

These statements point out that appropriate surgery has its own justification as an exception to the general criminal law. This means that normal medical procedures performed to an appropriate standard with the patient's consent will not be criminal offences.

In the non-criminal setting, medical intervention without legally valid consent can be seen as battery (assault in Scotland) or negligence. A battery occurs when there is any touching without a legally valid consent. Early case law in the US, such as *Mohr v Williams*,[48] accepted that no matter whether or not the touching is hostile, a battery has been constituted by touching without legally valid consent from the patient. In this case, an ear specialist, Williams, performed surgery on Mohr's right ear with her consent. After Williams began performing the operation he decided that Mohr's left ear rather than her right ear required surgery. Although the condition was not life threatening, Williams operated successfully on the left ear without having received permission from Mohr. Mohr sued in battery and was successful. The court held that the physician should have obtained the consent of the patient before operating on the other ear. However, in the UK case of *Wilson v Pringle*,[49] the Court of Appeal held that in order to constitute a battery, the touching must be 'hostile'. The main consideration is that there is generally acceptable physical touching in ordinary life, such as physical touching in crowded stores. In the medical context, since health care professionals' intention in providing medical treatment is almost always to benefit their patients, it could be argued that health care professionals' actions cannot be seen as battery under the 'hostile' touching condition, although this point has not been considered by UK courts. In some cases where healthcare professionals have been successfully sued for battery, they had conducted unnecessary treatment. For example, in the UK case of *Appleton v Garrett*,[50] the judge held that the dentist, Garrett, in order to gain personal profit, deliberately conducted unnecessary treatment on Appleton, while deliberately misleading Appleton that the treatment was necessary, since he knew that otherwise Appleton would not have consented to it. The consent Appleton had provided was not, therefore, based on the truth about the need for treatment and was accordingly not a legally valid consent. The court found Garrett liable in battery.

However, there are some medical treatments which do not require physical touching, such as when a doctor prescribes a drug. Given that the essence of battery is physical touching, battery is not an appropriate legal action in these

---

47 See note 42 at 891.
48 *Mohr v Williams*, 59 Minn. 261, 265; 104 N.W. 12, 15 (1905).
49 *Wilson v Pringle* [1986] 3 WLR 1.
50 *Appleton and Others v Garrett* [1996] PIQR P1.

cases if they take place without legally valid consent. In addition, there are some cases where the patient has given his or her consent to a certain medical intervention, but the process of obtaining consent is flawed to some extent, such as where the risks of this medical intervention have not been disclosed completely or adequately. In these cases, negligence would be the only available legal avenue for redress. The differences between the actions of battery and negligence were stated clearly in the UK case of *Chatterton v Gerson*,[51] which will be considered further below. Generally, if a person is competent and consent is given voluntarily, then once that person has given consent in the knowledge of the broad nature of the intervention, he or she has given a legally valid consent. Thus, if there has been inadequate information disclosure about risks, the consent is still legally valid, so there can be no action for battery, but the person performing the intervention could be sued for negligence.

The essential elements of a legally valid consent that will avoid liability for both battery and negligence on the part of the person performing medical procedures can be summarised as follows: competence, adequate information disclosure and voluntariness.

Competence

This term means the ability to perform a task. In the context of medical decisions, competence is the capacity that a patient must understand both the information presented and its relevance, and the reasonably foreseeable consequences of his or her decision, as well as to make a choice on this decision. Faden and Beauchamp argued that the function of a competence judgment is to 'distinguish persons from whom consent should be solicited from those from whom consent need not or should not be solicited'.[52]

There are two requirements for competence: (i) the capacity to understand relevant information and the potential risks of harm; and (ii) the capacity to make the decision as to whether or not to authorise a certain medical intervention. This capacity includes physical, psychological and legal requirements. Thus, consent must be given by a person who is deemed to be legally capable of consenting. The Mental Capacity Act 2005,[53] which applies in

---

51 *Chatterton v Gerson and Another* [1981] QB 432.
52 See note 32 at 288.
53 The Mental Capacity Act 2005 is an Act to make new provision relating to persons who lack capacity; to establish a superior court of record called the Court of Protection in place of the office of the Supreme Court called by that name; and to make provision in connection with the Convention on the International Protection of Adults signed at the Hague on 13 January 2000. It aims to provide a comprehensive framework for decision-making on behalf of adults aged 16 and over who lack capacity to make decisions on their own behalf in England and Wales. The full text of the Mental Capacity Act 2005 can be seen on the official website of the UK government, available at http://www.legislation.gov.uk/ukpga/2005/9/contents (last visited 4 July 2013).

England and Wales, noted that a person cannot be seen as competent to make decisions for herself/himself if s/he is unable:

(a) to understand the information relevant to the decision
(b) to retain that information
(c) to use or weigh that information as part of the process of making the decision or
(d) to communicate his decision (whether by talking, using sign language or any other means).[54]

Although there is a presumption that an adult is competent,[55] in practice, most judgments on competence can only be made in specific situations. A person can be capable of performing some tasks at one time, such as making decisions about proposed medical treatment, while not capable of accomplishing the same tasks at another time.[56] For example, in a UK case, *Re T*, Lord Donaldson MR highlighted the complexity of making a judgment on capacity as follows:

> Doctors faced with a refusal of consent have to give very careful and detailed consideration to the patient's capacity to decide at the time when the decision was made. It may not be the simple case of the patient having no capacity because, for example, at that time he had hallucinations. It may be the more difficult case of a temporarily reduced capacity at the time when his decision was made. What matters is that the doctors should consider whether at that time he had a capacity which was commensurate with the gravity of the decision which he purported to make. The more serious the decision, the greater the capacity required.[57]

Thus, competence cannot be evaluated without knowledge of the exact situation. Generally, in respect of medical interventions, the following requirements are essential to competence: capacity to understand the proposed interventions; capacity to weigh its risks and benefits; and capacity to make an autonomous decision based on relevant knowledge and information.[58]

Adequate information disclosure

This refers to the duty of the clinician to inform the patient of the nature of the proposed procedures and provide information relevant to the medical intervention, before seeking consent. The European Convention on Human

---

54 ibid section 3(1).
55 *Re MB (Medical Treatment)* (Court of Appeal) [1997] 2 FLR 426 at 436.
56 ibid at 289–90.
57 See note 39 at 113.
58 See note 52 at 291.

Rights and Biomedicine (ECHRB)[59] highlights that a patient should be given 'appropriate information as to the purpose and nature of the intervention as well as on its consequences and risks'.[60] The Explanatory Report on the ECHRB[61] emphasised that the information provided:

> ... must be sufficiently clear and suitably worded for the person who is to undergo the intervention. The patient must be put in a position, through the use of terms he or she can understand, to weigh up the necessity or usefulness of the aim and methods of the intervention against its risks and the discomfort or pain it will cause.[62]

The disclosure of relevant information is essential to the rules of consent, because adequate relevant information is the basis for the patient to make autonomous choices.[63] Ethically, if patients have a right to make decisions about proposed procedures, they must also have the right to be told what they need to know in order to make an informed assessment before deciding what to do. Thus, if they do not know all of the relevant information, their decision to give or refuse consent is problematic. Therefore, information disclosure is vital in the medical consent.

Having noted the significance of information disclosure to consent, it is necessary to address the legal standard for information disclosure. The general principle of information disclosure in UK law was set out in *Chatterton v Gerson* by Bristow J, who said that:

> In my judgment once the patient is informed in broad terms of the nature of the procedure which is intended, and gives her consent, that consent is real, and the cause of the action on which to base a claim for failure to go into risks and implications is negligence, not trespass. Of course if information is withheld in bad faith, the consent will be vitiated by fraud. Of course if by some accident, as in a case in the 1940s in the

---

59 Convention for the Protection of Human Rights and Dignity of the Human Being with regard to the Application of Biology and Medicine: Convention on Human Rights and Biomedicine was done at Oviedo, Spain (4 April 1997). The full text can be seen at the official website of the Council of Europe at http://conventions.coe.int/Treaty/en/Treaties/Html/164.htm (last visited 4 July 2013).

60 ibid Article 5.

61 The Explanatory Report on ECHRB was drawn up under the responsibility of the Secretary General of the Council of Europe, on the basis of a draft prepared, at the request of the Steering Committee on Bioethics (CDBI), by Mr Jean Michaud (France), Chairman of the CDBI. It takes into account the discussions held in the CDBI and its Working Group entrusted with the drafting of the Convention; it also takes into account the remarks and proposals made by delegations. The Committee of Ministers authorised the publication of this Explanatory Report on 17 December 1996.

62 ibid.

63 See note 8 at 121.

Salford Hundred Court where a boy was admitted to hospital for tonsil-lectomy and due to administrative error was circumcised instead, trespass would be the appropriate cause of action against the doctor, though he was as much the victim of the error as the boy. But in my judgment it would be very much against the interests of justice if actions which are really based on a failure by the doctor to perform his duty adequately to inform were pleaded in trespass.[64]

This principle was approved by a further two cases: *Hills v Potter*[65] and *Sidaway v Bethlem Royal Hospital Governors*.[66] It creates two different levels of information disclosure: one to avoid liability for battery; the other to avoid liability for negligence. This approach has been criticised for several reasons, such as that it 'reduces the role of battery in English law',[67] it 'excludes other relevant information such as alternative treatment, benefits of the proposed treatment and advice on the underlying ailment'[68] and that there is 'no inherent difference between information as to the nature of a procedure and the information as to its risks and consequences'.[69] Nevertheless, the current law is that once the broad nature of the procedure has been disclosed to the patient, negligence is the only possible legal claim. Thus, the specific level of information disclosure under the current law of negligence needs to be explored. There are several options that could be considered when setting a legal standard.

The subjective standard of disclosure focuses on what is of specific interest to a particular individual. The justification for this standard was provided by Justice Stanley Mosk in the US case of *Cobb v Grant*:[70]

A medical doctor, being the expert, appreciates the risks inherent in the procedure he is prescribing, the risks of a decision not to undergo the treatment, and the probability of a successful outcome of the treatment. But once this information has been disclosed, that aspect of the doctor's expert function has been performed. The weighing of these risks against the individual subjective fears and hopes of the patient is not an expert skill. Such evaluation and decision is a non-medical judgment reserved to the patient alone.[71]

---

64 See note 51 at 443.
65 *Hills v Potter* [1984] 1 WLR 641.
66 *Sidaway v Bethlem Royal Hospital Governors* [1985] 1 AC 871.
67 Wicks, E. (2007) *Human Rights and Healthcare* (Hart Publishing) at 80.
68 ibid at 81.
69 ibid.
70 *Cobb v Grant*, 8 Cal. 3d 229, 502 P.2d 1, 104 Cal.Rptr. 505 (1972).
71 ibid.

The subjective standard requires the discovery of the interests of each particular patient and the use of this information as a part of disclosure, so it is
potentially time-consuming. Given the limited time in medical practice
available to make disclosure, although this approach is probably the standard
which can provide a person with the maximum information s/he needs to
make an autonomous choice, it would be extremely difficult to meet.
Therefore, generally, there are two further alternative standards of information disclosure regarding medical interventions that could be required by
law: a prudent patient standard (reasonable patient standard) and a prudent
doctor (professional practice) standard.

Under the prudent patient standard, which is applied in some states in the
US, the law would require doctors to disclose all of the information which
would be considered relevant by a reasonable patient. This was proposed in
the US case of *Salgo v Leland Stanford Jr. Univ. Bd. of Trustees*.[72] In this case a
patient, Martin Salgo, awoke paralysed after aortography, having never been
informed that such a risk existed. He sued the physician for negligence in
performance of the procedure and failing to warn of the risk of paralysis. The
court noted that the physician has the duty to disclose 'any facts which are
necessary to form the basis of an intelligent consent by the patient to
proposed treatment', but that 'in discussing the element of risk a certain
amount of discretion must be employed consistent with the full disclosure of
facts necessary to an informed consent'.[73] Thereafter, the standard was developed in another influential case, *Canterbury v Spence*.[74] In this case, the patient
underwent a laminectomy for serious back pain. After this operation, he fell
off his hospital bed and then suffered major paralysis. He sued the physician
claiming that he had not informed him that there was about a 1 per cent risk
of paralysis after a laminectomy. The court stated:

> True consent to what happens to one's self is the informed exercise of a
> choice, and that entails an opportunity to evaluate knowledgeably the
> options available and the risks attendant upon each. The average patient
> has little or no understanding of the medical arts, and ordinarily has only
> his physician to whom he can look for enlightenment with which to
> reach an intelligent decision. From these almost axiomatic considerations
> springs the need, and in turn the requirement, of a reasonable divulgence
> by physician to patient to make such a decision possible.[75]

This statement made it clear that since the aim of information disclosure is
to provide relevant information to patients to enable them to make decisions

---

72 *Salgo v Leland Stanford Jr. Univ. Bd. of Trustees*, 154 Cal.App.2d 560, 317 P.2d 170 (1957).
73 ibid.
74 *Canterbury v Spence*, 464 F.2d 772, 150 USApp.D.C. 263 (1972).
75 ibid.

about their medical treatment, the disclosure should be able to be understood by an average patient who has little or no medical knowledge. After this case, the reasonable patient standard has gradually been accepted by courts in a number of countries.[76] In the UK, this standard was also accepted by Lord Scarman in the landmark UK case of *Sidaway v Bethlem Royal Hospital Governors*. In this case, Lord Scarman noted as follows:

> The doctor's duty arises from his patient's rights. If one considers the scope of the doctor's duty by beginning with the right of the patient to make his own decision whether he will or will not undergo the treatment proposed, the right to be informed of significant risk and the doctor's corresponding duty are easy to understand: for the proper implementation of the right requires that the doctor be under a duty to inform his patient of the material risks inherent in the treatment.[77]

Despite this, however, the other Law Lords held that the question whether an omission to warn a patient of inherent risks of proposed treatment constituted a breach of a doctor's duty of care was to be determined by applying the *Bolam* principle, which is also known as the prudent doctor, or professional practice, standard. This principle was established in the case of *Bolam v Friern Hospital Management Committee*.[78] In this case, the judge set out the principle that a doctor is 'not guilty of negligence if he has acted in accordance with a practice accepted as proper by a responsible body of medical men skilled in that particular art'.[79] Thus, in *Sidaway* the majority did not share Lord Scarman's view and did not support it. However, it has been considered more favourably in Commonwealth jurisdictions. For example, in an Australian case, *Rogers v Whittaker*,[80] Whittaker did not disclose to Rogers that an operation to correct the sight of her almost blind right eye had the potential risk to cause her left eye to lose sight, which would lead to total blindness. The High Court of Australia considered both the *Sidaway* case[81] and *Canterbury v Spence*,[82] and then applied the reasonable patient standard and explained the reasons for doing so as follows:

> The law should recognise that a doctor has a duty to warn a patient of a material risk inherent in the proposed treatment; a risk is material if, in the circumstances of the particular case, a reasonable person in the patient's position, if warned of the risk, would be likely to attach

76 See note 8 at 123.
77 See note 66 at 888.
78 *Bolam v Friern Hospital Management Committee* [1957] 1 WLR 582.
79 ibid at 587.
80 *Rogers v Whittaker* (1992) 175 CLR 479.
81 See note 66.
82 See note 74.

significance to it or if the medical practitioner is or should reasonably be aware that the particular patient, if warned of the risk, would be likely to attach significance to it. This duty is subject to the therapeutic privilege.[83]

In the UK, however, in the *Sidaway* case, Lord Diplock gave the *Bolam* principle a wide application as follows:

> ... no convincing reason has in my view been advanced before your Lordships that would justify treating the *Bolam* test as doing anything less than laying down a principle of English law that is comprehensive and applicable to every aspect of the duty of care owed by a doctor to his patient in the exercise of his healing functions as respects that patient.[84]

In addition, Lord Bridge, Lord Keith and Lord Templeman, although accepting that the risks of certain medical interventions should be evaluated with reference to the specific situation of the patient's subjective beliefs, fears and hopes, not expert skill, still held that the level of disclosure should be decided based on medical evidence, unless 'a patient's right to decide whether to consent to the treatment was so obvious that no prudent medical man could fail to warn of the risk save in emergency or some other sound clinical reason for non-disclosure'.[85] Thus, the English courts applied a medical professional practice principle to information disclosure. This requires disclosure of information that the medical professional, supported by other medical opinion, considers relevant.

However, since *Sidaway*, the *Bolam* test has been refined. In the case of *Bolitho v City and Hackney HA*,[86] the House of Lords modified the *Bolam* test, although not in the context of information disclosure. Lord Browne-Wilkinson held:

> ... in my view, the court is not bound to hold that a defendant doctor escapes liability for negligent treatment or diagnosis just because he leads evidence from a number of medical experts who are genuinely of opinion that the defendant's treatment or diagnosis accorded with sound medical practice ... the court has to be satisfied that the exponents of the body of opinion relied upon can demonstrate that such opinion has a logical basis. In particular in cases involving, as they so often do, the weighing of risks against benefits, the judge before accepting a body of opinion as being responsible, reasonable or respectable, will need to be

---

83 ibid at 490.
84 See note 66 at 893–94.
85 ibid at 872.
86 *Bolitho Appellant v City and Hackney Health Authority Respondents* [1998] AC 232.

satisfied that, in forming their views, the experts have directed their minds to the question of comparative risks and benefits and have reached a defensible conclusion on the matter.[87]

This statement showed that the courts still have the right and the duty critically to analyse the basis of the expert witnesses' evidence to ensure that the opinion itself is reasonable, not just that the experts are suitably qualified and credible, although Lord Browne-Wilkinson emphasised that 'it will very seldom be right for a judge to reach the conclusion that views genuinely held by a competent medical expert are unreasonable'.[88]

In addition, in *Pearce v United Bristol Healthcare NHS Trust*,[89] the standard of risk disclosure required to enable the patient to decide whether to accept the doctor's advice was considered. The consultant obstetrician in this case suggested to the patient, who was pregnant and had gone past the expected date of delivery and was extremely concerned for the safety of her foetus, that the safest course was to allow labour to begin naturally, but did not disclose that there was a small (0.1–0.2 per cent) risk of stillbirth. The risk unfortunately materialised. The woman sued the doctor for failure to disclose the risk. Although her claim was rejected both at first instance and by the Court of Appeal, Lord Woolf MR's judgment did argue that:

> ... if there is a significant risk which would affect the judgment of a reasonable patient, then in the normal course it is the responsibility of a doctor to inform the patient of that significant risk, if the information is needed so that the patient can determine for him or herself as to what course he or she should adopt.[90]

This statement appeared to advance the cause of the prudent patient standard. This more patient-centred trend has been continued in more recent cases. For example, in *Wyatt v Curtis*,[91] Sedley LJ suggested that Lord Woolf's explanation of Lord Bridge's statement in *Sidaway* on whether or not a risk is 'substantial' or 'grave' should be considered from the perspective of the patient not the doctor. He noted that:

> Lord Woolf's formulation refines Lord Bridge's test by recognising that what is substantial and what is grave are questions on which the doctor's and the patient's perception may differ, and in relation to which the doctor must therefore have regard to what may be the patient's perception.

87 ibid at 241–42.
88 ibid at 243.
89 *Tina Marie Pearce and Another v United Bristol Healthcare NHS Trust* [1999] ECC 167.
90 ibid at 167.
91 *Wyatt v Curtis* [2003] EWCA Civ 1779.

To the doctor, a chance in a hundred that the patient's chickenpox may produce an abnormality in the foetus may well be an insubstantial chance, and an abnormality may in any case not be grave. To the patient, a new risk which (as I read the judge's appraisal of the expert evidence) doubles, or at least enhances, the background risk of a potentially catastrophic abnormality may well be both substantial and grave, or at least sufficiently real for her to want to make an informed decision about it.[92]

In another case, *Chester v Afshar*,[93] Lord Steyn explicitly rejected medical paternalism as follows:

A surgeon owes a legal duty to a patient to warn him or her in general terms of possible serious risks involved in the procedure. The only qualification is that there may be wholly exceptional cases where objectively in the best interests of the patient the surgeon may be excused from giving a warning. This is, however, irrelevant in the present case. In modern law medical paternalism no longer rules and a patient has a prima facie right to be informed by a surgeon of a small, but well established, risk of serious injury as a result of surgery.[94]

Although Lord Steyn's statement did not clearly indicate whether the issue of determining if a risk is significant should be decided by the view of the patient, his rejection of medical paternalism could be viewed as evidence of the trend towards acceptance of a prudent patient standard in the UK. In another more recent case, *Birch v University College London Hospital NHS Foundation Trust*,[95] the patient had been warned of the 1 per cent risk of stroke of undertaking catheter angiography, but was not informed that there was an alternative procedure, an MRI scan, which has no risk of stroke. According to expert witnesses on behalf of the defendants, the doctor's duty was merely to disclose the risks relevant to catheter angiography, which had been done properly. However, Mr Justice Cranston agreed with Mrs Birch that the prudent doctor standard was not logically reasonable in this case. He firmly agreed with Lord Woolf MR's statement that the doctor's duty to inform of 'significant risks' would not be discharged until the patient was made aware that fewer or no risks were associated with another available treatment. He then argued that, although expert witnesses insisted the doctor had fulfilled the duty of disclosure, the failure to discuss these comparative risks 'could not be described in law as reasonable, responsible or logical'.[96] Therefore,

92 ibid.
93 *Chester v Afshar* [2005] 1 AC 134.
94 ibid at 143.
95 *Birch v University College London Hospital NHS Foundation Trust* [2008] EWHC 2237 (QB).
96 ibid at 73.

although the judgment in *Sidaway* is still not directly overruled, this (albeit limited) movement towards the acceptance of a prudent patient standard is, therefore, a continuing trend in English law, which may be welcomed in its potentially greater respect for patient autonomy.

Voluntariness

This refers to the patient's right to come to a decision freely, without undue influence, such as force, coercion or manipulation.[97] In general, coercion means that 'one party intentionally and successfully influences another by presenting a credible threat of unwanted and avoidable harm so severe that the person is unable to resist acting to avoid it'.[98] Manipulation refers to several forms of undue influence that are neither coercion nor reasonable persuasion.[99] At the ethical level, voluntariness indicates that an individual can make decisions regarding his or her treatment free from overwhelming external pressure and is exercising the right to self-determination. However, in medical interventions, external influence by those performing them may be a factor in the person's decision to give consent. For example, a patient may refuse to undergo certain medical procedures for reasons of fear or false belief, but he or she may agree to undergo this medical intervention following persuasion from the physician. In this case, it may well be the case that the patient's consent is given voluntarily, if this influence is not seen as improper, although the physician has externally influenced the patient's decision. Thus, the boundary of 'undue influence' is a significant issue in the evaluation of valid consent and should be considered carefully.

In UK case law, the voluntariness of patient involvement was considered in the case of *Re T (adult: refusal of medical treatment)*.[100] In this case, Miss T, a woman injured in a car accident when 34 weeks pregnant, told medical staff that she refused to consent to a blood transfusion which might be necessary following a Caesarean section. She refused blood transfusion, after being alone with her mother, who was a Jehovah's Witness. This faith does not accept blood transfusions. After Miss T became unconscious, her father and boyfriend applied to the court for assistance. The English Court of Appeal held that Miss T's mother had apparently influenced the decision of the daughter, who was not a Jehovah's Witness. The court denied the effectiveness of the Miss T's refusal of treatment as follows:

> ... although an adult patient was entitled to refuse consent to treatment irrespective of the wisdom of his decision, for such a refusal to be effective

97   See note 8 at 133–34.
98   See note 32 at 339.
99   See note 8 at 133.
100 See note 39.

his doctors had to be satisfied that at the time of his refusal his capacity to decide had not been diminished by illness or medication or by false assumptions or misinformation, that his will had not been overborne by another's influence and that his decision had been directed to the situation in which it had become relevant; that where a patient's refusal was not effective the doctors were free to treat him in accordance with their clinical judgment of his best interests ...[101]

Although the judge in this case failed to define undue influence in any detailed manner, this case illustrates the requirement of voluntariness in medical consent in English law.

In summary, if the decision is made by a patient who meets the requirement of competence, with adequate information disclosure from his or her medical professionals and without any form of undue influence, this consent would be seen as a legally valid consent. If people have difficulties in providing voluntary, informed consent arising from limitations of decision-making capacity (eg children), or situational circumstances (eg prisoners) or because they are especially at risk of exploitation (eg some under-valued ethnic minorities), they should be seen as vulnerable and additional scrutiny of their decisions or other protections would be required.[102] Generally, the requirements and standards of medical consent discussed above can be applied to human subjects in biomedical research; however, given the existence of some differences between medical treatment and research, there are additional specific rules concerning consent to take part in research. In the next section, these rules will be addressed.

General rules of consent in medical research

Currently, there are several international declarations and ethical guidelines on research involving human subjects, including: the World Medical Association (WMA) Declaration of Helsinki (Helsinki Declaration),[103] which

101 ibid at 96.
102 Iltis, A. S. (2009) 'Introduction: Vulnerability in Biomedical Research', *Journal of Law, Medicine and Ethics*, vol. 37, no. 1, pp. 6–11 at 7–8.
103 The WMA Declaration of Helsinki Ethical Principles for Medical Research Involving Human Subjects was adopted by the 18th WMA General Assembly, Helsinki, Finland, June 1964, and amended by the: 29th WMA General Assembly, Tokyo, Japan, October 1975, 35th WMA General Assembly, Venice, Italy, October 1983, 41st WMA General Assembly, Hong Kong, September 1989, 48th WMA General Assembly, Somerset West, Republic of South Africa, October 1996 and the 52nd WMA General Assembly, Edinburgh, Scotland, October 2000, 53rd WMA General Assembly, Washington 2002 (Note of Clarification on paragraph 29 added), 55th WMA General Assembly, Tokyo 2004 (Note of Clarification on paragraph 30 added), 59th WMA General Assembly, Seoul, October 2008. The full text of Helsinki Declaration can be seen on

is the most important statement of the principles guiding medical research; the International Ethical Guidelines for Biomedical Research Involving Human Subjects (CIOMS Guidelines),[104] drawn up by the Council for International Organisation for Medical Sciences (CIOMS) in collaboration with the World Health Organisation (WHO), which sets general standards for the ethical conduct of research in countries around world; the Universal Declaration on Bioethics and Human Rights;[105] and the Universal Declaration on the Human Genome and Human Rights,[106] both of which have been adopted by United Nations Educational, Scientific and Cultural Organization (UNESCO). In addition, the European regional convention, the Convention for the Protection of Human Rights and Dignity of the Human Being with Regard to the Application of Biology and Medicine: Convention on Human Rights and Biomedicine (Convention on Human Rights and Biomedicine),[107] is also an influential document on research involving human subjects.

According to these international declarations and ethical guidelines, there are two basic values that are central to current ethical and legal frameworks on biomedical research: the autonomy of the human subject and the wellbeing of the human subject. In order to protect the autonomy and wellbeing of human subjects, there are two critical steps in determining whether biomedical research involving them can be conducted in an ethical manner: obtaining potential subjects' valid consent and assessing risks and potential benefits to them. These two steps work at two different levels. At one level, individual research subjects should be fully informed about the nature, scope and risks of the research, and consent to participation should be voluntary. At another level, existing regulations require researchers to submit proposals for research

the official website of the World Medical Association (WMA) at http://www.wma.net/en/30publications/10policies/b3/index.html (last visited 4 July 2013).

104 The International Ethical Guidelines for Biomedical Research Involving Human Subjects were prepared by the Council for International Organizations of Medical Sciences (CIOMS) in collaboration with the WHO, Geneva (2002). The full text of the CIOMS Guidelines can be seen on the official website of the World Health Organization (WHO) at http://whqlibdoc.who.int/emro/2004/9290213639_annex2.pdf (last visited 4 July 2013).

105 The Universal Declaration on the Bioethics and Human Rights was adopted by UNESCO's General Conference on 19 October 2005. The full text of the Universal Declaration on Bioethics and Human Rights can be seen on the official website of UNESCO at http://portal.unesco.org/en/ev.php-URL_ID=31058&URL_DO=DO_TOPIC&URL_SECTION=201.html (last visited 4 July 2013).

106 The Universal Declaration on the Human Genome and Human Rights was adopted unanimously and by acclamation at UNESCO's 29th General Conference on 11 November 1997. The full text of the Universal Declaration on Human Genome and Human Rights can be seen on the official website of UNESCO at http://portal.unesco.org/en/ev.php-URL_ID=13177&URL_DO=DO_TOPIC&URL_SECTION=201.html (last visited 4 July 2013).

107 See note 59.

involving human subjects to expert committees, which must judge those proposals based on their adherence to current legal regulations and ethical guidelines for the protection of human subjects, as well as ensuring the validity of the process of information disclosure and consent.

Similar to the rules of consent in medical treatment, in the biomedical research context competence is a precondition of valid consent. However, all of the current international declarations and ethical guidelines provide additional rules designed to provide protection for vulnerable populations, for example, human subjects who are incompetent to give a valid consent. CIOMS Guideline 9 noted that:

> When there is ethical and scientific justification to conduct research with individuals incapable of giving informed consent, the risk from research interventions that do not hold out the prospect of direct benefit for the individual subject should be no more likely and not greater than the risk attached to routine medical or psychological examination of such persons. Slight or minor increases above such risk may be permitted when there is an overriding scientific or medical rationale for such increases and when an ethical review committee has approved them.[108]

According to the Helsinki Declaration there are three rules that need to be obeyed. First, 'if the research subject is legally incompetent, then the consent has to be given by the legally authorised representative'.[109] Secondly, there are other special protections for these vulnerable people, which are that minors and incompetents should not be included in research unless the research is necessary to promote the health of the population to which they belong, and the research could not be performed on legally competent persons instead. If the minor is able to understand the research, his or her assent is necessary in addition to the consent of the parents.[110] Thirdly, if the patient is not able to give consent, for example because he or she is unconscious, and in the absence of proxy consent, the research should be done only if the condition that prevents the obtaining of informed consent is a necessary characteristic of the research population.[111]

In the context of biomedical research on competent human subjects, voluntariness is another fundamental requirement. As has been pointed out above, the first principle of the Nuremberg Code highlighted that the human subjects' voluntary consent is an essential and absolute requirement for biomedical research. It placed the individual human subject as the decisive entity in biomedical research. However, this absolute requirement of

---

108 See note 104, Guidelines 9.
109 See note 103 Article 27.
110 ibid Article 27.
111 ibid Article 29.

individual informed consent would mean that individuals who cannot provide consent would be excluded from participation, which may lead to some negative effects. For example, excluding individuals from participation in biomedical research might result in losing the opportunity to test new drugs and medical treatments which might be relevant to a particular population, such as babies and young children. What is more, these individuals may also be excluded from some clinical research which might benefit them as individuals.[112] Thus, the absolute requirement of consent has been reconsidered by all other international declarations and ethical guidelines for biomedical research involving human subjects. These declarations all highlight the importance of freedom of choice and personal decision-making in informed consent, while allowing individuals who are not competent to be included in biomedical research under specific strict rules to seek to ensure their wellbeing is not compromised.

The main distinction between the general rules of consent for medical treatment and medical research is consideration of the extent of necessary information disclosure. In comparison with the legal requirements of information disclosure in medical treatment,[113] ethical declarations, guidelines and limited case law indicate that in the context of biomedical research involving human subjects, a higher standard of information disclosure is required. Most international declarations and conventions on biomedical research have attempted to describe the information that needs to be disclosed by researchers. For example, the Helsinki Declaration noted that:

> In medical research involving competent human subjects, each potential subject must be adequately informed of the aims, methods, sources of funding, any possible conflicts of interest, institutional affiliations of the researcher, the anticipated benefits and potential risks of the study and the discomfort it may entail, and any other relevant aspects of the study … Special attention should be given to the specific information needs of individual potential subjects as well as to the methods used to deliver the information.[114]

The UNESCO Universal Declaration on Bioethics and Human Rights noted the duty of disclosure as follows:

---

112 Noah, B. A. (2003) 'The Participation of Underrepresented Minorities in Clinical Research', *American Journal of Law and Medicine*, vol. 29, nos 2–3, pp. 221–45.
113 In UK, the case of *Sidaway v Bethlem Royal Hospital Governors* [1985] 1 AC 871 has showed the legal requirement on information disclosure is based on a professional practice standard, which now requires full disclosure.
114 See note 103 Article 24.

Scientific research should only be carried out with the prior, free and informed consent of the person concerned. The information should be adequate, provided in a comprehensible form and should include modalities for withdrawal of consent.[115]

Similarly, the CIOMS Guidelines, which defined informed consent in the biomedical research context as 'a decision to participate in research, taken by a competent individual who has received the necessary information; who has adequately understood the information; and who, after considering the information, has arrived at a decision without having been subjected to coercion, undue influence or inducement, or intimidation',[116] listed 27 pieces of essential information that need to be disclosed to inform the research subject 'in language or another form of communication that the individual can understand'.[117]

In addition, the need for a higher standard of information disclosure for medical research involving human subjects has also been pointed out in court judgments in some countries. For example, in the Canadian case of *Halushka v University of Saskatchewan*,[118] the judge noted the requirement of full information disclosure in biomedical research and explained this as follows:

> The duty imposed upon those engaged in medical research to those who offer themselves as subjects for experimentation is at least as great as, if not greater than, the duty owed by the ordinary physician or surgeon to his patient. The subject of medical experimentation is entitled to a full and frank disclosure of all the facts, probabilities and opinions which a reasonable man might be expected to consider before giving his consent... Failure to make full disclosure may vitiate any consent whether impliedly or expressly given; the undisclosed or misrepresented facts need not concern matters which directly cause the ultimate damage if they are of a nature which might influence the judgment upon which the consent is based.[119]

Similarly, in another Canadian case, *Weiss v Solomon*,[120] the judge of the Superior Court of Quebec noted that: 'The court must thus conclude that in a purely experimental research programme, the doctor must disclose all known risks, including those which are very rare or remote and a fortiori those whose consequences would be grave'.[121] However, in the UK, although

---

115 See note 105 Article 6 Consent (2).
116 See note 104 Commentary on Guideline 4.
117 See note 104.
118 *Halushka v University of Sask.* (1965) 52 W.W.R. 608, 53 D.L.R. (2d) 436.
119 ibid at 616–17.
120 *Weiss v Solomon* [1989] Carswell Que 72.
121 ibid at 109.

medical research involving human subjects has been addressed by law in the Medicines for Human Use (Clinical Trials) Regulations 2004 and the EU Clinical Trials Directive 2001/20/EC[122] through the requirement to inform clinical trial subjects of 'its nature, significance, implications and risks and appropriately documented',[123] there is no specific obligation set out concerning the degree or standard of information disclosure on the part of researchers. Whether a higher standard of information disclosure is required for potential research participants compared with patients is therefore uncertain.

It must also be noted that medical research involving human subjects is a broad term that encompasses a wide variety of research. It has been described as having two categories: therapeutic research and non-therapeutic research. Therapeutic research, which includes most clinical trials, can be distinguished from non-therapeutic research in that the former has a possibility of immediate benefit to the subjects, whereas the latter has no such intended potential.[124] This distinction has a historical basis, emerging after the Second World War in order to prevent future medical treatment and biomedical research abuses such as those committed during the war, under the assumption that research combined with patient care could be considered more ethical, as the patient benefited and physicians were guided by the patient's interests. Therapeutic research may benefit the participants as it not only aims to provide scientific knowledge, but also aims at healing or improving the participant's condition. Non-therapeutic research, which can be carried out on both patients and healthy subjects, will in all likelihood not be for the benefit of the research participant but for the benefit of others, such as future patients. The participant would need to accept the possibility of adverse effects and health risks, but the potential benefits, such as findings in connection with a new treatment, will be for others. While the Helsinki Declaration dropped the therapeutic/non-therapeutic research distinction in its 2008 version, it nonetheless provided separate principles on 'clinical research combined with professional care'. Section 31 of the Declaration states that 'the physician may combine medical research with medical care only to the

122 The Clinical Trials Directive (Directive 2001/20/EC of 4 April 2001) of the European Parliament and of the Council on the approximation of the laws, regulations and administrative provisions of the Member States relating to implementation of good clinical practice in the conduct of clinical trials on medicinal products for human use) is a European Union directive that aimed at facilitating the internal market in medicinal products within the European Union, while at the same time maintaining an appropriate level of protection for public health. The full text of this directive can be seen on the official website of EU, available at www.eortc.be/Services/Doc/clinical-EU-directive-04-April-01.pdf (last visited 4 July 2013).

123 ibid Article 2(j).

124 Liddell, K., Bion, J., Chamberlain, D., Druml, C., Kompanje, E., Lemaire, F., Menon, D., Vrhovac, B. and Wiedermann, C. J. (2006) 'Medical Research Involving Incapacitated Adults: Implications of the EU Clinical Trials Directive 2001/20/EC', *Medical Law Review*, vol. 14, no. 3, pp. 367–417.

extent that the research is justified by its potential preventive, diagnostic or therapeutic value and if the physician has good reason to believe that participation in the research study will not adversely affect the health of the patients who serve as research subjects'.[125] As has already been pointed out, there may be reasons to require a higher standard of information disclosure for medical research than for medical treatment. However, a distinction may also be made between therapeutic and non-therapeutic research. For example, in the US case of *Whitlock v Duke University*,[126] the court took the view that the standard of information disclosure in non-therapeutic research is stricter than in therapeutic research. Since the considerations and balance of interests are different, the court concluded that the standard of consent adopted by the Nuremberg Code required a greater degree of disclosure where research is considered non-therapeutic, and found the standard of care required for informed consent relating to medical treatment inapplicable to determine the responsibility for obtaining consent in a non-therapeutic context. In non-therapeutic research, the researcher is under a duty to disclose all risks which may reasonably be anticipated and not just the 'usual and most frequent' risks.[127] The standard of disclosure in non-therapeutic research requires disclosure of 'the possible effects upon the health and person of the subject'.[128]

Risk assessment in medical research

In the current medical ethical and legal frameworks, if these general rules of consent to medical research are met, any consent offered would be seen as valid and respectful of the autonomy of the individual. Apart from the issue of consent to participation, the other main concern of ethical and legal frameworks governing medical research is that of an assessment of the risks involved compared with the potential benefits.

In order to translate biomedical discoveries into practical medical treatment procedures or products, research involving human subjects is a necessary step, which offers the prospect of better lives for many people.[129] To take this further, some have argued that it is a moral obligation to undertake, support and even to participate in serious scientific research.[130] For example, Harris proposes that:

---

125 See note 103 Article 31.
126 *Whitlock v Duke University*, 637 F.Supp.1463 (M.D.N.C. 1986).
127 ibid at 1741.
128 ibid.
129 Koski, G. (2000) 'Risks, Benefits, and Conflicts of Interest in Human Research: Ethical Evolution in the Changing World of Science', *The Journal of Law, Medicine & Ethics*, vol. 28, pp. 330–31 at 330.
130 Harris, J. (2005) 'Scientific research is a moral duty', *Journal of Medical Ethics*, vol. 31, no. 4, pp. 242–48.

The argument concerning the obligation to participate in research should be compelling for anyone who believes there is a moral obligation to help others, and/or a moral obligation to be just and do one's share. Little can be said to those whose morality is so impoverished that they do not accept either of these two obligations.[131]

Research involving human subjects is helpful to scientific development, to the benefit of society in general and future patients in particular, so as a member of society, Harris considers that every individual should support and participate in biomedical research, at least if the research is directed toward preventing serious harm or providing significant benefits. Although it is too extreme to argue that research is a bigger priority than concern for the welfare and rights of human subjects, his argument has identified one important distinction between biomedical research and medical treatment. In medical treatment, the health care professional has a number of clear obligations: to seek to cure the patient; to alleviate his or her symptoms and to prevent illness or injury. This means that medical treatment is targeted to benefit the patient himself or herself. However, in the research context, promoting the human subject's wellbeing is not the primary focus, which is instead the improvement of the wellbeing of society and future patients by the creation of generalisable knowledge. Research focuses on benefiting the public as a whole, although it may also provide benefits to the research participant. The researcher has an obligation to ensure that the research findings are valid and replicable, and this has implications for the design and execution of the research.

There is no legal definition of 'medical research' in the UK,[132] although there is a definition of a 'clinical trial'.[133] The 'Supplementary Guidance Good Practice in Research and Consent to Research',[134] the professional guidance

131 ibid at 247.
132 In this book, the definition of 'biomedical research' excludes experimental treatment which refers to the use of untested innovative treatment on certain individual patients.
133 The Medicines for Human Use (Clinical Trials) Regulations 2004 Part 1 Regulation 2 noted that 'clinical trial' means any investigation in human subjects, other than a non-interventional trial, intended: (a) to discover or verify the clinical, pharmacological or other pharmacodynamic effects of one or more medicinal products; (b) to identify any adverse reactions to one or more such products; or (c) to study absorption, distribution, metabolism and excretion of one or more such products, with the object of ascertaining the safety or efficacy of those products. The full text of The Medicines for Human Use (Clinical Trials) Regulations 2004 can be seen on the official website of the UK government, available at http://www.legislation.gov.uk/uksi/2004/1031/contents/made (last visited 4 July 2013).
134 Supplementary Guidance Good Practice in Research and Consent to Research set out the good practice principles that doctors are expected to understand and follow if they are involved in research. It is the professional guidance of the General Medical Council (GMC). The full text of this can be seen on the official website of the GMC, available at

provided by the General Medical Council (GMC),[135] defined medical research as follows:

> Research ... refers to an attempt to derive generalisable new knowledge. Research aims to find out what is best practice by addressing clearly defined questions with systematic and rigorous methods. It includes studies that aim to generate hypotheses as well as those that aim to test them.[136]

This definition indicates that a medical researcher's primary aim is to benefit a broader population by producing reliable, statistically significant information through their medical research, while medical treatment is designed to benefit a specific individual, aims to restore the patient's health or prevent deterioration. The Helsinki Declaration also does not provide an explicit definition of medical research, but instead describes it by reference to the purpose of the research:

> The primary purpose of medical research involving human subjects is to understand the causes, development and effects of diseases and improve preventive, diagnostic and therapeutic interventions (methods, procedures and treatments). Even the best current interventions must be evaluated continually through research for their safety, effectiveness, efficiency, accessibility and quality.[137]

Similarly, in the US, the 'Ethical Principles and Guidelines for the Protection of Human Subjects of Research' (the Belmont Report)[138] also pointed out that medical treatment, which aims to provide diagnosis, preventive treatment or therapy to particular individuals, encompasses 'interventions that are designed solely to enhance the wellbeing of an individual patient or client

---

http://www.gmc-uk.org/static/documents/content/Research_guidance_FINAL.pdf (last visited 4 July 2013).

135 The GMC registers and regulates doctors in the United Kingdom. It has the power to revoke registration, or place restrictions on practice.

136 See note 134 Article 1.

137 See note 103 Article 1.

138 The Belmont Report is a report created by the former United States Department of Health, Education, and Welfare (which was renamed the Health Human Services Department) entitled 'Ethical Principles and Guidelines for the Protection of Human Subjects of Research', authored by Dan Harms, and is an important historical document in the field of medical ethics. The report was created on 18 April 1979 and gets its name from the Belmont Conference Center where the document was drafted. The full text of this can be seen on the official website of the Office of Human Subjects Research of the US, available at http://ohsr.od.nih.gov/guidelines/belmont.html#goc2 (last visited 4 July 2013).

and that have a reasonable expectation of success',[139] while medical research, which is usually described in a formal protocol that sets forth an objective and a set of procedures designed to reach that objective, is 'designed to test a hypo discussion, permit conclusions to be drawn, and thereby to develop or contribute to generalizable knowledge (expressed, for example, in theories, principles, and statements of relationships)'.[140]

The main consideration of a biomedical research design must be to include a research question which should be able to be answered reliably and efficiently, sufficient numbers of human subjects must be enrolled in a reasonable period and human subjects must comply with their allocated treatment. In theory then, the welfare of individual human subjects may be sacrificed to complete these targets when there is conflict. However, if researchers ignore the interests and wellbeing of human subjects, it may lead to unacceptable results, such as the medical experiments conducted by Nazi doctors in German concentration camps[141] during the Third Reich and the egregious experimentation undertaken in Unit 731[142] in the People's Republic of China. Therefore, the first basic principle of the Nuremberg Code[143] highlighted the importance of human subjects' voluntariness: '[T]he voluntary consent of the human subject is absolutely essential'.[144] The potential research participant 'should be so situated as to be able to exercise free power of choice, without the intervention of any element of force, fraud, deceit, duress, over-reaching, or other ulterior form of constraint or coercion'.[145] The first principle placed the wellbeing and protection of the individual at the centre of research ethics, and highlighted that neither the progress of medical science and technology nor potential benefit for society as a whole should be the determining factor of the ethics of research involving human beings.

In addition, compared with medical treatment, biomedical research may expose human subjects to a degree of additional risk to that inherent in

---

139 ibid.
140 ibid.
141 After the Second World War, a trial of the perpetrators of the Nazi experiments was held in Nuremberg, Germany and is reported as *United States of America v Karl Brandt et al*, which resulted in what has come to be known as the Nuremberg Code.
142 Unit 731 was a covert biological and chemical warfare research and development unit of the Imperial Japanese Army that undertook lethal human experimentation during the Second Sino-Japanese War (1937–1945) and the Second World War. However, for political reasons, Unit 731 avoided a procedure like the Nuremberg 'Doctor's Trial'.
143 The Nuremberg Code is a set of research ethics principles for human experimentation set as a result of the Subsequent Nuremberg Trials at the end of the Second World War. The record of this trial can be seen on the official website of the US, available at http://www.archives.gov/research/captured-german-records/microfilm/m889.pdf (last visited 4 July 2013).
144 Trials of War Criminals before the Nuremberg Military Tribunals under Control Council Law No. 10, vol. 2 (Washington, D.C.: US Government Printing Office, 1949) at 181.
145 ibid.

proven medical treatment. In the medical treatment setting, the patient takes the treatment for his or her health benefit. In the context of biomedical research, although such research could lead to potential benefits to biomedical science and human knowledge as a whole, as well as potential benefits to future patients, the direct and immediate benefits to participants in biomedical research may be less clear-cut. In contrast, human subjects may be exposed to a broad array of risks as a result of research participation.

Moreover, uncertainty is one of the main features of biomedical research. No matter how much animal and laboratory research has been conducted, the effect of biomedical research on human subjects cannot be known. Mason and Laurie identify the aim of randomised clinical trials as being 'to decide whether a new drug or other treatment is better than an existing one, or is preferable to none at all, the new treatment is given to a group of patients or healthy volunteers and not given to a group as similar a group as can be obtained'.[146]

Therefore, it may be concluded that since biomedical research involving human subjects is a necessary step which may lead to benefits to society as a whole, even though it may cause uncertain and additional risks of harm to its participants, we should allow it to be conducted. Nevertheless, we also bear responsibility for ensuring that the interests of those who participate in research are understood and protected. In other words, it could be suggested that biomedical research involving human subjects deserves specific rules, distinct from those that apply to medical treatment.

In order to ensure the welfare of human subjects, almost all the international declarations and conventions require the risk-benefit assessment to weigh the merits of proposed biomedical research and the potential impact on the rights, safety and welfare of participants. They clearly state that the risk to participants should be justified by the anticipated benefits to them and/or society, through risk-benefit assessments which are concerned with the probabilities and intensity of possible harm balanced against anticipated benefits. The research should be designed so that the researcher or research institution ensures that the potential benefits and risks are reasonably evaluated, and risks are minimised. The assessment of risks and potential benefits requires a careful appraisal of all available relevant data including, in some cases, alternative ways of obtaining the benefits sought in the research. For example, Article 16 of the Convention on Human Rights and Biomedicine, which provides special regulations for the protection of human subjects in scientific research, urges that it should be ensured that:

> The risks which may be incurred by that person are not disproportionate to the potential benefits of the research; the research project has been

146 Mason, J. K. and Laurie, G. T. (2011) *Mason and McCall Smith's Law and Medical Ethics* (8th edn, Oxford University Press) at 620.

approved by the competent body after independent examination of its scientific merit, including assessment of the importance of the aim of the research, and multidisciplinary review of its ethical acceptability.[147]

In addition, the first guideline of the CIOMS Guidelines relates to risk-benefit assessment and risk management. It points out that:

> The ethical justification of biomedical research involving human subjects is the prospect of discovering new ways of benefiting people's health. Such research can be ethically justifiable only if it is carried out in ways that respect and protect, and are fair to, the subjects of that research and are morally acceptable within the communities in which the research is carried out. Moreover, because scientifically invalid research is unethical in that it exposes research subjects to risks without possible benefit, investigators and sponsors must ensure that proposed studies involving human subjects conform to generally accepted scientific principles and are based on adequate knowledge of the pertinent scientific literature.[148]

This means that when, and only when, biomedical research involving human subjects provides adequate respect and protection for their welfare, can it be seen as ethically justifiable. Thus, providing adequate respect for, and protection of the welfare of, human subjects is also the first priority of the CIOMS Guidelines. Guideline 8 also refers to risk-benefit assessment and risk management. In general, the guideline requires that researchers must ensure that potential benefits and risks are reasonably balanced and that risks are minimised.[149] In respect of the different aims of therapeutic research and non-therapeutic research, CIOMS Guideline 8 sets distinctive standards on risk-benefit assessment in therapeutic research and non-therapeutic research.[150] In therapeutic research, since participants are involved in the expectation that it will be at least as advantageous to the individuals concerned as normal treatment, the risk must be justified 'in relation to expected benefits to the individual subject'.[151] This means that the risks should be less than, or approximately equal to, the risks of existing treatment, while the benefits should be better than existing treatment. On the other hand, in non-therapeutic research, which aims to gain generalisable knowledge expected to benefit society as a whole, risks must be 'reasonable in relation to the importance of the knowledge to be gained'.[152]

147 See note 107.
148 See note 104.
149 ibid.
150 ibid.
151 ibid.
152 ibid.

Risk-benefit assessment also has a legal basis in some countries. For example, the US Common Rule[153] requires that risks to human subjects should be minimised. Furthermore, risks associated with non-therapeutic research as well as being minimised must be 'reasonable in relation to anticipated benefits, if any, to subjects, and the importance of the knowledge that may reasonably be expected to result'.[154] Risks associated with therapeutic research must be in relation to the 'benefits of therapies subjects would receive even if not participating in the research'.[155]

The example of new drug research for people with acutely symptomatic schizophrenia provided in Chapter 1 also indicated another type of risk: these schizophrenic patients may pose risks to third parties, for instance if their behaviour is affected leading them to act violently toward others, such as their family. If this research is conducted while they are living in their homes, more third parties' interests could be exposed to risk of harm, such as neighbours, or people who may have daily contact with them. Despite the possibility that there may be third parties who could be adversely affected by the research, under the current ethical and legal frameworks of biomedical research, only the consent of the human subject is required. The interests of third parties cannot be protected by the rule of consent, which is the core principle in both legal and ethical frameworks on biomedical research. Another legal and ethical requirement for medical research is protecting the wellbeing of human subjects, which through the assessment of the risks and potential benefits of certain biomedical research is the overriding criterion for deciding whether or not certain research should be conducted. Nevertheless, the interests of third parties may not be sufficiently protected by this requirement either.

Kimmelman analysed the Tuskegee Syphilis case,[156] in which a study was designed to document the natural history of the disease by preventing about 400 men from obtaining treatment for their late stage syphilis. The men in question were told that they were being treated for 'bad blood'. Kimmelman illustrated that third parties' interests were at risk of harm as follows:

---

153 Title 45 CFR (Code of Federal Regulations) Part 46, can be seen on the official website of US Department of Health & Human Services, available at http://www.hhs.gov/ohrp/45CFRpt46faq.html (last visited 13 October 2010).

154 ibid 45 CFR § 46.111.

155 ibid.

156 From 1932 to 1972, 399 poor black sharecroppers in Macon County, Alabama were denied treatment for syphilis and deceived by physicians of the United States Public Health Service. In fact, government officials went to extreme lengths to ensure that they received no therapy from any source. As reported by *The New York Times* on 26 July 1972, the Tuskegee Syphilis Study was revealed as 'the longest non-therapeutic experiment on human beings in medical history'. More detail about this case can be seen in the 'Final Report of the Tuskegee Syphilis Study Legacy Committee', Tuskegee Syphilis Study Legacy Committee, available at http://www.hsl.virginia.edu/historical/medical_history/bad_blood/report.cfm (last visited 4 July 2013).

Normally, late-stage syphilis is not contagious. However, two circumstances surrounding this study suggest that family members, children, and the sexual partners of the male subjects may have been at risk of contracting syphilis. First, medical historians have speculated that some of the men in the study might not have been in the late stage of syphilis. If so, they would have been contagious. Second, persons in the early phases of the late stage syphilis are also contagious.[157]

In this research, relevant information was not provided to the research subjects, but it was also not provided to their family members or sexual partners, who could have been adversely affected by this research. Under current research guidelines, since this type of research would neither collect any information from or about persons other than the patients, nor would any other persons be asked to undergo any interventions relevant to the research, the researcher does not need to obtain consent from or provide any relevant information to persons other than the research subjects.

Furthermore, Resnik and Sharp also list some examples of research that may expose third parties to risks of harm, as follows:

> Vaccine research in which subjects are exposed to a biological agent that may pose a health hazard to others who come in contact with research subjects; studies that involve research interventions in settings occupied by multiple individuals such as a home, a school, or a community centre; research in settings in which third-party occupants may assume privacy, such as a home; research on mental illnesses associated with violent behaviour in which changes to ongoing treatment programs may present risks to persons living nearby; research on a localized environmental hazard that may impact all community residents; studies in which lactating women receive experimental medication that may be transmissible through nursing.[158]

In all of these types of research, certain third parties may suffer harm caused by the research, but their opinions would not be sought. Although the risks to third parties might be considered as part of the review of the effects of the study in general, current guidelines and regulations do not explicitly require institutional review boards (IRBs) or research ethics committees (RECs) to address such risks, and many IRBs/RECs tend to limit their deliberations to issues and concerns related to the guidelines and regulations.[159] Since IRBs/

---

157 Kimmelman, J. (2005) 'Medical Research, Risk, and Bystanders', *IRB: Ethics and Human Research*, vol. 27, no. 4, pp. 1–6 at 1.
158 Resnik, D. B. and Sharp, R. R. (2006) 'Protecting Third Parties in Human Subjects Research', *IRB: Ethics and Human Research*, vol. 28, no. 4, pp. 1–7 at 2.
159 ibid at 3.

RECs may not have sufficient time or appropriate expertise to assess risks to third parties in research, especially given the many demands and pressures of ethical review work, without such a requirement, it would be rare to conduct a risk-benefit assessment on the interests of third parties. Thus, the interests of third parties cannot be protected adequately under current research guidelines and legal requirements.

In summary, expanding knowledge on human health and the causes of disease, as well as promoting the development of biomedical science, is important. Obtaining the valid consent of human subjects and the assessment of risks and potential benefits of research are the two main measures that provide protection to human subjects. Nevertheless, some types of biomedical research may lead to new challenges to the legal and ethical frameworks of human subject protection, a problem that is particularly acute in the case of human population genetic research, which will be considered in the next chapter.

4 Human population genetic research and its harms

Human population genetic research

Human Population Genetic Research (HPGR) is also sometimes called 'population-based genetic research/study' or 'population genomic research/study'. It focuses on human genetic information at a group level. Collective human genetic information is the research target of human population genetic research.

The significance of human population genetic research

There are two different definitions of HPGR: a general one and a narrow one.

General HPGR is defined as '... a study which aims at understanding the nature and extent of genetic variation among a population or individuals within a group or between individuals across different groups'.[1] To be precise, the research object of general HPGR is the first type of genetic information mentioned above, which is non-differential human genetic information that is shared by all human beings.

At present, the most influential general human population genetic research is the Human Genome Project (HGP), which 'refers to the international 13-year effort, formally begun in October 1990 and completed in 2003, to discover all the estimated 20,000–25,000 human genes and make them accessible for further biological study. Another project goal was to determine the complete sequence of the 3 billion DNA subunits (bases in the human genome)'.[2] The UK House of Commons Science and Technology Committee

---

1 This definition stems from the United Nations Educational, Scientific and Cultural Organization's 'Bioethics and Human Population Genetics Research' (1995).
2 'About the Human Genome Project' can be seen on the official website of the Human Genome Project, available at http://www.ornl.gov/sci/techresources/Human_Genome/project/about.shtml (last visited 4 July 2013).

Report on Human Genetics outlined the HGP's possible outcomes in the following way:

- better understanding of human illness and the role of genetic influences in a great many conditions, including psychiatric and neurological disorders
- quicker and cheaper diagnoses of common diseases
- better understanding of the biochemical or physiological mechanisms involved in genetic disease: focusing on the mechanism involved may bring
- improved techniques in the design of drugs to produce chemicals that can fit precisely with molecules implicated in disease (pharmacogenomics)
- gene therapy
- germ-line therapy.[3]

Hence, the potential benefits of the HGP are numerous and significant. Connecting the DNA sequences of individual genes within the human genome to the various diseases and traits for which they encode will require thousands, even millions, of individual research subjects. Therefore, this research relies on the large-scale collection of genetic, genealogical and medical data from many individuals.[4] Meanwhile, the research spawned a range of concerns regarding human dignity,[5] privacy,[6] autonomy,[7] patents[8] and discrimination.[9]

3 UK House of Commons Science and Technology Committee, *Human Genetics: The Science and its Consequences*, Third Report (London, HMSO, 6 July 1995) pp. 31–51 paras 65–124. Quoted from Laurie, G. T. (2002) *Genetic Privacy: A Challenge to Medico-Legal Norms* (Cambridge University Press) at 87.
4 Greely, H. T. (1999) 'Iceland's Plan for Genomics Research: Facts and Implications', *Jurimetrics*, vol. 40, no. 2, pp. 153–92 at 157.
5 Brownsword, R. (2003) 'An Interest in Human Dignity as the Basis for Genomic Torts', *Washburn Law Journal*, vol. 42, pp. 413–87. Also see Caulfield, T. and Brownsword, R. (2006) 'Human Dignity: A Guide to Policy Making in the Biotechnology Era?', *Nature Reviews: Genetics*, vol. 7, pp. 72–76.
6 Ginsburg, D. H. (1999) 'Genetics and Privacy', *Texas Review of Law and Politics*, vol. 4, pp. 17–23. Also see Laurie, G. T. (2002) *Genetic Privacy: A Challenge to Medico-Legal Norms* (Cambridge University Press).
7 Smith, M. J. (2001) 'Population-based Genetic Studies: Informed Consent and Confidentiality', *Santa Clara Computer and High Technology Law Journal*, vol. 18, pp. 57–93. Also see Lawton, A. (1997) 'Regulating Genetic Destiny: A Comparative Study of Legal Constraints in Europe and the United States', *Emory International Law Review*, vol. 11, pp. 365–418.
8 Gold, E. R. and Caulfield, T. A. (2003) *Human Genetic Inventions, Patenting and Human Rights* (Health Law Institute of University of Alberta).
9 Spaak, T. (2006) 'Genetic Discrimination', *Minnesota Journal of Law, Science & Technology*, vol. 7, pp. 639–55. Also see Hellman, D. (2003) 'What Makes Genetic Discrimination exceptional?', *American Journal of Law and Medicine*, vol. 29, pp. 77–116. Also see Jungreis, R.

The narrow definition of HPGR focuses on community/group collective human genetic information, such as the Human Genome Diversity Project (HGDP).[10] According to international consensus, population genetic research aims to understand the nature and extent of genetic variation among a population or individuals within a group or between individuals across different groups.[11] This is the common understanding of human population genetic research and is the aspect that will be considered in this discussion. This type of HPGR focuses on a certain population, normally an isolated one. Studies such as the HGDP belong to this type of HPGR. The research object of this kind of HPGR is the third type of genetic information referred to above; that is, community or group collective human genetic information that is able to determine variation that could lead to knowledge about genetic disorders and possible cures, as well as the origin and migration patterns of peoples. In other words, unlike general HPGR, which emphasises the basic genetic equality of humans, the narrow HPGR project is directed at discovering DNA polymorphisms, emphasising the genetic difference between human groups.[12]

For example, the HGDP, proposed in 1991, is a collaborative research project that is being developed on a global basis under the auspices of the Human Genome Organisation. The 'Summary Document of the Human Genome Diversity Project', which is the official report of the HGDP International Planning Workshop, describes the project as follows:

> The overall goal of the project is to arrive at a much more precise definition of the origins of different world populations by integrating genetic knowledge, derived by applying the new techniques for studying genes, with knowledge of history, anthropology and language. More specifically the aims are: To investigate the variation occurring in the human genome by studying samples collected from populations that are representative of all of the world's peoples, and, ultimately, to create a resource for the

(2007) 'Fearing the Fear Itself: The Proposed Genetic Information Nondiscrimination Act of 2005 and Public Fears about Genetic Information', *Journal of Law and Policy*, vol. 15, pp. 221–47.

10 The Human Genome Diversity Project (HGDP) was started by Stanford University's Morrison Institute and a collaboration of scientists around the world. It is an international project that seeks to understand the diversity and unity of the entire human species. The official website of the HDGP is http://hsblogs.stanford.edu/morrison/human-genome-diversity-project/ (last visited 4 July 2013).

11 This definition stems from the United Nations Educational, Scientific and Cultural Organization's 'Bioethics and Human Population Genetics Research' (1995). It sometimes also is called 'population-based genetic research/study' or 'population genomic research/study'.

12 Sleeboom-Faulkner, M. (2006) 'How to Define a Population: Cultural Politics and Population Genetics in the People's Republic of China and the Republic of China', *BioSocieties*, vol. 1, pp. 399–419 at 401–2.

benefit of all humanity and for the scientific community worldwide. The resource will exist as a collection of biological samples that represents the genetic variation in human populations worldwide and also as an open, long-term, genetic and statistical database on variation in the human species that will accumulate as the biological samples are studied by scientists from around the world.[13]

The HGDP, which targets genes from certain populations, especially isolated and indigenous ones which are unusually homogenous, made genetic and medical research easier and genes from such populations were considered valuable. In 1991, one of HGDP's initiators, Cavalli-Sforza, highlighted the importance of genetic research on these populations:

> Isolated human populations contain much more informative genetic records than more recent, urban ones. Such isolated human populations are being rapidly merged with their neighbors, however, destroying irrevocably the information needed to reconstruct our evolutionary history. Population growth, famine, war, and improvements in transportation and communication are encroaching on once stable populations. It would be tragically ironic if, during the same decade that biological tools for understanding our species were created, major opportunities for applying them were squandered.[14]

The 'Summary Document of Human Genome Diversity Project' describes the values of the HGDP as follows:

> 1 The main value of the HGD Project lies in its enormous potential for illuminating our understanding of human history and identity. 2 The resource created by the HGD Project will also provide valuable information on the role played by genetic factors in the predisposition or resistance to disease. 3 The HGD Project will bring together people from many countries and disciplines. The work of geneticists will be linked in an unprecedented way with that of anthropologists, archaeologists, biologists, linguists and historians, creating a unique bridge between science and the humanities. 4 By leading to a greater understanding of the nature of differences between individuals and between human populations, the HGD Project will help to combat the widespread popular fear

---

13 Summary Document of Human Genome Diversity Project, full text can be seen on the official website of the HGDP, available at http://hsblogs.stanford.edu/morrison/files/2011/03/Alghero.pdf (last visited 5 July 2013).
14 Cavalli-Sforza, L., Wilson, A. C., Cantor, C. R., Cook-Deegan, R. M. and King, M. C. (1991) 'Call for a Worldwide Survey of Human Genetic Diversity: A Vanishing Opportunity for the Human Genome Project', *Genomics*, vol. 11, p. 490.

and ignorance of human genetics and will make a significant contribution to the elimination of racism.[15]

Therefore, HPGR, such as the HGDP, has become an important type of human genetic research which may result in great benefits.

Concerns about human population genetic research

HPGR on target groups on the one hand 'can generate valuable knowledge about genetic disorders, possible cures, and the origin and migration patterns of distinctive peoples'.[16] On the other hand, it also may 'pose distinctive risks and disadvantages for targeted groups and may even resurrect now-discredited "scientific" theories of race and human capacity'.[17]

It has therefore inspired a debate between proponents who argue that research on certain groups, especially isolated groups, should be vigorously advocated to gain more knowledge about the origins of human life,[18] and opponents of such research, who argue that results of such research could be seen as 'scientific' proof to support several types of discrimination and which may pose significant risks for the target groups.[19]

In the context of HPGR, the real research target is not individual human genetic information, but community or group collective human genetic information. Nevertheless, this type of genetic information must be sourced from individual members of a particular group or community. Not only does a member of the group or community have a personal interest in the use of the information resulting from his or her involvement, so too does the group or community as a whole. This is entirely different from the traditional Western approach to the control of information, which generally vests in the person to whom the information belongs, or to whom it relates.[20] The traditional core value of Western ethics and law has been 'the rights of the individual to determine for herself the course of her life, with minimal interference by others'.[21] However, community or group collective human genetic information relates not only to the person from whom it is derived, but also to the whole community or group.

15 See note 13.
16 Tsosie, R. and McGregor, J. L. (2007) 'Genome Justice: Genetics and Group Rights', *Journal of Law, Medicine & Ethics*, vol. 35, no. 3, p. 352.
17 ibid.
18 See note 14.
19 Weijer, C. (1999) 'Protecting Communities in Research: Philosophical and Pragmatic Challenges', *Cambridge Quarterly of Healthcare Ethics*, vol. 8, pp. 501–13 at 502.
20 Laurie, G. (2002) *Genetic Privacy: a Challenge to Medico-Legal Norms* (Cambridge University Press) at 93.
21 ibid.

As McGregor has said: 'given the public's view about the power of genetics, genetic research has many risks associated with it'.[22] She argued that the disclosure of negative information or research results of HPGR could lead to risks of harm to the group as a whole, both externally and internally.[23] While these concepts of external and internal harm will be explored in greater detail later in this work, for the moment it can be noted that external harms may arise where there is the possibility of exposing a community or group to stereotyping and/or stigmatisation, including damaging effects on employment and insurance opportunities. It has been argued that HPGR may also lead to potential internal harms to target group, which would include effects upon group members' perceptions of the group. For example, Tsosie identified 'cultural harms' as the violation of groups' rights to their own culture in the context of HPGR.[24]

Genetic research which focuses on population groups in the Western world has raised concerns about protection of group rights or community rights. In the 1990s, a research project on the genetics of cancer in Ashkenazi Jews illustrated the problem well:

> Streuwing and colleagues reported work on the frequency in Ashkenazi Jews of one particular mutation (185delAG) in the BRCA1 gene associated with a high risk of developing breast and ovarian cancer. Samples for the project were collected from databanks established for Tay-Sachs disease and cystic fibrosis screening. Since identifying information was removed from all samples, the NIH Office of Human Subjects Review did not require individual informed consent. The investigators found that 0.9% of Ashkenazi Jews carry the mutation, a much higher rate than in the general population.[25]

In this project, all of the DNA samples were collected without any personal identifying information, which is to say that the DNA samples were analysed anonymously. Thus, except for any physical harm which might be caused by the collection procedures, there were no direct risks to individuals who participated in these projects, even in respect of discrimination or stigmatisation. However, the community may be put at risk. The results of these studies could generate a substantial negative influence on the whole community of Ashkenazi Jews, and have repercussions not only for individuals whose

22 McGregor, J. L. (2007) 'Population Genomics and Research Ethics with Socially Identifiable Groups', *Journal of Law, Medicine and Ethics*, vol. 35, pp. 356–70 at 362.

23 ibid.

24 Tsosie, R. (2007) 'Cultural Challenges to Biotechnology: Native American Genetic Resources and the Concept of Cultural Harm', *Journal of Law, Medicine & Ethics*, vol. 35, no. 3, pp. 396–411.

25 ibid.

genetic information was used but also for those whose personal information was not used. As Lehrman noted with concern:

> Such findings, which have already led to Jewish groups being targeted as a potential market for commercial genetic tests, could create the perception that Jewish people are unusually susceptible to disease ... As a result ... anyone with a Jewish-sounding name could face discrimination in insurance and employment as companies struggle to keep down health-care costs.[26]

Owing to the possibility of discrimination, US Jewish leaders asked the National Human Genome Research Institute to discuss developing guidelines for the conduct of genetic research on Ashkenazi Jews.[27] Another example is that of the Nuu-chah-nulth people of Vancouver Island, Canada, who were shocked to learn that the genetic samples they had given to a researcher in the early 1980s to discover the genetic cause of rheumatoid arthritis were shared with many researchers and used for purposes beyond those to which the tribe had consented.[28] The research uncovered the spread of lymphotropic viruses by intravenous drug use. That discovery imposed risks on the group as a whole, stigmatising the group and altering the perception of the group about itself.

Thus, although human genetic information is not entirely different from other types of information in respect of human beings, in the context of HPGR, community or group collective human genetic information is arguably unique, and the interests of the community or group require special consideration in bioethics and legal regulation. The uniqueness of community or group collective human genetic information is that it can be gained from individual members, but in conjunction with results obtained from others may reveal information about a particular group or community.

Potential risks of harm of HPGR

Many of the risks of harm that may be caused by HPGR seem to be similar to those raised by general genetic research, since they are also related to the disclosure of negative information or research results rather than physical harms. However, the issues arising from HPGR have some differences too. HPGR, as with the HGDP, 'provides no information on individual phenotypes – the only information provided about each sample is the population name, its geographical location in degrees of latitude and longitude, and the

---

26 Lehrman, S. (1997) 'Jewish leaders seek genetic guidelines', *Nature*, vol. 389 at 322.
27 ibid.
28 Dalton, R. 'Tribe Blasts "Exploitation" of Blood Samples', available at http://www.nature.com/nature/journal/v420/n6912/full/420111a.html (last visited 4 July 2013).

sex of each individual'.[29] This means that the information collected by HPGR will not lead to risks of harm to individual participants in exactly the same way as other types of genetic research might, since the information sought in HPGR is not individual, subject-identifiable information. The target genetic information of HPGR is group or community collective genetic information, which is carried by individuals in the target group. However, the collective genetic information of the target group is the result of thousands of years of evolution; thus, the interests affected by research into it cannot be seen as a matter relating solely to individuals, even though it relies on samples taken from individual members. Rather, some scholars have argued that group or community collective genetic information relates to the interests of the whole group. For example, McGregor has pointed out that there are two types of harms that may be caused by research: tangible harms and dignitary harms. Both of them can be suffered by either the individual or the group.[30] According to her, tangible harms to 'a group include stereotyping or stigmatizing which can result in loss of social, political, or economic opportunities',[31] while dignitary harms to a group 'undermine the value and worth of the group in the eyes of others and the group itself',[32] which may include 'disrespectful or humiliating treatment of the group or community, or treating them as less than or subordinate to others'.[33] The disclosure of negative information or research results of HPGR could lead to risks of harm to the group as a whole, both externally and internally. Some examples of external and internal harms were briefly noted in the introduction but this issue will be explored further here.

External harms

Abuse of group or community genetic information might threaten national security and the survival of certain groups or communities. For example, there was a theory that severe acute respiratory syndrome (SARS), of which there was an outbreak in the People's Republic of China (PRC) in the spring of 2003, might have been a man-made biological weapon, because 'there is no vaccine for this virus, its make-up is unclear, it has not been very widespread and the population is not immune to it'.[34] Although there was no clear evidence to support this view, it raised the issue of concerns about population targeted bio-weapons based on population genetic research. In developing this type of

---

29 Cavalli-Sforza, L. (2005) 'The Human Genome Diversity Project: Past, Present and Future', *Nature Reviews: Genetics*, vol. 6, pp. 333–40 at 335.
30 See note 22 at 363.
31 ibid.
32 ibid.
33 ibid.
34 'Sars Biological Weapon?', *News 24* website, available at http://www.news24.com/World/News/Sars-biological-weapon-20030411 (last visited 4 July 2013).

bio-weapon, scientists would try to exploit medical advances by identifying distinctive genes carried by the target population, and then create a genetically modified bacterium or virus. The distinctive genes carried by certain populations is the exact research target of HPGR; thus, the abuse of genetic samples collected by HPGR or the inappropriate disclosure of HPGR results could perhaps lead to this kind of devastating consequence. Imagine that there is a HPGR project involving a Chinese ethnic minority – Miao nationality – which currently has a population of more than 7 million. The group's collective genetic information is disclosed to scientists who use that information to produce a kind of virus or bacterium which is more likely to infect and harm Miao people. The development of this biological profile is based on HPGR, which revealed the unique predisposition of Miao people. If this kind of virus or bacterium is hard to destroy or protect against and the effects cannot easily be treated, the survival of the Miao nationality would be seriously threatened. The risk of harm, which might be caused by abuse of the research results of HPGR or inappropriate disclosure of the group's collective genetic information, is relevant to the interests of the whole group, even the security of a whole country. Thus, the concerns about the risk of harms that may be caused by HPGR cannot simply be equated to those that may arise in other biomedical research involving individual human subjects. Although this type of bio-weapon targeted on a certain population is alarming, some would argue that this is an unrealistic scenario. However, there have been reports that this type of bio-weapon may become a reality. For example, in a front-page report in the London *Sunday Times* of 15 November 1998, the newspaper stated that:

> Israel is working on a biological weapon that would harm Arabs but not Jews, according to Israeli military and Western intelligence sources. The weapon, targeting victims by ethnic origin, is seen as Israel's response to Iraq's threat of chemical and biological attacks.[35]

According to the article, this secret Israeli programme was based on research targeted on a small town southeast of Tel Aviv, conducted by the Institute for Biological Research in Nes Tsiona, which is the main research facility for Israel's clandestine arsenal of chemical and biological weapons.[36] Despite this, there is no clear evidence to support the existence of genetic based types of bio-weapons at present. However, if they were to be developed, this type of bio-weapon could be a serious threat to national security and national population survival, since it would kill or harm some parts of the population but not others.

Perhaps more likely, however, is the possibility that HPGR can expose a whole community or group and all of its members to stigmatisation.

35 Mahnaimi, U. and Colvin, M. 'Israel Planning "Ethnic" Bomb as Saddam Caves In', *The Sunday Times* (15 November 1998).
36 ibid.

Stigmatisation of certain groups could include claims that a certain population is prone to particular diseases, such as schizophrenia, or behavioural problems, such as alcoholism. The public's views of genetic determinism and reductionism could exacerbate this discrimination. If a HPGR result revealed that Miao nationality people have a genetic disposition for alcoholism, for example, each member of the Miao might face the risk of higher automobile liability insurance premiums than other people, based on the perceived risk of higher numbers of car accidents as a result of the misuse of alcohol. As opposed to genetic testing of an individual in medical research, which may have a negative effect on the individual and possibly his or her family members, the potential risks of harm in HPGR could affect a broader range of people. Further, the discrimination caused by individual genetic research is often relevant to inappropriate disclosure of or access to the individual's and his or her family members' personal information or privacy. These risks of harm in this kind of research can be regulated by personal data protection regulations which protect the confidentiality and privacy of individual genetic information. What is more, some kinds of genetic research can be conducted anonymously and disclosure of genetic research results could also avoid the disclosure of personal identities of human subjects. However, HPGR aims to identify information about a specific human population; thus, it cannot avoid disclosing information about a specific group or community and the HPGR result may lead to negative effects for the target group. This disclosure would be likely to be a part of any report of the scientific research findings, which is the normal outcome of scientific research, even though these research findings could be the basis of discrimination against a whole group.

There are other derivative negative effects on the group as a whole that may be caused by HPGR. For example, negative effects could include economic ones: 'downgrading the group or community's bond rating, making it more expensive to borrow money'.[37] Legal and political claims can also be threatened. In the PRC, for example, there are some special benefit policies and special legislation for ethnic minorities, which might be threatened if, for instance, HPGR proves that the target group is not in fact related historically or geographically. One could also imagine claims that ethnic minorities are not really ethnic minorities at all, since their origins can be traced to alternative ancestries than those that had been previously believed to be the case.

Internal harms

Internal harms are the potential risks of harm which may occur inside the target groups of HPGR. They include the group's self-conception of genetic determinism and self-stigmatisation. For example: 'we Jews are defective because our genes make us prone to cancer' and/or 'we American Indians are

37 See note 30.

defective because our genes make us prone to alcoholism'.[38] Given that psychosocial stress and the disruption of family life are recognised and widely accepted by researchers as harms[39] and are regarded as legitimate risks to be considered and minimised by institutional review boards (IRBs) in some countries,[40] consistency dictates that community or group stress and the disruption of a group or community's constitution or core culture should also be treated as significant research-related harms in the context of HPGR, since target groups of HPGR almost always have their own unique cultural sensitivities. The powerful identification of individual members with their group also means that group harms can have significant individual effects.

In order to discuss group internal harms, it is significant at the outset to make clear what a group is. What constitutes a group is not only problematic in the context of HPGR, but also in the recognition of group entities and interests by law. Although conceptually uncertain, it is evident that local, state and national political entities, religious groups, cultural groups, corporate groups, minority groups, indigenous and tribal groups, and a myriad of others have distinctly recognised and protected interests in law.[41]

'Group' is a common term that occurs frequently in legal publications. In fact, like many other common terms, such as dignity and rights, there is no consensus on what constitutes a group even in the context of international law, although several studies have attempted to define it and use various terms to describe it, such as 'people', 'community', 'communality', 'social group' – and the most prevalent one – 'minority'.[42]

There is a related definition of what constitutes a 'people'. The following definition was provided by experts of the United Nations Education, Scientific and Cultural Organization (UNESCO) in 1990:

A group for the rights of peoples in international law, including the right to self-determination, has the following characteristics:

1. A group of individual human beings who enjoy some or all of the following common features: (a) a common historical tradition; (b) racial or ethnical identity; (c) cultural homogeneity; (d) linguistic unity; (e) religious or ideological affinity; (f) territorial connection; (g) common economic life.

38 ibid.
39 See note 20.
40 NIH Office of Protection from Research Risks (1993) 'Human Genetic Research' in *Protecting Human Research Subjects: Institutional Review Board Guidebook* (US Government Printing Office, Washington D.C.).
41 Underkuffler, L. S. (2007) 'Human Genetics Studies: The Case for Group Rights', *Journal of Law, Medicine and Ethics*, vol. 35, pp. 383–95 at 386.
42 Goldman, O. Q. (1994) 'Need for an Independent International Mechanism to Protect Group Rights: A Case Study of the Kurds', *Tulsa Journal of Comparative and International Law*, vol. 2, pp. 45–89 at 47.

2. The group must be of a certain number who need not be large (e.g., the people of micro state), but must be more than a mere association of individuals within a state.
3. The group as a whole must have the will to be identified as a people or the consciousness of being a people – allowing that groups or some members of such group, though sharing the foregoing characteristics, may not have the will or consciousness.
4. Possibly, the group must have institutions or other means of expressing its common characteristics and will for identity.[43]

Another related concept is 'minority group'. The most widely accepted definition of a minority group is 'a group which is numerically inferior to the rest of the population of a state and in a non-dominant position, whose members possess ethnic, religious or linguistic characteristics which differ from those of the rest of the population and who, if only implicitly, maintain a sense of solidarity, directed towards preserving their culture, traditions, religion or language'.[44]

Although the terms 'people' and 'minority' are closely related to group, 'minority' emphasises their political situation, while 'people' focuses more on the social situation of a group.

Other theorists also provide explanations as to what is a group in particular contexts. For example, Thomas Pogge argued that an ethnic group has the following three features: the members of this group must identify themselves as descendants of members of a historical society, which is a broad concept of society, including tribes, principalities and others; this group has a unified culture, or partial culture, among which its members can be connected, through a continuous history; and the group must contain most of the persons who, within the relevant state, are taken to share the group's descent and culture.[45] Natan Lerner, in an analysis of group recognition in international law, stressed the purposes and goals of the group, the connections and distinctions between the group and other relative groups, the history and permanence of the group, the naturalness or spontaneity of the group, and the voluntariness of group membership.[46] There are other definitions of a group,

---

43 UNESCO Meeting of Experts on Future Study of the Rights of Peoples (Paris, February 1990).
44 This definition is provided by Francesco Capotorti, a Special Rapporteur of the United Nations Sub-Commission on Prevention of Discrimination and Protection of Minorities, available at http://oppenheimer.mcgill.ca/IMG/pdf/definitions_droit_des_minorites_ethniques.pdf (last visited 4 July 2013).
45 Pogge, T. (1997) 'Group Rights and Ethnicity' in *Ethnicity and Group Rights: Nomos XXXIX*, I. Shapiro and W. Kymlicka, eds. (New York University Press, New York) pp. 187–221 at 193–94.
46 Lerner, N. (2003) *Group Rights and Discrimination in International Law* (The Hague: Kluwer Law International) at 36.

too, which focus on shared normative understandings, the importance of the group to personal identity, and whether the wellbeing of group members is at least in part determined by group wellbeing.[47]

These definitions all reflect some features of a group, but none of them has been universally accepted as an explanation to make it clear what a group is. However, through all those efforts, scholars and legal practitioners have developed two widely accepted criteria for defining a group; one of which is subjective while the other is objective. The subjective criterion is the group and its members' self-perception of the group's distinctiveness, and the desire of the individual members of the group to identify themselves as a group. The objective criterion is the existence of objective characteristics which distinguish the group from the remainder of the population, such as history, geography, ethnicity, economics, language and religion. It is important to keep in mind that neither of these two criteria is sufficient on its own to constitute a group. Only if a group fulfils both of these two criteria can it be seen as an independent group.[48]

If something leads to negative effects on members of a group, this could also cause harm to the constitution of the group itself. In this situation, the interest of the group as a whole would also be harmed, not only its individual members. Some scholars have argued that 'the most common and damaging risk of harm to communities is community disruption', and in respect of genetic research, that 'the disruption is usually at the stage of publication and release of the research results or secondary use of existing specimens'.[49] HPGR is just this kind of research which may cause intra-group harms to the target group. For example, HPGR specific to an ethnic minority in the PRC might prove that this group has no genetic difference from other Chinese people. This result may lead the group members to reassess their origins and relationships to one another. This may threaten 'group members' self-identity and the identity of the group as a whole, as well as causing cultural harms to spiritual traditions and to their sense of who they are and where they are from, all of which upset their historical narrative'.[50] Some HPGR, such as that looking into migration pattern research, can also challenge or disrupt a group's cultural or spiritual values. For example, the cultural narratives of Miao nationality people in the PRC say that they are the descendants of a butterfly and a bubble; thus Miao people believe that they are distinct from other people. The HPGR's result might, however, show that they have no essential biologically based distinction from other people. Under current

---

47 See note 41 at 386.
48 See note 42 at 46–47.
49 Freeman, W. L. and Romero, F. C., 'Community Consultation to Identify Group Risk' in R. J. Amdur and E. A. Bankert, eds., *Institutional Review Board: Management and Function* (Sudbury, MA: Jones and Bartlett Publishers, 2005). Quoted from note 37 at 363.
50 See note 30.

research guidelines, this type of risk of harm would not even need to be disclosed to the individual human subjects. This means that the target group and its members could suffer risks of harm to which they have not consented; indeed, the risk has not even been disclosed to them.

Since HPGR aims to discover variation that could lead to knowledge about genetic disorders, possible cures and the origin and migration patterns of target groups, the results of HPGR may challenge or disparage target groups' spiritual traditions, historical narratives or traditional beliefs, which can be defined as cultural harms. Rebecca Tsosie, as noted earlier, defined 'cultural harms' as the violation of groups' rights to their own culture.[51] Her definition was based on the theory of Avishai Margalit and Halbertal Moshe[52] on culture, which defined culture as the 'material, spiritual, and artistic expression of a group that defines itself',[53] and maintains that 'human beings have a right to culture – not just any culture, but their own'.[54] The target groups of HPGR are almost all ethnic minorities or isolated groups in rural areas of developing countries. Their rights to their own culture, including a comprehensive way of life by which a group defines itself, have been accepted in international human rights law. For example, Article 27 of the International Covenant on Civil and Political Rights (ICCPR) reads as follows:

> In those States in which ethnic, religious or linguistic minorities exist, persons belonging to such minorities shall not be denied the right, in community with other members of their group, to enjoy their culture, to profess and practice their own religion, or to use their own language.[55]

HPGR results, for example, those that provide evidence that an historical spiritual leader of a certain group does not genetically belong to that group, could lead to cultural harms. In addition, the result of HPGR as scientific proof to challenge group identity and group members' self-understanding could also be defined as causing cultural harms. The group members' self-consciousness is crucial to a group's coherence. HPGR results which question the historical narratives of the target group may decrease group

---

51 See note 24.
52 Margalit, A. and Moshe, H. (1994) 'Liberalism and the Right to Culture', *Social Research*, vol. 61, no. 3, pp. 491–510.
53 ibid at 497–98.
54 ibid at 499.
55 International Covenant on Civil and Political Rights, adopted and opened for signature, ratification and accession by General Assembly resolution 2200A (XXI) of 16 December 1966, entry into force 23 March 1976. The full text is available on the official website of the Office of the High Commissioner of Human Rights, available at http://treaties.un.org/doc/Publication/UNTS/Volume%20999/volume-999-I-14668-English.pdf (last visited 5 July 2013).

members' belief and pride in the group tradition and culture, which can also lead to negative effects on the group's cultural rights.

Some scholars have argued that cultural harm, such as undermining a group's beliefs about its origins, is not a real risk which needs to be disclosed in the research protocol and when seeking consent; therefore, the risks of cultural harms caused by HPGR should equally not be taken into account. For example, Reilly said that:

> Should a potential subject be warned that one or more findings may challenge his religious beliefs? This strikes me as beyond the appropriate boundaries of the duty to warn, for it suggests that scientists must censor their inquiries if conducted in the shadow of religion. When Galileo trained his telescope on the heavens and saw four moons orbiting Jupiter, he set in motion forces that would destroy the narratives built around a geocentric universe – no doubt upsetting the world views of a lot of people.[56]

This example is inappropriate, however, in the context of HPGR. Admittedly, in general, scientific research does not need to take into account existing ideology and public beliefs. However, this argument cannot apply to HPGR, which is specifically conducted on certain groups. HPGR needs the target group and its members to participate voluntarily. If the research results may cause one of the potential risks that could challenge the common group belief, such as the narrative origins of the group, I would argue that the group and its members do have the right to be informed of that risk before deciding on whether or not to participate. If the target group and its members decide not to participate in this research, this potential risk, which is specific to them, would not arise.

In summary, HPGR could lead to additional risks of harm, which is group harm, other than those raised by other genetic research. All of the international declarations and ethical guidelines on research involving human subjects have noted that the welfare of the individual research subject must take precedence over all other interests. It needs to be highlighted that the welfare of target groups in HPGR should also be considered.

The application of human subject protection to HPGR

The application of consent to HPGR

In 1914, in the US, Justice Cardozo argued that '[e]very human being of adult years and sound mind has a right to determine what shall be done with

---

56 Reilly, P. R. (1998) 'Rethinking Risks to Human Subjects in Genetic Research', *American Journal of Human Genetics*, vol. 63, pp. 682–85 at 684.

his [or her] own body'.[57] This influential statement paved the way for the development of the importance of individual autonomy and consent in the medical setting. The primary legal and ethical considerations in biomedical research have traditionally revolved around the individual subject, ranging from issues as to how a piece of research will affect a human subject to whether the human subject will have the opportunity to provide voluntary and sufficiently informed consent. In brief, given the competence of the human subject to give a valid consent, consent is a two-step process in biomedical research: first, researchers present appropriate information to the human subject; secondly, the human subject is free either to agree or refuse to participate in a given biomedical research project, based upon this information disclosure.

As we have seen, HPGR is research on specific groups which can generate valuable knowledge. As has been discussed above, the acceptability of non-therapeutic research without direct and immediate benefits to participants has historically been based on a requirement that the research subject consents to exposure to risks of harm which may be caused by the research, with full disclosure of relevant information to enable him or her to make a decision on whether or not to participate. Consent is also important in HPGR. However, the application of the current approach to consent to participation in biomedical research to the specific context of HPGR is problematic.

Under the ethical justification of respect for individual autonomy, in non-therapeutic research the subject who may suffer harm caused by the research should make the decision as to whether or not to participate. In most other biomedical research, the potential risks of harm would be posed to the individual human subject, so again the human subject would make the decision on research participation, based on the consideration of his or her own interests. Thus, in these types of research, under current research guidelines, the simple consent of individual human subjects based on the consideration of their own interests is ethically and legally justifiable.

In HPGR, the research objective is obtaining the collective genetic information shared by members of a target group. Therefore, it could be argued that the target group or community of HPGR is the research subject of HPGR, and it is the group which should make the decision on whether or not participate. However, the current dominant ethical principle of 'respect for persons' is secured through individual consent. The moral basis of consent as currently understood in law is an individualised model of autonomy. This means that current research protections are not aimed at protecting populations, communities, groups, or other possible third party victims.

---

57 *Schloendorff v Soc'y of N.Y. Hosp.*, 105 N.E. 92, 93 (N.Y. 1914), abrogated on other grounds by *Bing v Thunig*, 143 N.E.2d 3 (N.Y. 1957).

In addition, the uniqueness of genetic information is that the genetic samples obtained from human genetic research subjects contain not only his or her genetic information, but also genetic information about his or her blood relatives, and even potentially genetic information about the group of which he or she is a member. However, HPGR, which targets specific groups, can be conducted with the participation of only some of the members of the group. Nonetheless, the potential risk of harm could be created for every member of the target group, and even the group itself.

Thus, the individual human subject has no overwhelming superior moral justification to give consent to participate in HPGR than any other member of the group who may be affected, other than the fact that he or she must undergo the procedure upon his or her body to allow a blood sample to be taken. Individuals have no superior rights to consider issues concerning the welfare of the group, although they may wish to take them into account for themselves as part of the information process before giving consent to participate. The issue of information disclosure will be returned to later. However, for the moment, current ethical and legal frameworks of consent help support autonomy and self-determination, protect the vulnerable and promote the welfare and equality of human beings; but this focuses primarily on individual rights and does not always see individuals as part of wider social orders and community.[58] The application of current individualistic ethical frameworks of consent for medical research to HPGR is problematic.

Chapter 3 discussed the concept of relational autonomy as part of a reconsideration of the individualised Western idea of autonomy. It examined the idea that an individual's decision-making depended on his or her position within social networks. It argued that individuals may wish to take account not only of personal interests, but also the welfare of his or her group which could be influenced by the decision. Applying this relational autonomy model to HPGR would provide one means of greater protection of the interests of target group, as well as recognising the need for such issues to be considered as part of an individual's decision-making process. Based on the relational autonomy model, I will suggest that ways to incorporate this model might include two important developments: adding the risks of harm to the target group or community as a whole as one aspect of ethical review of the project, before seeking participants, and adding the risks of harm to the target group as a whole as relevant information that needs to be disclosed to potential participants. One further issue that arises is the need for cultural sensitivity.

58 Gostin, L. (1991) 'Ethical Principles for the Conduct of Human Subject Research: Population-Based Research and Ethics', *Journal of Law, Medicine and Ethics*, vol. 19, no. 3–4, pp. 191–201 at 191.

Adequacy of information disclosure

The rule of consent in the medical treatment context has a different purpose than it does in the biomedical research context. In general, because there might be a greater potential for harm in biomedical research, it may be considered that there must be more relevant information disclosed to the research subject than to a patient. Thus, many international declarations, ethical guidelines and national legislation on biomedical research provide a list of items of information that must be disclosed to the potential human subject. For example, the following are those elements of information considered relevant to the vast majority of research projects in US federal legislation:

> (1) A statement that the study involves research, an explanation of the purposes of the research, and the expected duration of the subject's participation, a description of the procedures to be followed, and iden- tification of any procedures which are experimental; (2) A description of any reasonably foreseeable risks or discomforts to the subject; (3) A description of any benefits to the subject or to others which may reason- ably be expected from the research; (4) A disclosure of appropriate alternative procedures or courses of treatment, if any, that might be advantageous to the subject; (5) A statement describing the extent, if any, to which confidentiality of records identifying the subject will be maintained; (6) For research involving more than minimal risk, an explanation as to whether any compensation and an explanation as to whether any medical treatments are available if injury occurs and, if so, what they may consist of, or where further information may be obtained; (7) An explanation of whom to contact for answers to perti- nent questions about the research and the research subject's rights, and whom to contact in the event of a research related injury to the subject; and (8) A statement that participation is voluntary, refusal to partici- pate will involve no penalty or loss of benefits to which the subject is otherwise entitled, and the subject may discontinue participation at any time without penalty or loss of benefits to which the subject is otherwise entitled.[59]

From this list of information that needs to be disclosed, it can be shown that existing legal regulations and ethical guidelines concentrate on immediate risks to individual research participants and do not explicitly require researchers to consider potential harms to non-participants.

---

59 Title 45 CFR § 46.116, Title 45 CFR (Code of Federal Regulations) Part 46, can be seen on the official website of the US Department of Health & Human Services, available at http://www.hhs.gov/ohrp/45CFRpt46faq.html (last visited 13 October 2010).

Nonetheless, HPGR is a good example of the argument that when research involving human subjects places non-participating members of specific groups or communities at risk, these potential harms should be considered by persons conducting, reviewing and participating in the research. Compared with other types of harm that research may cause, the risks of harm from HPGR are collective and could be suffered by all members of the group, not simply individual participants. For this reason, I would argue that potential researchers should demonstrate respect for the diverse social and cultural traditions of many communities and acknowledge that research findings can disrupt social relationships within and between communities. These considerations suggest that in order to protect certain groups or communities from HPGR-related harm, the scope of information disclosure should be expanded to risks at group level, not limited to the immediate risks to individual participants. Thus, the information disclosure requirements in existing legal regulations and ethical guidelines are inadequate in HPGR, since only potential risks of harm to individual participants would normally be disclosed, while risks of harm that may potentially be suffered by the target group as a whole are not required to be disclosed.

In fact, there are rare examples in Western genetic research which indicate that information disclosure concerning wider risks than those to participants themselves, under what might be considered a relational model of autonomy, would be appropriate. For example, a study of 30 women on the breast cancer BRCA1/2 mutation showed that the dilemma relevant to information disclosure on issues which may affect others, in this case female relatives, was not whether or not to inform participants of these kinds of factors, but how to tell them.[60] In this study, over 90 per cent of participants' intention to participate was in order to obtain information for their relatives. Hence, the authors concluded that 'we need to ground consent upon an ethic that takes into account the social nature of human beings'.[61] This example indicated that individual benefits or risks of harm are not the only factors which influence individual decision-making, especially in the context of genetic research. The interests of relatives or families may also be essential. In such cases, the potential interests of their relatives would be the determinative factor influencing their decision on whether or not to participate in certain kinds of genetic research. Although this example related to the issues of families in genetic research, it may be reasonable to require researchers to provide information about potential effects on a group of other people as well as the participants; it would enable potential participants to consider such issues as part of their own risk-benefit analysis before they are asked to consent.

60 Hallowell, N., Foster, C., Eeles, R., Ardern-Jones, A., Murday, V. and Watson, M. (2003) 'Balancing Autonomy and Responsibility: The Ethics of Generating and Disclosing Genetic Information', *Journal of Medical Ethics*, vol. 29, no. 2, pp. 74–79.
61 ibid at 78.

The interests which should be considered in consent

Since the research target groups or populations of HPGR are usually ethnic minorities or isolated groups in rural areas in developing countries, in some of these groups or populations, such as in the PRC, the understanding of the nature of a person may be in line 'with more relational definitions of the person found in other societies ... which stress the embeddedness of the individual within society and define a person by his or her relations to others'.[62] In these areas, where the notion of persons as individuals is not dominant, the individual consent process may not be suitable, and there may be a need to widen the focus from the individual to the family or to the community, and to accept that their involvement may be a cultural expectation. For example, in India and West Africa, great respect and deference may be given to clinicians, healers and elders.[63] Clinton also indicates that:

> ... Indians and many non-Westerners, often have a very different view of the nature of their rights and legal relationships... human beings are born into a closely linked and integrated network of family, kinship, social and political relations. One's clan, kinship, and family identities are part of one's personal identity and one's rights and responsibilities exist only within the framework of such ... networks.[64]

The model of relational autonomy also concluded that individual decisions might be influenced by external considerations, without such influences necessarily amounting to improper, or undue, influence. In addition, the cultural sensitivities of some developing countries are also conducive to the adoption of relational autonomy. HPGR projects are almost always conducted on target groups from isolated rural areas of developing countries, where cultural ideologies are different from Western ones. For example, in a traditional Chinese group or community, the group or community is the background to personal acts and decisions. When facing decision-making issues relevant to group collective interests, it may be a cultural expectation that individual members of target group for HPGR would wish to rely on the opinion of group or community leaders, or group or community leaders would make the final decision directly. Although it is not argued in this

---

62 Christakis, N. A. (1988) 'The Ethical Design of an AIDS Vaccine Trial in Africa', *The Hastings Center Report*, vol. 18, no. 3, pp. 31–37 at 34.

63 ibid; Xu, X., Yang, J., Chen, C., Wang, B., Jin, Y., Fang, Z., Wang, X. and Weiss, S. T. (1999) 'Familial Aggregation of Pulmonary Function in a Rural Chinese Community', *American Journal of Respiratory and Critical Care Medicine*, vol. 160, no. 6, pp. 1928–33.

64 Clinton, R. N. (1990) 'Rights of Indigenous Peoples as Collective Group Rights', *Arizona Law Review*, vol. 32, no. 4, pp. 739–48 at 742.

discussion that a group member should be compelled to participate in HPGR if approval of the research was given by a group leader, or that individual consent should not be sought from potential participants, what is at issue here is the need for respect for cultural sensitivity to enable the involvement of others than participants in decision-making and consideration of the welfare of those in the group who are not actively participating. In this respect, HPGR participation would be considered as a group collective affair or a collective interest. Thus, cultural sensitivities would also be an important factor to be considered in HPGR. The issue of cultural sensitivities in HPGR will be discussed in more detail in Chapters 5 and 6.

In HPGR, adopting a relational autonomy model would be even more appropriate. Unlike the situation of most medical treatment which primarily has consequences for the individual, since the research target in HPGR is group collective genetic information, the main risks of harm would be group harms which may affect the group as a whole as well as each group member. A relational autonomy model, as has been discussed above, requires that the interests of all relevant parties should be considered in the decision-making process. Applying a relational autonomy model in HPGR would require researchers to disclose information about both individual risks and potential group harms posed by HPGR, because the interests of the group could be affected by the decision whether to participate, and whether or not target groups and other group members would be negatively affected could be a determinative factor to the decision-makers.

Accordingly, the current Western research ethical and legal frameworks of consent have not sufficiently addressed the harms that may be suffered by the target groups of HPGR. The individualistic frameworks can neither fit into the cultural sensitivities of target groups in HPGR from some developing countries, nor properly provide for disclosure of the main risks of harm that may be posed by HPGR. In HPGR, the relational autonomy-based consent model is superior to the highly individualised autonomy based consent model, particularly in developing countries like the PRC where collective decision-making is not uncommon.

Recently, some scholars have discussed group protection measures as supplements to individual informed consent.[65] They have argued that a group or community/population ought to have moral status in HPGR, especially in respect of research in developing countries, for the following reasons: (i) people do not view themselves atomistically, but as members of one or more communities that constitute their values and self-understanding; (ii) a variety of communities are already given the authority to make binding decisions on behalf of individual members on

---

65 Weijer, C. and Anderson, J. A. (2002) 'A Critical Appraisal of Protections for Aborginal Communities in Biomedical Research', *Jurimetrics*, vol. 42, pp. 187–98.

certain issues; and (iii) the primacy of the individual versus the community varies from one community to the next.[66] However, although there is a clear need for alternative models which include group consideration, it could be argued that there are concerns with models that take the group as the unit of ethical concern. It is arguable that it might be problematic to determine the boundaries of the group or community and to find a mechanism for balancing interests within a group. The most essential ethical issue here is whether or not 'individuals and their claims of right will be crushed beneath the greater weight of groups and their claims of right'.[67] Other scholars have argued that group consent is hard to obtain in practice. There are three main difficulties: (i) the extent of the affected parties' participation in decision-making; (ii) the identification of the parties whose consent should be sought if collective consent procedures were adopted; and (iii) the veto power problem: the possibility of a group veto power over individual decisions to participate or not would make collective consent extremely difficult to support.[68] The alternative to the ethical principle and rule of individualistic consent, such as 'respect for community' or 'group consent', will be discussed in detail in the next chapter. However, while supporting group and community involvement in reviewing HPGR, it needs to be emphasised that this discussion does not intend to substitute group consent for individual consent, but to supplement individual consent with additional considerations concerning the interests of the target group, based on the relational autonomy model.

The application of risk-benefit assessment to HPGR

Compared with clinical research, in most cases genetic research cannot produce direct and immediate benefits to human subjects. This characteristic is even more apparent in HPGR. Thus, in the risk-benefit analysis of HPGR, the risks of harm should be considered more carefully. It should not only consider the risks and potential harms to each member of the target group, but also the risks and potential harms to the group or community as a whole and all of its members.

Recognising that additional protections are needed in the research context, all of the international declarations and conventions, such as the Helsinki

---

66 ibid at 192–93.
67 Jones, P. (1999) 'Human Rights, Group Rights and Peoples' Rights', *Human Rights Quarterly*, vol. 21, no. 1, pp. 80–107 at 92.
68 Varelius, J. (2008) 'On the Prospects of Collective Informed Consent', *Journal of Applied Philosophy*, vol. 25, no. 1, pp. 35–44.

Declaration,[69] the CIOMS Guidelines,[70] as well as some national legislation, such as that in the US, require IRBs or research ethics committees (RECs) to ensure that research is conducted ethically and with the fully informed consent of the participants. IRBs or RECs provide the initial approval of the proposed research and then conduct a continuing review of the research to ensure ongoing compliance with institutional policies and procedures. Under the terms of the Helsinki Declaration, ethical review committees must 'take into consideration the laws and regulations of the country or countries in which the research is to be performed as well as applicable international norms and standards but these must not be allowed to reduce or eliminate any of the protections for research subjects set forth in this Declaration'.[71] Ethical review committees are responsible for reducing unnecessary risks for the participants in research and for guarding against the exploitation of those subjects. US federal common law also notes that the specific role of the IRBs is to assure the protection of research subjects and 'to ascertain the acceptability of proposed research in terms of institutional commitments and regulations, applicable law, and standards of professional conduct and practice'.[72] Thus, one of the core functions of RECs or IRBs is to review the potential risks of harm that may be caused by research to ensure that the interests of human subjects are protected.

However, considering the criteria for IRBs' or RECs' approval of biomedical research involving human subjects, the essential risks of harm that may be caused by HPGR may not be identified by them. For example, the US Common Rule noted that IRBs must ensure that:

> Risks to subjects are reasonable in relation to anticipated benefits, if any, to subjects, and the importance of the knowledge that may reasonably be

69 The WMA Declaration of Helsinki Ethical Principles for Medical Research Involving Human Subjects was adopted by the 18th WMA General Assembly, Helsinki, Finland, June 1964, and amended by the 29th WMA General Assembly, Tokyo, Japan, October 1975, 35th WMA General Assembly, Venice, Italy, October 1983, 41st WMA General Assembly, Hong Kong, September 1989, 48th WMA General Assembly, Somerset West, Republic of South Africa, October 1996 and the 52nd WMA General Assembly, Edinburgh, Scotland, October 2000, 53rd WMA General Assembly, Washington 2002 (Note of Clarification on paragraph 29 added), 55th WMA General Assembly, Tokyo 2004 (Note of Clarification on paragraph 30 added), 59th WMA General Assembly, Seoul, October 2008. The full text of the Helsinki Declaration can be seen on the official website of the World Medical Association (WMA) at http://www.wma.net/en/30publications/10policies/b3/index.html (last visited 4 July 2013).
70 The International Ethical Guidelines for Biomedical Research Involving Human Subjects were prepared by the Council for International Organizations of Medical Sciences (CIOMS) in collaboration with the WHO, Geneva, 2002. The full text of the CIOMS Guidelines can be seen on the official website of the World Health Organization (WHO) at http://whqlibdoc.who.int/emro/2004/9290213639_annex2.pdf (last visited 4 July 2013).
71 See note 69.
72 45 C.F.R. § 46.107(a) (2005).

expected to result. In evaluating risks and benefits, the IRB should consider only those risks and benefits that may result from the research (as distinguished from risks and benefits of therapies subjects would receive even if not participating in the research). *The IRB should not consider possible long-range effects of applying knowledge gained in the research (for example, the possible effects of the research on public policy) as among those research risks that fall within the purview of its responsibility.*[73] (emphasis added)

According to these criteria, IRBs are only requested to consider the risks of harm which can be clearly foreseen, and these are focused on individual participants. These types of risks might befall anyone: physical harms, hurts or injuries and psychological harms including pain and suffering. It might be suggested that IRB members will tend to identify the risks of harm they themselves might expect to experience if they were to take part in the proposed research. However, the target groups of HPGR are ethnic minorities and isolated groups in rural areas of developing countries. IRB members are almost always at a social and cultural distance from them; thus, they are not likely to have a cultural awareness of the target groups. Consequently, they are not likely to recognise the circumstances and traditions of these groups, so they may not be able appropriately to identify the possible and potential harms that may occur to certain groups correctly, especially internal or cultural harms.

Similar to the focus on individual autonomy in current ethical and legal guidelines on informed consent, with regard to welfare, the basic ethical principle of 'respect for persons' results in the concentration of IRBs and ethical review committees on individual human subjects. For example, the human subject in the US Common Rule is defined as 'a living individual about whom an investigator (whether professional or student) conducting research obtains data through intervention or interaction with the individual, or identifiable private information'.[74] Thus, according to this definition, the risks of harm IRBs need to consider are the risks of harm that individual participants may suffer. In the context of HPGR, existing ethical guidelines do not require an assessment of risks of group harm to be addressed in the ethical review process.

In fact, it is worth noting that a number of scholars have indicated their concerns about the interests of groups and communities in research ethics. For example, as far back as the National Bioethics Advisory Commission's (NBAC) first meeting, Emanuel argued that the three principles, 'respect for persons, beneficence, and justice' and their related guidelines do not

---

73 45 C.F.R. § 46.111(a)(2) (2005).
74 45 C.F.R. § 46.102(f).

adequately address the interests of communities.[75] Levine also argued that the Belmont Report overemphasised individual rights and failed to talk about the community. He noted:

> In each of its publications, it [the National Commission] seems to embrace an atomistic view of the person. The person is seen as a highly individualistic bearer of duties and rights; among his or her rights, some of the most important are to be left alone, not to be harmed, and to be treated with fairness. Except, perhaps, in its report on research involving children, there is little or no reference to persons in relationship to others or as members of communities.[76]

On the other hand, the consumerist movement swept America in the early 1970s and concern for individual rights was very much a part of the *zeitgeist*. The Belmont Report was undoubtedly also influenced by these larger societal forces. Nonetheless, the failure of the Belmont Report to deal adequately with families and communities does not, Levine argues, render it useless: 'Having said this, I do not think the Commission's recommendations are obsolete ... [I]t is usually quite appropriate to view investigator-subject relationships as relationships between strangers. Thus, in general an individualistic ethics is appropriate'.[77] Along with the development of biomedical science and technology, especially the prevalence of population genetics, the NBAC came to realise the need to protect groups or communities. For example, the NBAC's specific recommendation on stored human biological materials indicated that:

> Research using stored human biological materials, even when not potentially harmful to individuals from whom the samples are taken, may be potentially harmful to groups associated with the individual. To the extent such potential harms can be anticipated, investigators should to the extent possible plan their research so as to minimize such harm and should consult, when appropriate, representatives of the relevant groups regarding study design. In addition, when research on unlinked samples that poses a significant risk of group harms is otherwise eligible for exemption from IRB review, the exemption should not be granted if IRB review might help the investigator to design the study in such a way as to avoid those harms.[78]

75 Childress, J. F. (2000) 'Nuremberg's Legacy: Some Ethical Reflections', *Perspectives in Biology and Medicine*, vol. 43, pp. 347–61 at 356.

76 Levine, R. J. (1998) *Ethics and Regulation of Clinical Research* (2nd edn, Yale University Press) at 13.

77 Weijer, C. (1999) 'Protecting Communities in Research: Philosophical and Pragmatic Challenges', *Cambridge Quarterly of Healthcare Ethics*, vol. 8, pp. 501–13 at 503.

78 National Bioethics Advisory Commission, *Research Involving Human Biological Materials: Ethical Issues and Policy Guidance* (Rockville, Maryland, 1999) available at http://bioethics. georgetown.edu/nbac/hbm.pdf (last visited 4 July 2013).

This recommendation seems to indicate the NBAC's awareness of the possibility of specific research protocols posing a risk to a specific group, and its concern that, if this risk can be anticipated, it should be disclosed during the informed consent process. However, this has not been reflected in current ethical guidelines, such as the Declaration of Helsinki, nor in legal regulation. Nevertheless, HPGR may pose some risks of internal group harm, which are hard to recognise or identify by people who are outside the group. Thus, under current frameworks, similar risks posed to target groups in HPGR would very probably not be taken into account in the risk-benefit analysis of IRBs/RECs.

In summary, HPGR may lead to specific risks of harm to the target groups. However, existing legal and ethical frameworks on human subject protection, such as consent and risk-benefit assessment, are ill-equipped to provide a comprehensive solution to avoid the potential risks of harm posed by HPGR.

In addition to these concerns, the target groups or communities in HPGR are also distinguished from participants in many other types of biomedical research. They are almost always deliberately selected as target groups because they are in isolated groups or communities in rural areas of developing countries, which may lead to the potential for vulnerability in HPGR participation. Thus, the next chapter will go on to consider the issues of protecting target groups as potentially vulnerable populations in HPGR.

5   Group protection in human population genetic research

Since human population genetic research (HPGR) aims to identify specific aspects of the diversity of the human genome, target groups are often ethnic minorities or isolated groups in rural areas of developing countries, whose members are believed to share the same community or group collective human genetic information. This chapter will suggest that these target groups should be considered to be vulnerable in respect of HPGR, and need specific protections.

The vulnerability of target groups in HPGR

Vulnerability itself is a complex and ambiguous concept. Although several influential national laws and international declarations concern special protection for vulnerable groups, such as racial minorities, ethnic minorities or groups with disadvantaged economic and social resources,[1] the specific aims of these documents did not focus on HPGR, so the definition and scope of vulnerability of these groups in this context has not been addressed.[2] Despite the available codes of research ethics and regulations describing certain individuals and groups as vulnerable, little consensus exists on what this actually means, even in the context of human subject protection in biomedical research.

The World Medical Association's Declaration of Helsinki (Helsinki Declaration),[3] for example, noted that: '[s]ome research populations are

---

1 For example, the Helsinki Declaration and the CIOMS Guidelines all have specific regulations on vulnerable population protection.

2 Iltis, A. S. (2009) 'Introduction: Vulnerability in Biomedical Research', *Journal of Law, Medicine and Ethics*, vol. 37, no. 1, pp. 6–11 at 7.

3 The WMA Declaration of Helsinki Ethical Principles for Medical Research Involving Human Subjects was adopted by the 18th WMA General Assembly, Helsinki, Finland, June 1964, and amended by the 29th WMA General Assembly, Tokyo, Japan, October 1975,

particularly vulnerable and need special protection. These include those who cannot give or refuse consent for themselves and those who may be vulnerable to coercion or undue influence'.[4] It also points out that 'the particular needs of the economically and medically disadvantaged must be recognized'.[5] According to this explanation, the target groups of HPGR, ethnic minorities and isolated groups in developing countries, which often go hand in hand with limited social resources, poverty, low level of education, little familiarity with genetic research and lack of access to health care, should be seen as vulnerable.

Guideline 13 of the International Ethical Guidelines published by the Council of International Organizations of Medical Sciences (CIOMS) entitled 'Research Involving Vulnerable Persons' noted that: '[s]pecial justification is required for inviting vulnerable individuals to serve as research subjects and, if they are selected, the means of protecting their rights and welfare must be strictly applied'.[6] The meaning of vulnerable people was also addressed in the commentary on this guideline as follows: '[v]ulnerable persons are those who are relatively (or absolutely) incapable of protecting their own interests. More formally, they may have insufficient power, intelligence, education, resources, strength, or other needed attributes to protect their own interests'.[7] It also listed several types of populations and individuals who could be seen as constituting vulnerable groups, including 'some ethnic and racial minority groups'.[8] In addition, in the reference and commentary on Guideline 12 it was noted that:

> Not only may certain groups within a society be inappropriately over-used as research subjects, but also entire communities or societies may be overused. This has been particularly likely to occur in countries or

---

35th WMA General Assembly, Venice, Italy, October 1983, 41st WMA General Assembly, Hong Kong, September 1989, 48th WMA General Assembly, Somerset West, Republic of South Africa, October 1996 and the 52nd WMA General Assembly, Edinburgh, Scotland, October 2000, 53rd WMA General Assembly, Washington 2002 (Note of Clarification on paragraph 29 added), 55th WMA General Assembly, Tokyo 2004 (Note of Clarification on paragraph 30 added), 59th WMA General Assembly, Seoul, October 2008. The full text of the Helsinki Declaration can be seen on the official website of the World Medical Association (WMA) at http://www.wma.net/en/30publications/10policies/b3/index.html (last visited 4 July 2013).

4 ibid Article 9.

5 ibid.

6 The International Ethical Guidelines for Biomedical Research Involving Human Subjects were prepared by the Council for International Organizations of Medical Sciences (CIOMS) in collaboration with the WHO, Geneva, 2002. The full text of the CIOMS Guidelines can be seen on the official website of the World Health Organization (WHO) at http://www.cioms.ch/publications/guidelines/guidelines_nov_2002_blurb.htm (last visited 4 July 2013).

7 ibid.

8 ibid.

communities with insufficiently well developed systems for the protection of the rights and welfare of human research subjects. Such overuse is especially questionable when the populations or communities concerned bear the burdens of participation in research but are extremely unlikely ever to enjoy the benefits of new knowledge and products developed as a result of the research.[9]

Article 8 of the Universal Declaration on Bioethics and Human Rights,[10] adopted by the United Nations Educational, Scientific and Cultural Organization (UNESCO), is entitled 'Respect for human vulnerability and personal integrity'. This Article noted that:

> [I]n applying and advancing scientific knowledge, medical practice and associated technologies, human vulnerability should be taken into account. Individuals and groups of special vulnerability should be protected and the personal integrity of such individuals respected.[11]

It can be seen from this Article that this declaration made a claim as to the necessity of special protection for vulnerable individuals and groups in biomedical research, but it did not explain the meaning and scope of human vulnerability.

In addition to the international declarations and ethical guidelines above, some national laws or ethical guidelines also mention the vulnerability of certain groups. For example, the US National Commission's Belmont Report[12] includes 'racial minorities, the economically disadvantaged, the very sick, and the institutionalized'[13] in its list of vulnerable populations. The Common Rule, the core of the US human subject protection regulation, did not define vulnerability, but it mentioned 'economically or educationally disadvantaged persons'[14] as vulnerable populations, which is a general characteristic of target groups of HPGR in developing countries.

9 ibid at Guideline 12.
10 The Universal Declaration on Bioethics and Human Rights was adopted by UNESCO's General Conference on 19 October 2005. The full text of the Universal Declaration on Bioethics and Human Rights can be seen on the official website of UNESCO at http://portal.unesco.org/en/ev.php-URL_ID=31058&URL_DO=DO_TOPIC&URL_SECTION=201.html (last visited 4 July 2013).
11 ibid Article 8.
12 National Commission for the Protection of Human Subjects of Biomedical and Behavioural Research, 'The Belmont Report, Ethical Principles and Guidelines for the protection of human subjects of research'. The text can be found on the official website of US National Institution of Health, available at http://www.hhs.gov/ohrp/humansubjects/guidance/belmont.html (last visited 5 July 2013).
13 ibid.
14 45 CFR § 46.107.

From the above, it can be seen that despite broad agreement that the vulnerable have a claim to special protection, the definition and scope of vulnerable persons or populations are not clear. In addition, the pattern of defining vulnerability in international declarations and ethical guidelines, or national legal regulations and ethical guidelines, is to focus on particular populations, for example prisoners, children or ethnic minorities. This pattern has been criticised as it may lead to the implication that individuals who are members of these populations are inherently vulnerable in all types of biomedical research. For example, the National Bioethics Advisory Commission (NBAC) argued that 'vulnerability is sensitive to context and individuals may be vulnerable in one situation but not in another'.[15] Thus, the NBAC suggested that vulnerability should be defined in terms of situations in which individuals might be considered vulnerable, rather than in terms of groups or populations. The situation of the vulnerability of target groups in HPGR is similar. Ethnic minorities or groups who live in poverty or with fewer social resources may be categorised in international declarations and ethical guidelines as 'vulnerable groups', but this does not prove that these groups are necessarily vulnerable in HPGR. The concept of the vulnerability of target groups in HPGR has been defined so broadly and inconsistently[16] that it is tempting to conclude that it is incapable of providing any meaningful ethical guidance.

Coleman has pointed out that the core of fully understanding vulnerability is determining the nature of the human subject's vulnerability; that is, what are vulnerable human subjects actually vulnerable to?[17] He argued that vulnerability should be linked to the basic principles that underlie society's regulation of human subject research, as reflected in regulatory standards and internationally agreed-upon ethical guidelines.[18] According to this framework, a vulnerable person or group can be seen as an individual or a group at risk of being enrolled in research in violation of one or more of the interests defined by regulations and ethical guidelines. Vulnerability should be examined from three distinct perspectives – consent-based, risk-based and justice-based.[19] Consent-based and risk-based vulnerabilities make more sense when conceptualised as individual issues, but justice-based vulnerabilities are hard to understand as anything other than a population-based concern.[20]

---

15 National Bioethics Advisory Commission (NBAC), 'Assessing Risks and Potential Benefits and Evaluating Vulnerability", Ethical and Policy Issues in Research Involving Human Participants, Vol. I: Reports and Recommendations (Bethesda, Maryland, 2001) at 87.

16 See note 2 at 7–8.

17 Coleman, C. H. (2009) 'Vulnerability as a Regulatory Category in Human Subject Research', *Journal of Law, Medicine and Ethics*, vol. 37, no. 1, pp. 12–18 at 14.

18 ibid at 15.

19 ibid.

20 ibid at 16.

There are several reasons to agree with this understanding of vulnerability in human subject research. First, avoiding these three kinds of vulnerability is the baseline of permitting researchers and research institutions to invite human subjects to participate in their research, since their research may cause risks of harm to the participants without any compensating benefits, medical or otherwise. According to principles such as 'respect for autonomy', 'beneficence' and 'justice', the following conditions should be fulfilled before conducting research: the institutional review boards (IRBs) or research ethics committees (RECs) must determine that the risks of the study are reasonable in relation to its total anticipated benefits (both direct benefits to subjects and potential long-term benefits to society), that the risks have been minimised to the extent reasonably possible and that the subjects will be able to provide voluntary, informed consent. If an individual or a certain group is identified as vulnerable, his or her interests will be more susceptible to violation than those of other individuals or groups. Thus, in order to clarify the nature of vulnerability of target groups in HPGR, we should explore what these groups are vulnerable to from these three distinct aspects: consent-based, risk-based and justice-based. Secondly, the division of authority and responsibility between IRBs or RECs, research subjects and legislators within this framework is clear. It can be seen that the conditions mentioned above require human subjects to determine whether or not to participate in the research; meanwhile, IRBs or RECs should decide whether or not the risks of the study are reasonable in relation to the total anticipated benefits, as well as whether the risks have been minimised to the extent reasonably possible; then, the legislators stipulate the legal requirements for the implementation of the research subject's consent and the ethical review conducted by IRBs or RECs. Coleman has argued that the roles of individuals and IRBs or RECs are not well balanced:

> At one extreme, we could let competent adults participate in any type of research, regardless of the study's objective risk-benefit ratio, on the theory that autonomous individuals have the right to take whatever risks they find personally acceptable. We do not have such a system: if the study does not offer a net social benefit, then the IRB is not supposed to approve it, even if a fully informed subject would be willing to participate. At the other extreme, we could require IRBs to determine that participating in research would be in the individual best interests of all the subjects in a study ...[21]

Neither of these two extreme situations is acceptable. As Coleman continues: 'we defer to individuals' choices to take research-related risks for idiosyncratic reasons – but only if they are genuinely capable of acting autonomously, and only if the risks are "worth it" from a societal point of view'.[22]

---

21 ibid at 15.
22 ibid.

As a result, a reasonable division of authority between ethical review agents and research participants should respect competent individual participants' decisions to participate in research, but only if the risks of harm are deemed reasonable in relation to the importance of the knowledge to be gained from a societal point of view.

According to this framework, the risks to vulnerable individuals or groups can arise from different sources. First, consent-based vulnerabilities can create or exacerbate barriers to obtaining sufficiently informed consent to research, potentially violating the requirement that consent to the research risks be voluntary. Secondly, risk-based vulnerabilities may enhance the level of risks associated with subjects' participation in human subject research, thereby calling into question the study's underlying risk-benefit ratio. Finally, justice-based vulnerabilities can raise concerns about the distribution of the benefits and burdens of the research, and these distributional concerns may also be relevant to the risk-benefit analysis.[23]

According to these concerns, it can be suggested that target groups of HPGR are vulnerable in respect of consent, benefit-risk assessment or exploitation, because of a low educational level, lack of economic and social resources, cultural sensitivities and an absence of effective and adequate legal regulations and ethical guidelines in most developing countries.

Consent-based vulnerability of target groups in HPGR

Consent-based vulnerability refers to the diminished ability to protect one's own interests, leading to a compromised capacity to give sufficiently informed or voluntary consent. This diminished ability may render a particular individual or group more susceptible to impaired decision-making, coercion or undue influence in research.

In the context of HPGR, there are several factors which may lead to the consent-based vulnerability of target groups. Target groups and their members may have difficulty giving valid consent and protecting their own interests and could thus be classed as vulnerable.

HPGR aims to study isolated populations to find out the impact of their history on their genetic make-up, so target groups of HPGR are often located in isolated areas, where transportation is inconvenient; the members of target groups are relatively homogeneous with respect to ethnic group, environment, occupation and diet, and the groups will have existed for several thousand years with a stable population. For example, Arizona State University (ASU) conducted several research projects on the Havasupai tribe, which is a small tribe numbering a few hundred people living in an isolated community in the Grand Canyon, which is accessible only by foot, mule or helicopter.[24] The

23 ibid.
24 *Tilousi v Arizona State University Board of Regents*, No. 04-CV-1290-PCT-FJM (2005).

Harvard University research in the Anhui province of the People's Republic of China (PRC) was also conducted on isolated groups in rural areas.[25] It is quite normal that the members of target groups in HPGR are less-educated than the majority population and unfamiliar with the implications and possible consequences of genetic research. For instance, according to the Second National Agricultural Census by the National Bureau of Statistics of the PRC,[26] at the end of 2006, the total of the rural labour force numbered 478,520 persons, occupying 90.1 per cent of the total labour force resources; however, among these rural labourers, 6.8 per cent had no formal education, 49.5 per cent had junior middle school education level and 32.7 per cent had primary school education.[27] It showed that 89 per cent of the population in the rural areas in the PRC have fewer than nine years of education. This low educational situation might have a negative influence on their understanding of information disclosed and their evaluation of the potential risks of harm in HPGR.

These groups or individuals may have limited health literacy and may not appropriately understand the exact meaning of sample collection procedures or the possible outcomes of the research project. For example, in 1984, a US physician, Dr Arthur Bosley, who conducted medical research in developing countries, told of the dilemma he faced in the application of informed consent.[28] According to his report, in most developing countries, 'the germ theory of disease causation is yet to be accepted, particularly among the not so-educated members of the population'.[29] What is more, most of the people in these countries thought that a blood test was a good thing, because 'if your blood is good, then you are all right'. Thus, if Dr Bosley wished to invite patients attending the clinic to undergo a blood test, they would consent readily.[30] In addition, information about HPGR, including the risks involved,

---

25 Pomfret, J. and Nelson, D., 'In Rural China, a Genetic Mother Lode' *Washington Post* (20 December 2000).

26 The Second National Agricultural Census by the National Bureau of Statistics of PRC. According to the State Council's decision, the PRC launched the Second National Agricultural Census. The time reference for point items is 31 December 2006. The time reference for period items is 1 January to 31 December 2006. The objects of the census focused on the PRC rural households, urban agricultural production households, agricultural holdings, villagers' committees, and township and town governments. The main contents include conditions for agricultural production, agricultural production and management activities, utilisation of agricultural land, rural labour force and employment, rural infrastructures, rural social services, rural households' livelihood, as well as the situation of the township, villagers' committees, community environment and other aspects. The full text and data of this census (in Chinese) can be seen on the official website of the National Bureau of Statistics of the PRC, available at http://www.stats.gov.cn/tjgb/nypcgb/qgnypcgb/index.htm (last visited 4 July 2013).

27 ibid.

28 Ekunwe, E. O. and Kessel, R. (1984) 'Informed Consent in the Developing World', *Hastings Centre Report*, vol. 14, no. 3, pp. 22–24 at 22.

29 ibid at 23.

30 ibid.

may be difficult to understand. The majority of members of target groups in HPGR may not be able to read and write. Even those who can read may not understand all the medical terms that such information is bound to contain. If the consent form is in a normal Western style, which often lists possible risks over multiple pages, but does not explain them in common terms or spell out the seriousness, probability or consequences of each possible risk in simple terms, the difficulty can be exacerbated. If the target groups are in developing countries, whose members are not aware of the potential risks of harm of biomedical research, even if they agree to participate in it,[31] these difficulties increase even further.

Any decision whether or not to participate in scientific research that is based on incomplete understanding or misunderstanding of research information or on an inaccurate assessment of potential risks of harm is ethically and may be legally problematic. In fact, normal competent people sometimes do participate in research studies without a good understanding of the study purpose and risks, even in non-HPGR projects. Competent individuals may sometimes consent to research without fully understanding each sentence of the consent form; however, these individuals often have background knowledge on research, can realise the scope of risks approximately and are capable of making an appropriate evaluation of potential risks. Thus, they may be deemed capable of understanding the research information sufficiently. It could therefore be argued that understanding may be correlated with educational level[32] but the person's social and cultural context will also play an important role.

The members of target groups of HPGR may be less capable of understanding, and hence more vulnerable to impaired decision-making, because of their lack of education, cultural orientation, or limited health and medical knowledge. In other words, target groups do not have the experience to weigh up the advantages and disadvantages as they are unused to making these kinds of decisions. Target groups of HPGR and their members who do not understand what the purpose of HPGR is may not know what they are actually consenting to and may misunderstand or not realise the risks of participation. Thus, they are vulnerable when making a decision on whether or not to participate in HPGR. Therefore, explanations with adequate accuracy and articulation, easily understood by people with a low level of education, are essential requirements both for the ethical conduct of this type of biomedical research and for the protection of subjects' interests. In the context of HPGR, as in any other research, the burden is on the researchers

31 Lynoe, N., Sandlund, M., Jacobsson, L., Nordberg, G. and Jin, T. (2004) 'Informed Consent in China: Quality of Information Provided to Participants in a Research Project', *Scandinavian Journal of Public Health*, vol. 32, no. 6, pp. 472–75.

32 Grady, C. (2009) 'Vulnerability in Research: Individuals with Limited Financial and/ or Social Resources', *Journal of Law, Medicine and Ethics*, vol. 37, no. 1, pp. 19–27 at 21.

and research institutions to inform individuals in a way that ensures that the target groups and their members can appreciate the risks and requirements of participation while minimising the possible impact of educational or cultural barriers that may distort understanding.

The second possible type of consent-based vulnerability is that if medical services or other goods are offered in connection with participating in an HPGR, these may be so attractive that members of target groups, especially with limited economic and social resources, will irrationally disregard the risks and requirements of the research. These attractive offers are referred to as 'undue inducements' in biomedical research. According to Emanuel, there are four elements to undue inducement, and each of these four elements is necessary for undue inducement to exist:

> (1) An Offered Good – Individuals are offered something that is valuable or desirable in order to do something. (2) Excessive Offer – The offered good must be so large or in excess that it is irresistible in the context. (3) Poor Judgment – The offer leads individuals to exercise poor judgment in an important decision. (4) Risk of Serious Harm – The individual's poor judgment leads to sufficiently high probability that he or she will experience a harm that seriously contravenes his or her interests.[33]

According to this account, it could be argued that HPGR may only offer some free common medicine or access to limited primary healthcare treatment, which can be seen as normal compensation for research participation and would not lead to the undue influence of potential participants. In fact, just as happened in the Harvard project in the PRC, in order to recruit participants from rural areas of developing countries, researchers might seek to provide some medical services or standing drugs for free. In 2001, *Outlook Weekly* published a survey on the Harvard case, describing one of the participants, Chu Mianzhai, whose whole family had twice taken these kind of free 'physical examinations', given blood samples and received a little money as compensation for loss of working time, as well as two packages of instant noodles.[34] The first time, on 5 November 1996, the family gave a blood sample for which they were given 10 yuan each as compensation. The second time, on 10 March 1997, they gave more blood and were given 20 yuan each. Chu also received a bottle of medicine for his high blood pressure. A similar situation also arose in the case of Havasupai. In this case, taking part in the research would result in access to some free summer school for students from

33 Emanuel, E. J. (2005) 'Undue Inducement: Nonsense on Stilts?', *The American Journal of Bioethics*, vol. 5, no. 5, pp. 9–13 at 9.
34 Xiong, L. and Wang, Y., 'Meiguo Hafei Daxue zai Anhui de jiyin yanjiu xiangmu' ['Harvard University's genetic research project in Anhui Province'] (in Chinese), *Outlook Weekly* (26 March 2001).

the tribe.[35] Thus, the question arises whether target groups of HPGR should be considered vulnerable to undue inducement if such benefits were offered.

An example, provided by McGregor, of an impecunious mother with a very sick child and a lecherous millionaire can illustrate that whether or not something is an undue inducement should be decided by the specific situation of the subject, although the example is not in the context of research:

> The millionaire proposes to the impecunious mother that he will pay for the medical treatment that her child needs if she will become his mistress.[36]

This hypothetical situation satisfies the first element of undue inducement: an irresistible offer. The offer to fund the treatment of a very sick child is not an excessive one for a millionaire, but it is an irresistible one for the child's mother, given her inability to pay for the treatment. Poor judgment is less obvious, because from the perspective of the child's welfare, accepting the offer is reasonable, but on the other hand, accepting unwanted sexual interactions would generally not be seen as reasonable. To some extent, whether or not this leads to a serious harm would be decided by the subject's circumstances and values (for example, if the mother here was a prostitute, she might think this exchange is not a serious harm).[37] Thus, undue inducement would occur where an attractive offer distorts the individual's ability to make rational decisions for himself or herself, according to his or her own values and preferences. Such offers may be especially irresistible to those individuals who lack economic and social resources. That is to say, the main concern of undue inducement is that individuals are offered some good that, effectively without reference to their better judgment, makes them assume risks of harm that compromise their welfare.[38]

In the context of HPGR, considering the level of economic development and actual living conditions of most target groups, their members may be vulnerable in the face of what may appear to others to be small and reasonable offers. Indeed, HPGR conducted in some developing countries may offer payments or primary health care service to the Western standard as part of research participation, such as free health care or other benefits such as free housing etc. However, these offers could be enticing enough to impair decision-making, such that members of target groups participate in HPGR disregarding risks or not giving risks appropriate weight in the decision-making process. In the Harvard case, an individual participant Chu and his family lived in Toutuo, an impoverished village in Yuexi district with an average

---

35 See note 24.
36 McGregor, J. (2005) '"Undue Inducement" as Coercive Offers', *The American Journal of Bioethics*, vol. 5, no. 5, pp. 24–25 at 24.
37 ibid.
38 See note 33.

annual wage of less than 2000 yuan.[39] Thus, although 10 yuan or 20 yuan can be seen as a small sum and normal compensation in medical research, compared with the low annual wages of target group members in HPGR, the compensation offered might amount to an undue influence.

From the above case, we can appreciate that seemingly simple offers could be a decision-impairing inducement rendering members of target groups in HPGR incapable of appropriately considering research risks. In this situation, they have fulfilled the definition of the CIOMS that they are 'relatively or absolutely incapable of protecting their own interests'.[40] But it should be noted that, with sufficient recognition of vulnerability of target groups in HPGR, it is the main task of the RECs to protect against unacceptable risks. Studies with an inappropriate risk-benefit ratio should not be open to research participants in the first place.

In addition, there are also other concerns about the potential vulnerability of target groups of HPGR, especially in developing countries, such as the PRC. In the PRC, medical care in each county is administered through a three-tier (county, township, village) service network, which was established a quarter of a century ago to provide medical services for all residents.[41] It is quite convenient and efficient to conduct biomedical research through collaboration with this medical care service network. Meanwhile, in pursuing a better future for their personal career, some physicians in developing countries like to conduct collaborative HPGR with Western research institutions. In these HPGRs, they may dispatch personnel to be trained in foreign research institutions, experience how foreign researchers conduct HPGR and even publish co-authored journal articles.[42] However, these physicians are also practitioners in the health service network of the country; thus, they are relied on by the local people. HPGR conducted by these local physicians may provide a misconception to members of target groups of HPGR that the project is risk-free and might be good for their health. This situation would exacerbate the consent-based vulnerability of target groups of HPGR and there might be a risk of undue influence if local doctors encourage participation.

Risk-based vulnerability of target groups in HPGR

Risk-based vulnerability refers to a situation where the risks to subjects are not reasonable, compared with the potential benefits of the research.

39 See note 34.

40 See note 6.

41 Xu, X., Yang, J., Chen, C., Wang, B., Jin, Y., Fang, Z., Wang, X. and Weiss, S. T. (1999) 'Familial Aggregation of Pulmonary Function in a Rural Chinese Community', *American Journal of Respiratory and Critical Care Medicine*, vol. 160, no. 6, pp. 1928–33 at 1929.

42 Chu, J. (2000) 'Chinese Human Genome Diversity Project: A Synopsis' in *Genetic, Linguistic and Archaeological Perspectives on Human Diversity in Southeast Asia*, J. Li, M. Seielstad and C. Xiao, eds. (Singapore: World Scientific Publishing) pp. 95–105.

According to Coleman, risk-based vulnerability may be 'jeopardized if some subjects are at risk of greater than usual harms from participating in research'.[43] For example, if the primary risk of an HPGR is the potential disclosure of the genetic evidence of the origin of ethnic or isolated group, the target group can be considered vulnerable if it has its own narrative origin stories which have been believed to be the foundation of its collective identity.

In general, IRBs or RECs should address risk-based vulnerability and require additional safeguards to protect the subjects' interests. In the context of HPGR, however, the situation is more complicated. The potential risks of harm caused by HPGR include external harms, such as group discrimination and group stigmatisations as well as internal harms, such as group self-conception of genetic determinism and self-stigmatisation. External harms might perhaps be assessed by IRBs or RECs, although they are not usually required to do so, but internal harms, which are specific to an ethnic or isolated group, are difficult to identify correctly by any agent outside of the specific group. Foster, Sharp et al provided an example from the Indian Health Service (IHS) Headquarters IRB, which can illustrate this point:

> ... the Indian Health Service (IHS) Headquarters IRB has 28 members, 20 of whom are Native Americans (including MD- and PhD-level researchers, health professionals, and laypersons from Native communities). Despite its unique composition, however, the IHS IRB sometimes is unable to predict what a specific Native community views as the primary risks to itself. Two recent examples include worries about the use of genetic research into migration history to attack tribal sovereignty and concerns about the use of mitochondrial DNA and Y chromosome research in claims about who is or is not 'Indian'. These risks were identified only by community review, not by any IRB.[44]

In this case, the IHS IRB included many American Indian and American Native (AI/AN) members, which reflected the IRB's regard for the sensitivity of indigenous communities. However, even here there have been instances where the IHS IRB has failed to identify potential risks of internal group harms that were of concern to members of the target population, such as culturally specific harms. The reason why the IHS IRB, with its unique composition and wide range of experiences with AI/AN communities, failed to identify such potential risks may include the following two aspects: first, the members from certain target groups often fully understand their

43 See note 17 at 16.
44 Foster, M. W., Sharp, R. R., Freeman, W. L., Chino, M., Bernsten, D. and Carter, T. H. (1999), 'The Role of Community Review in Evaluating the Risks of Human Genetic Variation Research', *American Journal of Human Genetics*, vol. 64, pp. 1719–27 at 1724.

socio-cultural traditions, but they may lack sufficient knowledge of biomedical research and sufficient training on the proper conduct of ethical review. Secondly, ordinary IRB or REC members, owing to a deficiency in knowledge of the cultural background of target groups, could not correctly identify the potential risks of internal group harms or give them sufficient weight. Therefore, unless IRBs include target group representatives with appropriate training on ethical review, and there is sufficient community consultation and investigation of group cultural sensitivity, IRBs may be unable to assess these potential risks correctly.

The absence of sufficient understanding of the cultural sensitivities of target groups by researchers may also lead to a failure to address these risks of harm in their research protocol or not providing adequate information disclosure on these risks. For example, in the Havasupai Indian Tribe case,[45] ASU researchers collected more than 200 blood samples from tribe members for research on diabetes and genetics in 1990. The consent form described the project as studying 'the causes of behavioural/medical disorders',[46] but in the pre-research communications with tribal leaders, it was agreed that the samples should be used in research focused on diabetes. However, the researchers used the samples in several other research projects unrelated to diabetes, sharing them with other researchers, and publishing several articles based on data from tribal members' blood samples.[47] Among these research publications, 'some of the papers generated from the blood samples dealt with schizophrenia, inbreeding and theories about ancient human population migrations from Asia to North America'.[48] The focus on schizophrenia raised stigmatisation issues for the tribe along with concerns related to a cultural belief that inbreeding brings harm to one's family. Furthermore, evolutionary-genetics research suggested that, contrary to the tribe's own origin story, its ancestors migrated across the Bering Sea, creating the possibility of cultural harms.[49] Although the core legal question of the Havasupai case was whether the downstream uses of the samples fell within the scope of the donors' informed consent, it also illustrates that the unique cultural beliefs of a target group might be a barrier to researchers and IRBs or RECs actually identifying potential risks of harm that may be caused by research to target groups and their members. It also implied the responsibility of researchers to ensure that the study population's perspectives are understood and considered. Thus, isolation and specific cultural sensitivities can increase the risk-based vulnerability of target groups in HPGR.

45 See note 24.
46 ibid.
47 ibid.
48 ibid at 5.
49 Mello, M. M. and Wolf, L. E. (2010) 'The Havasupai Indian Tribe Case: Lessons for Research Involving Stored Biologic Samples', *The New England Journal of Medicine*, vol. 363, no. 3, pp. 204–7 at 204.

Justice-based vulnerability of target groups in HPGR

This kind of vulnerability concerns the violation of the principle of justice in research ethics. The concern that target groups of HPGR are particularly vulnerable to exploitation is a consideration of justice-based vulnerability.

Exploitation is a complex concept which has been explained in several different ways. Generally, there are two elements considered to be essential to exploitation: (1) using people as mere means for the ends of others (a Kantian sense of exploitation);[50] and/or (2) taking unfair advantage of people.[51] Thus, exploitation usually occurs 'when wealthy or powerful individuals or agencies take advantage of the poverty, powerlessness, or dependency of others by using the latter to serve their own ends (those of the wealthy or powerful) without adequate compensating benefits for the less powerful or disadvantaged individuals or groups'.[52]

In the context of HPGR, target groups who are usually poor, less-educated and lacking social and economic resources, may not understand that they might be used as means to others' ends, or might agree to participate in an exchange without realising its inherent unfairness. As noted previously, researchers or research institutions may provide some free primary drugs or simple treatment in exchange for the genetic samples and consent forms signed by participants. These participants may not even realise that the outcome of the research may not benefit them and will have no (positive) meaning for them. Thus, they are likely to become 'mere means' of HPGR. This could lead to justice-based vulnerability in this situation as they cannot realise they might be exploited by others. Identifying whether or not researchers are in fact taking unfair advantage of target groups in HPGR is more complex. The core issue here is to assess whether the level of benefit which the researchers or research institutions will get is fair or unfair. Exploitation would be identified if benefits are unfair, and would not require the existence of actual harm to have occurred.

In addition, the isolated locations raise another possible source of vulnerability for target groups of HPGR. They have rare opportunities to obtain offers provided by HPGR researchers, such as free primary health care services, common drugs or trivial amounts of cash. Fewer choices and limited bargaining power may exacerbate the justice-based vulnerability of target groups in HPGR. For example, a research institution affiliated to a university, such as the research organisation in the Harvard case in the PRC, could offer several summer course places to students of ethnic minorities or isolated groups in rural areas in developing countries in exchange for 1000 genetic samples and signed consent forms from these groups.

50 See note 32 at 23.
51 ibid.
52 Macklin, R. (2003) 'Bioethics, Vulnerability, and Protection', *Bioethics*, vol. 17, nos 5–6, pp. 472–86 at 475.

Although this offer costs only a trivial amount for the research institution, it could be immensely attractive to target groups, because without this offer they will have no other such opportunity. Thus, target groups probably feel that they have to take this offer. Meanwhile, compared with the risks of harm, such as the internal and external harms that may be caused by HPGR that have been discussed above, several summer course places may be perceived as an inadequate benefit. Therefore, target groups of HPGR might be considered to have been exploited if they accept this offer.

On the other hand, some might argue that although from the perspective of a neutral observer, this offer is inadequate, nevertheless, for target groups, several summer course places at a top university could be a reasonable recompense for their participation in HPGR. To those target groups, even this arguably unfair benefit is an option that could let several students of these groups gain further education. Thus, they may question whether these target groups are being exploited. The following example can illustrate why to use the viewpoint of the vulnerable groups as the standard of fairness is problematic. If a rich man from a developed country offers an extremely poor man a substantial pay-off to induce this poor man to be his or her slave, this substantial pay-off could help the poor man to afford to give his whole family a better life. He has no alternative way to gain a better life for his family. However, no matter this substantial pay-off is actually trivial, or is not important to the rich man, to be a slave is a violation of primary human rights, so the rich man would not make slavery right. Thus, this is obvious exploitation. Therefore, it requires a neutral standard of fairness to be used as a tool for distinguishing between fair and unfair benefits, thereby protecting vulnerable parties from exploitation. In the context of HPGR, the objective baseline of fairness should be drawn by the ethical review committees with the involvement of target group representatives, based on the specific economic and cultural context of certain target groups. Without a neutral standard of fairness, target groups may be vulnerable to exploitation in HPGR. However, it needs to be highlighted that what the author intends to argue here is to avoid exploitation, so if the undue inducement issue could be solved, the fair benefit sharing with the donors, including both target group and individual participants, of DNA samples should be provided.

The justice-based vulnerability of target groups in HPGR is also relevant to the background conditions in the developing countries where the HPGR is conducted. The background conditions include lack of effective legal regulations and ethical guidelines on human subject protection together with poor law enforcement, inadequate experience of or capacity for conducting ethical and scientific reviews of proposed research, poor local infrastructure, untrained personnel and limited technical capacity for conducting the proposed research itself. Most developing countries have no stringent rules on the basic requirements of research involving human subjects, such as informed consent or the welfare of human subjects, not to mention effective legal regulations and ethical guidelines on human subject research. This situation has led to several troubling examples of research trials in developing countries. For example, the Pfizer incident in Nigeria during an epidemic of meningitis in children in 1996 illustrates these issues, although it involved clinical research, rather than HPGR. Pfizer, an American multinational pharmaceutical company, conducted a trial of an antibiotic at the site of the outbreak of a meningitis epidemic in the northern state of Kano, where 15,000 people were alleged to have died from these epidemics. Kano is a typical poor area in a developing country, so even the Kano Infectious Diseases Hospital, where the trials took place, was reported to be at the time a poor, dirty hospital with few beds, poor power supply, and no clean water. Pfizer conducted the clinical trials in Kano to investigate whether the oral form of Trovan was more effective and efficient in treating children infected with meningitis than other existing treatments, including Ceftriaxone, the gold standard treatment. Pfizer's Trovan had not been previously tested in children. However, about 200 infected children participated in the Kano trials. Of these, 100 took Trovan while another 100 were put on Ceftriaxone. Eleven children died in the trials, five of whom were on the experimental drug, Trovan, given orally, while the other six were on injections of Ceftriaxone. There were also other children involved in the trials who suffered seizures, or became paralysed. While there is no evidence that Trovan was responsible for the deaths and injuries to children, the trials were conducted within a period of two weeks and Pfizer left immediately thereafter.[53] This case was first publicised by *The Washington Post* in an investigative article on the conduct of clinical trials by developed country researchers in developing countries. According to the report, there was no informed consent, no follow-up of the children after conclusion of the trial and no parents of the children had been adequately informed about the trial. What is more, there was no approval of the research protocol by an independent ethics review committee – there was no ethics committee in the hospital at the time of the trial.[54] There were no legal regulations or ethical guidelines in Nigeria at the time of the trial requiring Pfizer to obtain any such approval. When charges of unethical conduct were made, Pfizer alleged that apart from the goals of obtaining information about the efficacy of the drugs, 'another major reason for conducting the trials was to provide humanitarian services to the infected victims who were obviously in need of medical assistance at the time'.[55]

53 Onyemelukwe, C. (2008) 'Research Involving Humans in African Countries: A Case for Domestic Legal Frameworks', *African Journal of International and Comparative Law*, vol. 16, no. 2, pp. 152–77 at 155–56.

54 ibid at 157.

55 ibid at 156.

This case highlights the common situation of lack of effective legislation and regulations on biomedical research governance and human subject protection in developing countries.[56] It has been suggested that researchers and research institutions have all too often defended their apparent double standards of research ethics in research conducted in developing countries. On the one hand, they apply a higher standard of research ethics in their own countries according to the relevant legal regulations and ethical guidelines, as well as undertaking strict implementation of those rules. On the other hand, these researchers and research institutions have proposed and accepted a less demanding standard of research ethics in developing countries, where effective and adequate legal regulations and ethical guidelines on human subject protection is lacking.[57] They may also argue that they have offered participants free physical tests – even free treatments such as drugs – which are needed by these participants and would benefit them. However, it can be argued that those researchers and research institutions take unfair advantage of their wealth in economic and social terms. Accordingly, Macklin suggests that whole communities or countries may be vulnerable to exploitation, particularly if 'investigators or sponsors are from a powerful industrialized country or a giant pharmaceutical company and the research is conducted in a developing country'.[58] Therefore, the absence of specific regulations and standards for HPGR together with poor law enforcement in most developing countries make target groups of HPGR particularly open to justice-based vulnerability.

Consequently, what is significant to note about HPGR in developing countries is that even if the relational autonomy model is applied, which lets individual participants take into account the interests of the group and other group members when considering whether to consent to participate, given the vulnerability of the target groups stated above, it is possible that this would not be sufficient to take account of the need to protect all of those who had interests at stake. Thus, it is reasonable to suggest that additional protection for target groups in HPGR, such as the involvement of the target group as a whole in some way, is needed. Nevertheless, it also needs to be reiterated that arguing for group involvement in a review of HPGR does not mean advocating group consent instead of individual consent. The following section will nevertheless propose that the target group, or its representatives, could and should be involved in the protection of the group's interests.

---

56 The situation of lack of effective legislation and regulations in the PRC would be set as an example to be discussed in more detail in the next chapter.
57 Kottow, M. H. (2003) 'The Vulnerable and the Susceptible', *Bioethics*, vol. 17, nos 5–6, pp. 460–71 at 466.
58 See note 52 at 474.

Justifications for protection of groups in HPGR

Critiques of group protection in HPGR

The suggestion that the group as a whole should be protected in HPGR has been criticised, since some researchers have doubted that HPGR may lead to potential harms for the group as a whole. They have argued that the actual human groups under study, human demes, are unidentifiable before research begins, since it is only when genetic relationships have been established as a result of the HPGR study that such a group can be said to exist;[59] thus, there is no group collective interest to be harmed in HPGR. Furthermore, the idea of a group as a rights-holder has been met with scepticism or outright rejection by some researchers, ethicists and legal scholars. The opponents of group protection in HPGR have argued that it is hollow rhetoric to set up a group as an independent entity to be protected from the risks of harm in HPGR.[60] Their arguments almost always focus on the argument that groups lack moral standing and that seeking to obtain prior group permission is not possible in HPGR.

To explain these criticisms in more detail, Juengst argues that there are two different understandings of a group in HPGR. First, the term 'target groups' in HPGR refers to genetic populations or human demes; in his opinion, this type of group has no moral standing and cannot be approached for group consent or group permission, since these groups are unidentifiable until the research itself has been conducted.[61] Human demes or genetic populations are groups which are 'picked out, described, and compared in the course of population-genomics research';[62] thus, they are not identical with named social groups which might perhaps deserve respect as an independent entity. Since they are the nameless demes which are created by researchers of genetic research, as well as 'the results of mixed lineages that make hash of most of our familial origin stories and social groupings',[63] Juengst considers that these human demes are 'not autonomous, self-identified human groups, and it would be dangerous to devise a system that suggested that demes should be invested with special social value or identity'.[64] Juengst goes on to state that:

> ... given our species' long history of using putative genetic relationships as the basis for nepotism, tribalism, racism, and aggression, aspiring to

---

59 Juengst, E. T. (1998) 'Groups as Gatekeepers to Genomic Research: Conceptually Confusing, Morally Hazardous, and Practically Useless', *Kennedy Institute of Ethics Journal*, vol. 8, no. 2, pp. 183–200 at 183.

60 Gostin, L. O. (1991) 'Ethical Principles for the Conduct of Human Subject Research: Population-Based Research and Ethics', *Journal of Law, Medicine and Ethics*, vol. 19, pp. 191–201.

61 ibid at 187.

62 ibid at 196.

63 ibid.

64 ibid.

invest human demes with special moral standing seems wrong-headed in the first place. If we are right in our convictions that our biological roots should be irrelevant to the ways in which humans regard each other, promoting our demes as groups with interests of their own makes no more sense than reviving old eugenic attempts to reify the concepts of 'race,' 'genetic stock,' or 'germ plasm.'[65]

He concluded that the genetic concept of a human group should just be a tool that helps in organising scientific data in HPGR, but not a way of classifying the members of the human species.[66] Thus, if a human deme does indeed mean the same as the target group of HPGR, there is neither moral standing of group collective interests, nor would seeking group consent or group approval in HPGR be possible or necessary.

Secondly, even if the group refers to self-identified groups, morally authoritative social groups, then in most cases we could approach them for permission; however, Juengst insists that group permission in HPGR has its internal limitations. In the first place, the problem of how to define the group still exists, which has also been described as the 'nesting' of local and larger communities. The example of the Mohawk,[67] provided by Sharp and Foster, can illustrate this problem well. In the US and Canada, individuals who consider themselves Mohawk may have distinct understandings on what a Mohawk community consists of. Some may base this understanding on factors such as whether members reside in a discrete local community, located on a single reservation. However, several of these reservation-based communities define themselves collectively, for example as 'a part of the League of Iroquois, a political and religious organization comprised of six culturally related American Indian communities'.[68] Thus, they argued that nesting all the members of a self-identified group is a hard obstacle. Sharp and Foster warned that 'the nesting problem results from the possibility that the concerns of local communities may fail to correspond with those of communities at broader levels of inclusiveness'.[69] Juengst argues that the practice of nesting local groups within larger social categories, as well as cross-cultural immigration, would lead to group consent not having the moral reach to decide for potential participants in HPGR.[70] He also points out that there are resource issues if groups are seen as the right-holders:

65 ibid at 189.
66 ibid.
67 Sharp, R. R. and Foster, M. W. (2000) 'Involving Study Populations in the Review of Genetic Research', *Journal of Law, Medicine and Ethics*, vol. 28, pp. 41–51 at 47.
68 ibid at 47.
69 ibid.
70 See note 59 at 196.

Accepting them [groups as right-holders] would significantly complicate the work of population genomicists. If groups have interests that require protections like those of individual subjects, a layer of research arrangements would be necessary that our individually-oriented biomedical research ethic is ill-prepared to define or delimit. What would it mean for a group's collective permission to be 'informed' and 'voluntary'? If group consent is required, are other protections, such as the right to withdraw from research, or to confidentiality, also important for groups? How should the 'researcher-group' relationship be managed administratively? Moreover, if the logic behind the argument for group rights in population-genomics research is accepted, it is likely to be applied to other biomedical spheres as well.[71]

Sharp and Foster described the costs and demands on researchers when formal community approval is required to indicate the same point.[72] They further argued that the practice of group consent is also problematic. They summarised this in terms of 'the dispersion of community':

A related objection to group consent, one that also can be extended to other forms of community review, notes how features of a study population's geographical distribution can undermine the effectiveness of involving communities in the review process. It has been argued that the dispersion of individual members and the lack of frequent social interactions between members of a study population combine to limit the effectiveness of community review.[73]

Using these reasons, the opponents of group protection in HPGR have suggested that there is no group collective interest that needs to be protected from the risks of harm in HPGR, nor could group consent be reasonably obtained and any purported group consent would lack moral and legal validity.

Perspective on groups as right-holders

On the other hand, with respect to target groups of HPGR, there are several scholars who consider that a group should be seen as a right-holder in HPGR.

First, in HPGR, the effect on individuals' purely private interests, which are the most significant potential risks of harm in other types of genetic research, could be protected by anonymising samples. However, the wider

71 ibid at 184–85.
72 See note 67 at 49.
73 ibid at 47–48.

risks of harm that may arise from HPGR, such as stigmatisation of groups, as has been discussed, can only threaten individual participants' welfare through their group identities.[74] Thus, the advocates of group protection support their argument from the necessity of respect for group identity. For example, Gostin argues that:

> The importance of group identity, and of treating social communities with dignity and respect, is increasingly well recognized. Human beings gain security, happiness, and enjoyment by forming networks based upon their special national or sub-national characteristics. Respect and beneficence for populations requires researchers to observe choices made by local communities, and to avoid any activity which stigmatizes, demeans, harms, or disintegrates human populations, intentionally or inadvertently.[75]

In addition, as discussed in Chapter 4, members of target groups of HPGR tend to identify themselves through and with certain groups to which they belong, and not as isolated existential individuals. Therefore, members of target groups in HPGR are more likely largely to accept their group's values and priorities as their own, and accordingly they tend to be protective of their group's interests as reflective of their own interests. This tendency seems to support the practice of interests of the group as a whole should be considered in HPGR by both researchers and ethical review committees.

Secondly, it has been morally and legally accepted that certain human groups can practise collective decision-making. Even those who envision human groups as simply free associations of atomistic contractors have to recognise the moral authority of many kinds of groups to make collective decisions about the best interests of their members.[76] For example, Sanders points out that:

> Group organizations have a particular legitimacy or standing to assert rights on behalf of their members, which gives them certain advantages over individuals seeking redress for rights violations. They are the best bodies to seek affirmative action programs, initiate test-case litigation, handle educational programs, engage with the media, lobby governments, and choose spokespeople for the group.[77]

---

74 Foster, M. W., Eisenbraun, A. J. and Carter, T. H. (1997) 'Communal Discourse as a Supplement to Informed Consent for Genetic Research', *Nature Genetics*, vol. 17, pp. 277–79.
75 See note 60 at 192.
76 Sanders, D. (1991) 'Collective Rights', *Human Rights Quarterly*, vol. 13, no. 3, pp. 368–86.
77 ibid at 369.

In fact, as the proponents of group protection further argue, the concept of autonomy, or self-governance, which is widely accepted and adopted by international human rights declarations, such as the United Nations International Covenant on Civil and Political Rights,[78] in defence of individual freedom, has its roots in efforts to protect the ability of particular human groups to govern themselves.[79] For example, Michael McDonald supports the community as an independent entity of value in this way:

> What the liberal takes as basic and unquestionable is the idea that the individual is the measure of everything; hence, the liberal believes that correct normative principles treat the individual as the fundamental unit of value ... Individuals are regarded as valuable because they are choosers and have interests. But so also do communities make choices and have values. Why not then treat communities as fundamental units of value ...?[80]

Many scholars would agree that if we do not let groups be the entity to make decisions on issues related to group identity, it would undermine both the integrity and the autonomy of those groups that enjoy the moral standing to make such decisions.[81] For example, Underkuffler points out that on both a theoretical and a practical level, the assumed anti-group bias in the Western tradition is fraught with weaknesses. She illustrated that all of the negative assertions about group collective interests and rights in Western ethics are based on the proposition that 'all moral value is rooted in the well-being of individual human beings'.[82] Thus, she argues that if one accepts the moral value of distinctly collective interests, the group collective interests would have their own moral value as well. On this view, it is normal to entitle a group to be an independent right-holder to 'protect distinctly collective

78 The United Nations International Covenant on Civil and Political Rights (ICCPR) is a multilateral treaty adopted by the United Nations General Assembly on 16 December 1966, and in force from 23 March 1976. It commits its parties to respect the civil and political rights of individuals, including the right to life, freedom of religion, freedom of speech, freedom of assembly, electoral rights and rights to due process and a fair trial. As of October 2009, the Covenant had 72 signatories and 166 parties. The full text of the ICCPR can be seen on the official website of the UN, available at http://www.hrweb.org/legal/cpr.html (last visited 4 July 2013).

79 Buchanan, A. E. (1991) 'Right to Self-Determination: Analytical and Moral Foundations', *Arizona Journal of International and Comparative Law*, vol. 8, no. 2, pp. 41–50 at 50.

80 McDonald, M. (1991) 'Should Communities Have Rights: Reflections on Liberal Individualism', *Canadian Journal of Law and Jurisprudence*, vol. 4, pp. 217–37 at 237.

81 Dinstein, Y. (1976) 'Collective Human Rights of Peoples and Minorities', *International and Comparative Law Quarterly*, vol. 25, no. 1, pp. 102–20.

82 Underkuffler, L. S. (2007) 'Human Genetics Studies: The Case for Group Rights', *Journal of Law, Medicine and Ethics*, vol. 35, pp. 383–95 at 384.

interests, such as larger societal recognition and respect for the group's decision-making mechanisms, rights, and powers'.[83] She further argues that:

> From the point of view of what rights do, there is no structural reason why legal rights – which guarantee particular states of affairs in law – cannot be afforded to groups as well as to individuals. Indeed, the idea that Western jurisprudence shuns group rights is, itself, an obvious conceptual fallacy. In international law, governments – which recognize and enforce individual rights – are themselves groups with recognized legal status. In addition, groups of all kinds are recognized in a myriad of circumstances. Binding international agreements and non-binding international declarations recognize group rights in the contexts of cultural property, education, religion, and genocide. National, ethnic, religious, and linguistic minorities, as well as indigenous peoples, are afforded group rights.[84]

Using this argument, the justification for group collective rights in international law seems strong.

Justifications for protection of groups in HPGR

In the first place, in respect of Juengst's first problem, which is that target groups of HPGR refer either to human demes or social identified groups, it is clear that the target groups will already have been identified by the researchers in the context of HPGR. As has already been said, they are almost always ethnic minorities or isolated groups in rural areas of developing countries, whose members share the same community or group collective human genetic information. Even if the result of a particular research project is that the target group is not in fact a group given their genetic make-up, this in itself could also lead to cultural harms to the target group, as was discussed in Chapter 4. Hence, nesting problems cannot be an argument against offering protection to groups in HPGR.

Indeed, a great many arguments and supporting evidence can be found to provide a justification for group collective rights in international law and human rights law. For example, Article 1 of the ICCPR[85] states that:

> All peoples have the right of self-determination. By virtue of that right they freely determine their political status and freely pursue their economic, social and cultural development.[86]

---

83 ibid.
84 See note 82 at 384–85.
85 See note 78.
86 ibid Article 1.

No matter how 'peoples' are defined, they must be collectives consisting of more than one individual. There are also examples, such as the UN's nation-building efforts in East Timor and other countries' recognition of East Timor as a sovereign nation, which can illustrate that the UN and other countries regard self-determination as a right belonging to an abstract 'East Timorese people', which is a group as a whole.[87] In this case, self-determination is regarded as a collective right independent of the rights of any individuals who make up this group, so the right of self-determination was implemented in good faith for the benefit of this abstract group. Since the right belonged to an abstract group above and beyond any of its individual members, the implementation of the self-determination right was not a matter that was determined by reference to any of the individuals, but rather to the abstract group. Thus, although not each individual of East Timor voted to be part of a sovereign nation, according to the collective ideas of the group, East Timor became a sovereign nation.

Additionally, in the context of medical law, there are also arguments concerning collective human rights to public health which have been used to advance health rights in a globalised world. For example, Meier pointed out that although the United Nations International Covenant on Economic, Social and Cultural Rights (ICESCR)[88] endorsed the right to health and declared the obligation of states to provide the 'highest attainable standard' of health for all,[89] this highest attainable standard is for each individual, while the 'right to health has been ineffective in compelling states to address burgeoning inequalities in underlying determinants of health, focusing on individual medical treatments at the expense of public health systems'.[90] Distinct from individual human rights that need to be enforced by personal action, collective rights operate at a societal level, considering the wellbeing of the whole public, which can only be enjoyed by the whole society of people and cannot be fulfilled solely through individual rights mechanisms.[91]

87 Fan, H. (2007) 'The Missing Link between Self-Determination and Democracy: The Case of East Timor', *Northwestern University Journal of International Human Rights*, vol. 6, no. 1, pp. 176–95.

88 The United Nations International Covenant on Economic, Social and Cultural Rights (ICESCR) is a multilateral treaty adopted by the United Nations General Assembly on 16 December 1966, and in force from 3 January 1976. It commits its parties to work toward the granting of economic, social and cultural rights (ESCR) to individuals, including labour rights and rights to health, education and an adequate standard of living. The full text of the ICESCR can be seen on the official website of the UN, available at http://www.ohchr.org/EN/ProfessionalInterest/Pages/CESCR.aspx (last visited 5 July 2013).

89 ibid Article 12(1): 'The States Parties to the present Covenant recognize the right of everyone to the enjoyment of the highest attainable standard of physical and mental health'.

90 Meier, B. M. (2007) 'Advancing Health Rights in a Globalized World: Responding to Globalization Through a Collective Human Right to Public Health', *Journal of Law, Medicine and Ethics*, vol. 35, no. 4, pp. 545–55 at 545.

91 ibid at 551.

According to Meier, collective health rights could be a new type of independent human right, which would mean that the abstract society or state, not each individual, would be the right-holder.

Thirdly, proponents of group protection also argue that there are real interests at stake for human groups in HPGR. This issue has already been addressed, but it is worth reconsidering here. Edlin has explained that some genetic epidemiological research may lead to risks of harm to participants and their group members. Such research, aimed at identifying genes associated with disease, for example, may find that a certain group carries a relatively greater genetic propensity for alcoholism. This may be interpreted as universally predictive for the group, which could lead to further harms, such as discrimination, stigmatisation and even self-stigmatisation.[92] What is more, Sawyer and Hartl have argued that most HPGR, such as the comparative genealogical efforts of the molecular anthropologists, would pose significant risks to groups. According to them, the genetic differences that most contemporary molecular anthropologists use to assess the relatedness of human groups consist of medically irrelevant molecular variations in the non-coding regions of the DNA, which are then compared with the DNA for functional genes. Single mutations are quick to accumulate and can be used quite precisely to establish ancestries.[93] Identifying these genomic hallmarks of particular groups would produce more sensitive gene-based tools for identifying members of target groups, which may raise the risks of the harm of racism or discrimination. Moreover, Tsosie also illustrated this point by the example of the Havasupai Tribe, referred to earlier:

> ... in a case brought by the Havasupai Tribe and its members over the use of blood samples, handprints, and genealogy information initially taken by researchers at Arizona State University for a diabetes project. These materials were then allegedly used by researchers at ASU and other institutions for a multitude of unauthorized purposes, including research into the frequency of mental health disorders and the origin of human populations. Consequently, the affected members sued for damages under several legal theories. However, underlying all of these claims was the allegation that this unauthorized use of genetic resources and data not only injured the individuals who gave samples, but also caused a collective harm to the Havasupai Tribe and the cultural and spiritual beliefs of its members.[94]

92 Edlin, G. (1987) 'Inappropriate Use of Genetic Terminology in Medical Research: A Public Health Issue', *Perspectives in Biology and Medicine*, vol. 31, pp. 47–56.
93 Sawyer, S. A. and Hartl, D. L. (1992) 'Population Genetics of Polymorphism and Divergence', *Genetics*, vol. 132, pp. 1161–76.
94 Tsosie, R. (2007) 'Cultural Challenges to Biotechnology: Native American Genetic Resources and the Concept of Cultural Harm', *Journal of Law, Medicine and Ethics*, vol. 35, no. 3, pp. 396–411 at 396.

She further pointed out that most of the concerns about biotechnology raised by indigenous peoples should be regarded as 'cultural claims' that rest on a concept of 'cultural rights'. Although the standard model used to evaluate cultural claims suggests that 'such rights ought to be adjudicated within pluralistic societies according to a secular model of rights that respects individual claims to autonomy, equality, and liberty', in certain situations 'special' rights for particular groups to ensure their equal treatment in society can also be accepted.[95] According to her, HPGR is one of those special situations that deserve the recognition of group rights.

Nevertheless, there remain significant problems in suggesting that target groups of HPGR should be deemed to be rights-holders in a legal sense. In fact, it would be difficult to regard a target group as a rights-holder, even if such a group could be identified for a specific HPGR project. As Hartney noted:

> ... not all goods (or interest) generate rights ... Goods (or interests) may generate duties (e.g., of protection) but these duties do not correlate with rights, unless there is some specific moral reason for protecting these good. There is an importance deference here between legal and moral rights. In order to determine whether a certain legal rights exists, one determines first whether the law has imposed a legal duty on someone, and then whether that duty can be interpreted as owed to somebody; since the law can create duties for all sorts of reasons, including relatively unimportant, and the importance of this thing or of the reason for the legal duty do not tell us whether there is a right to it. On the other hand, a moral right implies a good (or interest) sufficiently important that it warrants protection by duties on others. Thus, there are no unimportant moral duties, and an estimate of the importance of the good or interest in question is central to the determination of the existence of a moral right. We have all sorts of legal rights which do not correlate with any moral right.[96]

This statement indicated that there is a difference between recognising a group as a legal entity, such as the East Timorese people mentioned above, and recognising that a group has interests that can be harmed. In the context of HPGR, undoubtedly a target group may have interests, as they may be harmed, but it does not indicate that target groups should be the right-holders. In HPGR, it is difficult to argue how a target group could hold rights or enforce them in the context of HPGR. Therefore, it can only be

---

95 ibid at 401–2.
96 Hartney, M. (1991) 'Some Confusions Concerning Collective Rights', *Canadian Journal of Law and Jurisprudence*, vol. 4, pp. 293–314 at 304.

suggested that the interests of target groups should be taken into account and protected in HPGR.

Furthermore, the idea that a group could be the holder of a legally enforceable right to decide whether HPGR can proceed, would not least face the dilemma of creating conflicts between individuals and groups, whether it were to give the group a right of veto to research proceeding, or to allow group consent to override individual refusal of consent. Doing so would challenge the baseline of respect for fundamental individual rights. Despite this, it is reasonable to argue that issues relevant to collective interests could and should be considered in HPGR, even though a group or community approval of HPGR could not be a substitute for the decisions made by individual members. Accordingly, it needs to be emphasised that group consent is not the only way to recognise the concept of group or community interests in HPGR. As will be proposed in more detail later, the recognition of the possibility of group harms might be achieved in a number of alternative ways. These would include group involvement in the design and review of research before individuals are asked to participate, taking group collective views into account by IRBs and RECs, asking representatives of target groups to be involved in the ethical review process and subsequent monitoring of the research and providing them with appropriate training and support to enable them to do so effectively.

Protection of groups in HPGR

Protection of groups

At present, most guidelines for the protection of groups or communities in research have been drafted for research involving specific indigenous peoples, such as American Indians, Alaska Natives, Inuit Peoples, Australian Aborigines and Maori People. There are three main considerations of these guidelines. First, indigenous peoples are often geographically isolated and have their own unique histories, cultures, beliefs and traditions. The members of these indigenous people often distinguish themselves as a unique and independent group from the dominant ones. Secondly, it has been accepted as a common political aspiration by several international political declarations that indigenous peoples have their own rights to self-determination and autonomy. There are increasingly arguments that the responsibility for governance should belonged to the groups or communities themselves. For example, Article 3 of the United Nations Declaration on the Rights of Indigenous Peoples[97] confers on

---

97   The United Nations Declaration on the Rights of Indigenous Peoples was adopted by the United Nations General Assembly during its 62nd session at UN Headquarters in New York City on 13 September 2007. It is worth noting that this declaration is not a legally binding instrument under international law. The full text of this declaration can be seen on the official website of the UN, available at http://www.un.org/esa/socdev/unpfii/en/declaration.html (last visited 4 July 2013).

indigenous peoples the right of self-determination and states that 'by virtue of that right they freely determine their political status and freely pursue their economic, social and cultural development'.[98] Article 4 of the Declaration also provides that 'in exercising their right to self-determination, indigenous peoples have the right to autonomy or self-government in matters relating to their internal and local affairs'.[99] Thirdly, indigenous peoples are increasingly concerned that research may adversely affect them and their values.

Therefore, there are several guidelines that have been drafted for the protections of indigenous peoples in research. For example, in Australia, the National Health and Medical Research Council drafted the Guidelines on Ethical Matters in Aboriginal and Torres Strait Islander Research[100] in 1991; and the Aboriginal Health Research Ethics Committee of South Australia drafted the Ethical Considerations for Health Related Research Involving Aboriginal People[101] in 1998. In the US, the American Indian Law Centre published a Model Tribal Research Code[102] in 1999.

In addition, there are also some guidelines to protect communities beyond indigenous peoples, including the CIOMS Guidelines for Epidemiological Research,[103] and Canada's Tri-Council Working Group on Ethics document, Code of Conduct for Research Involving Humans,[104] which articulate guidelines to protect a variety of collective interests of groups.

According to the reviews of the Australian National Health and Medical Research Council[105] and the American Indian Law Centre,[106] the requirements for the protection of a group or community can be organised into five themes. If they are to provide adequate protection to a target group or community in

98   ibid Article 3.

99   ibid Article 4.

100 See Guidelines on Ethical Matters in Aboriginal and Torres Strait Islander Health Research 1991. The full text of the guidelines can be seen on the official website of the National Health and Medical Research Council, available at http://www.nhmrc.gov.au/_files_nhmrc/file/publications/synopses/withdrawn/e11.pdf (last visited 4 July 2013).

101 See Ethical Considerations for Health Related Research Involving Aboriginal People 1998. The full text of the guidelines can be seen on the official website of the Aboriginal Health Research Ethics Committee of South Australia, available at http://www.research.murdoch.edu.au/ethics/hrec/Policies/WAAHIEC%20guidelines.pdf (last visited 14 December 2010).

102 American Indian Law Centre, *Model Tribal Research Code*, available at http://www.ihs.gov/Research/pdf/mdl-code.pdf (last visited 4 July 2013).

103 International Ethical Guidelines for Epidemiological Studies 1991 can be seen on the official website of the CIOMS, available at http://www.cioms.ch/publications/guidelines/1991_texts_of_guidelines.htm (last visited 4 July 2013).

104 Code of Conduct for Research Involving Humans can be seen on the website of the Tri-Council Working Group, available at http://www.ethics.ubc.ca/code/july97/ (last visited 4 July 2013).

105 See note 100.

106 See note 102.

HPGR, however, there are several shortcomings in each theme, which need to be addressed.

Consultation in protocol development

Almost all of the guidelines require that researchers respect the culture of the community, suggesting widespread agreement about the need for consultation early in the research development process.[107] For example, the Guidelines on Ethical Matters in Aboriginal and Torres Strait Islander Health Research noted that:

> 1. In the preparation of the research proposal, the researcher has sought advice not only from State, Territory and Federal Aboriginal and Torres Strait Islander Health agencies, but also from local community-controlled Aboriginal and Torres Strait Islander health service and agencies.
> 2. The Aboriginal and Torres Strait Islander community, or appropriate community controlled agency able to represent the Aboriginal and Torres Strait Islander group which is the focus or context of research, has indicated that the research being proposed will be potentially useful to the community in particular or Aboriginal and Torres Strait Islanders in general, and will be conducted in a way that is sensitive to the cultural and political situation of that community.[108]

However, none of these guidelines provides guidance on how to cope with circumstances when it may be unclear who represents a particular group or community. In addition, none addresses the problem of oppressed individuals within a group or community.

Consent process and informed consent

Most of the research guidelines require that informed consent be obtained from individual research subjects and from community leaders on behalf of the community. For instance, the Guidelines on Ethical Matters in Aboriginal and Torres Strait Islander Health Research, the regulations of which on informed consent have also been applied by the Ethical Considerations for Health Related Research Involving Aboriginal People noted that:

> 3. The researcher has obtained written documentation of consent from the communities in which it is proposed to conduct research and where this has not been possible, the reasons should be documented.

---

107 Weijer, C. and Anderson, J. A. (2002) 'A Critical Appraisal of Protections for Aboriginal Communities in Biomedical Research', *Jurimetrics*, vol. 42, pp. 187–98 at 195–96.
108 See note 100, Articles 1 and 2.

In such circumstances, informed consent should be shown to have involved: (a) provision of information in a form accessible to community members and able to be readily understood by them. This information should have included details of the collection and analysis of data, and the drafting and publication of reports. It should also list any potential costs to the community as well as potential benefits; (b) face-to-face discussions with community groups and individuals concerned wherever possible and where this has not been possible, the reasons should be documented; (c) the allowance of sufficient time for the community and the individuals concerned to assimilate and respond to the information offered; (d) demonstration of a process for obtaining free consent from individuals as well as written evidence of consent by the community-at-large; (e) provision of information to participants that consent may be withdrawn at any time.[109]

However, there is no guideline considering the situation that the target group has the cultural tradition of collective decision-making, thus no guideline provides for a specific, clear mechanism for obtaining community permission if needed. Besides, these guidelines do not address the issue of consent to changes in research design. If consent is required for the research to proceed, then it would seem logical that major changes in the agreed-upon protocol should also be agreed to by the community.[110] The same problem occurs in respect of withdrawal of consent.

Involvement in the conduct of research

Some research guidelines suggest that community members be trained to help conduct the research, and some think that they should be employees of the research and receive fair compensation for their work.[111] For example, the Guidelines on Ethical Matters in Aboriginal and Torres Strait Islander Health Research stated in relation to community involvement that:

4. Members of the Aboriginal and Torres Strait Islander community being studied will be offered the opportunity to assist in the research and will be paid for the assistance, and the funds to support that assistance are included in the research budget proposal. Specifically, Aboriginal and Torres Strait Islander women, as advised by the community, will be involved when research deals with women's and children's issues; and the

---

109 See note 100 at Article 3.
110 Weijer, C., Goldsan, G. and Emanuel, E. J. (1999), 'Protecting Communities in Research: Current Guidelines and Limits of Extrapolation', *Nature Genetics*, vol. 23, pp. 275–80 at 278.
111 See note 107 at 196.

specific cultural and social needs of Aboriginal and Torres Strait Islander men would be similarly recognised.[112]

However, it is rare to see the requirement that group or community representatives be involved in the conduct and ethical review of research.

Access to data and samples

Because of the historical exploitation and abuse suffered by aboriginal communities in Australia and the US, the need for group or community consent for future use of data is urgent.[113] However, current guidelines only provide regulations on the secondary use of personal identifiable and sensitive information. For example, the Code of Conduct for Research Involving Humans, provided by the Tri-Council Working Group in Canada, noted that:

> Article 3.4 If identifying information is involved, REB approval must be sought for secondary uses of data. REB approval is not required for access to non-identifying data.
> Article 3.5 Depending on the sensitivity of the information and on feasibility, the REB may also require that a researcher's access to secondary use of data be dependent on: (a) the informed consent of those who contributed data; or (b) an appropriate strategy for informing the participants; or (c) consultation with a representative group of those who contributed data.[114]

There are seldom statements on the related requirement of storage of research samples and data.[115] Such requirements would refer to the need for researchers and communities to discuss where data or samples will be stored, whether or not any will be destroyed, and who ultimately controls them after the completion of the research.[116] Guidelines are almost all silent on this issue.

Dissemination and publication of research results

Most of the guidelines require that a draft report be circulated for comment before publication, that the participation of the community be acknowledged and that the consent of the community be sought concerning whether the

---

112 See note 100 at Article 4.
113 ibid.
114 See note 104.
115 Most developing countries put these requirements in their domestic data protection law. However, because of jurisdiction, these requirements cannot be used to protect target groups in HPGR in developing countries.
116 See note 110 at 278.

community is identified in the final report.[117] For example, Canada's Tri-Council Working Group on Ethics document noted that:

> ... participants have the right to know whether they will be identified directly or indirectly in publications resulting from the research. It is important that prospective participants know whether or not they will be given an opportunity to comment on research findings prior to publication. (Affording participants an opportunity to review and comment on research results is one way of building a stronger trust relationship between researchers and participants.) In some cases (e.g., when there has been a history of alleged misrepresentation), individuals or groups may be unwilling to participate unless they are guaranteed the right to review research results and even have their comments incorporated in resulting publications. Reviewing research results with participants may also improve the quality of research (e.g., in terms of correcting mistaken impressions on the part of researchers or by including a more comprehensive perspective) and also help protect the researcher (e.g., against claims of libel).[118]

These requirements point toward 'a tension between the acknowledgement requirement and protecting the identity of the community in research where confidentiality is a particular concern'.[119]

While there are, therefore, shortcomings in the coverage of individual guidelines, their existence nevertheless illustrates the possibility of taking into account collective risks posed by HPGR. The need for the involvement of target groups or their representatives in identifying issues of concern to them and reducing vulnerability are also highlighted. The question of vulnerability, however, deserves some further consideration.

Protection of vulnerable groups

If we accept that target groups of HPGR are vulnerable, several influential national legislation and international declarations advocate special protection for vulnerable groups in biomedical research, such as the Helsinki Declaration, the CIOMS Guidelines and the Universal Declaration on Bioethics and Human Rights; however, there has not been a specific approach focused on HPGR and group issues. In the US, federal regulations stipulate that IRBs are charged with the task of protecting human research subjects from coercion and unreasonable risk, and assessing a variety of scientific and ethical

---

117 ibid note 107 at 197.
118 See note 104.
119 See note 107 at 195.

factors in research.[120] IRBs must also pay attention to the emerging interest in the inclusion of vulnerable minority populations in research, including the trend of biomedical research that focuses exclusively on minority populations. The confluence of this new emphasis on the role of vulnerable ethnic minorities or isolated groups and some increased willingness on the part of these populations to participate in order to obtain health care or economic benefits, raises some difficult scientific and ethical questions for IRBs. The research community should proceed with caution, focusing primarily on human subject protections and special protection for vulnerable groups, but IRBs should also evaluate questions of protocol design and scientific validity as they affect the inclusion of target groups.

In order to do so it can be proposed that specific regulations to ensure that the interests of vulnerable groups in HPGR are properly considered are essential. Hurst has argued that the 'concept of vulnerability ... serves to identify groups of individuals that do, in fact, need and merit this special care in the application of criteria for ethical research'.[121] She also argued that the actions required for special protection would need to be tailored to the sort of risks to be avoided and to the source of the specific vulnerability, as follows:

(1) Breach of confidentiality: as researchers or healthcare providers may be at greater risk, IRBs should share in the duty of protection, and could require specific anonymisation of data to limit colleagues' access to their personal information. (2) Unfavourable risk/benefit ratio: vulnerable populations are, for example, terminally ill patients, so IRBs share in the duty of protection; their risk/benefit ratio should be specifically examined by researchers and IRBs rather than assumed to be the same as for other potential subjects. (3) Being enrolled without valid consent: consent is sought at that time only for those parts of the protocol that are truly urgent; the remaining problems with consent at that time can be compensated by including a requirement that an independent clinician confirm that enrolment is not contrary to the potential subject's interest. (4) Being denied the benefit of research: participants in developing countries who lack access to healthcare are excluded from an important part of the social benefits of research; although IRBs are not alone in bearing some responsibility for this, it is among the points they should examine in general, and thus also for the purposes of protecting the vulnerable; minimization: reasonable availability aims to minimize this problem; compensation: fair benefits aim to compensate it [the benefit of research].[122]

120 See 45 CFR § 46.101(a).
121 Hurst, S. A. (2008) 'Vulnerability in Research and Health Care: Describing the Elephant in the Room', *Bioethics*, vol. 22, no. 4, pp. 191–202 at 197.
122 ibid at 198.

This approach concentrates on the responsibility of IRBs, which have a moral and legal function to protect vulnerable populations. However, the actual situation of HPGR conducted in developing countries is that there is rarely legislation or ethical guidelines which require the existence of IRBs or RECs to conduct ethical review on research involving human beings. Therefore, although huge sums of money have been invested in these kinds of activities, such as EDCTP,[123] many difficult issues remain, both with the set-up and the running of RECs. It is suggested here that developing countries without IRBs or RECs in place should set them up and ensure that they are governed by appropriate legal regulations concerning review. Furthermore, members of target groups in HPGR, with proper training on ethical review, should be part of IRBs or RECs in order to provide a level of consideration and protection of group interests. As a result, in order to provide adequate and appropriate protections to vulnerable target groups of HPGR the existing guidance on research involving human beings needs to be reconsidered.

Attempts to protect groups in HPGR

There have been several attempts to revise the guidelines to protect groups in genetic research. For example, there has been the suggestion that a fourth principle of 'respect for communities' should be added to 'respect for persons', 'beneficence' and 'justice' – the three basic ethical principles which were referred to in the Belmont Report.[124] In addition, Sharp and Foster have developed an account of 'community review' that includes groups' interests in the research process. Both of these approaches have pointed out some of the unique issues of research with groups or communities and the need to devise strategies to bring communities into the process and provide insight into the risks that the proposed research might pose to communities or groups. In addition, Michael Parker, who conducts research on the ethics of collaborative global health research, also raised concerns on ethical issues in HPGR in developing countries and provided some practical suggestions. The following section will analyse these proposals.

---

123   The European and Developing Countries Clinical Trials Partnership (EDCTP) was created in 2003 as a European response to the global health crisis caused by the three main poverty-related diseases of HIV/AIDS, tuberculosis and malaria. These three diseases account for over 6 million deaths each year, with the greatest burden of disease in sub-Saharan Africa, where besides ravaging lives, they impede development and cause poverty. More details of the EDCTP can be seen on the official website of the EDCTP, available at http://www.edctp.org/ (last visited 4 July 2013).

124   Weijer, C. (1999), 'Protecting Communities in Research: Philosophical and Pragmatic Challenges', *Cambridge Quarterly of Healthcare Ethics*, vol. 8, pp. 501–13.

A fourth ethical principle: 'respect for communities'

Since existing ethical frameworks, such as that established by the Belmont Report, ignore the interests of community in research, some scholars have argued that the basic principles need to be reconsidered. For example, Childress has argued that a new meaning of 'person' in the principle of 'respect for persons' is necessary. He noted that:

> Any serviceable account of biomedical ethics in a liberal society requires a central place for the principle of respect for autonomy. However, its demands are often unclear because of the complexity of personal actions and values, and because it is not the only source of moral guidance. In fact, the richest resolutions of debates in bioethics presuppose attention to the claims of other ethical principles as well as a fuller interpretation of selves in time and community.[125]

What is more, according to Weijer, the communitarian argument 'has been successful in establishing two claims: first, that self-determination is impossible unless we presuppose an individual located within a community (otherwise choice can never "get off the ground"); second, that the interests of the individual may include the continuation of certain communal practices'.[126] He argued that according to these two claims and Childress's assertion, it can be concluded that the existing framework of ethical principles needs to be enriched. He then analysed several attempts which were intended to accomplish this. For example, Levine called for a principle of 'respect for culture', and stated that: 'Perhaps instead we should recognize the validity of certain forms of cultural relativism and have each culture decide how it should show respect for its own persons'.[127] McCarthy suggested that attention should be paid to respect for the family and the community of the research subjects, noting that contemporary Western principles stress individual liberty and place less emphasis on the rights and dignity of the community, while many third world countries have much to teach developed nations about community values.[128]

Weijer then argued for the creation of a new ethical principle: respect for communities. He suggested that there are at least three arguments that support the development of this 'fourth principle':

125 Childress, J. F. and Fletcher, J. C. (1994) 'Respect for Autonomy', *Hastings Centre Report*, vol. 24, no. 3, pp. 33–34 at 34.
126 See note 124 at 505.
127 Levine, R. J. (1982) 'Validity of Consent Procedures in Technologically Developing Countries' in *Human Experimentation and Medical Ethics: Proceedings of the XV CIOMS Round Table Conference*, Bankowski, Z. and N. Howard-Jones, eds. (Geneva: Council for International Organizations of Medical Sciences) at 16–30.
128 McCathy, C. (1993) 'A North American Perspective' in *Ethics and Research on Human Subjects: International Guidelines*, Bankowski, Z. and R. J. Levine, eds. (Geneva: Council for International Organizations of Medical Sciences) at 208–11.

... First, even if the continuation of some communal practices is in the interest of the individual, community interests are separable from individual interests. Indeed, individual and community interests may even conflict ... Second, an ethical principle does not merely serve the purpose of capturing existing moral debate; in other words, principles are not merely descriptive. Ethical principles also serve to acknowledge the moral status of players ... A new ethical principle, respect for communities, would similarly accord moral status to the community and require that the wishes and interests of the community be taken seriously ... Third, the principle of respect for communities can be justified as other ethical principles have been. The sorts of justification required to establish a new principle depend on just what one thinks ethical principles are ... Concerns about the community in research, and ultimately moral rules regarding the proper treatment of the community, may be loosely collected under the placeholder 'Be sure and think about the community' – the principle of respect for communities.[129]

According to him, the principle of respect for communities would 'obligate researchers to respect the values and interests of the community in the research and, wherever possible, to protect the community from harms'.[130]

After making his case for the need for this new principle, Weijer went on to discuss how it would be implemented. He found that 'clear guidelines exist for research involving first nations communities, and the guidelines must be respected and ought to be enforced',[131] through careful observation of existing research guidelines for researchers working in communities, both at the international and the domestic level. The guidelines include the CIOMS's two sets of guidelines: International Ethical Guidelines for Biomedical Research Involving Human Subjects and International Guidelines for Ethical Review of Epidemiological Studies; the US Department of Health and Human Services regulations pertaining to standards for international research; as well as other guidelines for research in first nation communities, such as the National Health and Medical Research Council Guidelines on Ethical Matters in Aboriginal and Torres Strait Islander Research in Australia, the American Indian Law Centre's Model Tribal Research Code in the US and Canada's Tri-Council Working Group on Ethics document, Code of Conduct for Research Involving Humans. However, he also concluded that 'difficult challenges lay in the way of developing guidelines for research on other sorts of communities'.[132]

---

129 See note 126 at 505–6.
130 Weijer, C. and Anderson, J. A. (2002) 'A Critical Appraisal of Protections for Aboriginal Communities in Biomedical Research', *Jurimetrics*, vol. 42, pp. 187–98 at 192.
131 See note 126 at 510.
132 ibid.

One advantage of Weijer's proposed fourth principle of respect for communities is that it clarifies the reasons why communities and groups require separate consideration, since the interests and potential risks for communities are separate from those potentially posed for each individual within the community. Thus, in his revision of individualistic research ethics, he highlighted the significance of community interests. This proposal goes further than simply the provision of some special measures to protect a community through the process of informed consent. Thus, this revision is targeted at challenging the individualism of current research ethics through emphasis on the interests of community, not just at making some supplementary adjustments to current requirements for individual informed consent, although his premise on personhood is still focused on the isolated individual without consideration of his or her other social relationships and context.

There are, however, some disadvantages. First, he was not able to identify a clear pattern of the use of the word 'community'. Having investigated existing research guidelines he found that there were different ways to use the word 'community'. Moreover, these research guidelines only extended to 'aboriginal communities', such as American Indians, Alaskan Natives, Inuit Peoples and other indigenous peoples, but did not comment on how to protect other kinds of communities.

Secondly, he failed to establish the relationship between the fourth principle and the other three principles. Thus, if there is conflict between individual and communal choices, for example between the principle of respect for persons and respect for communities, he offers no practical approach to resolve it.

Thirdly, he failed to provide a practical strategy for implementation of the fourth principle in research. He merely states:

> The protections are arranged chronologically, beginning with the issues pertaining to consultation with the community on research design and ending with issues arising from the dissemination and publication of research findings. The order is as follows: consultation in protocol development, consent process and informed consent, involvement in research conduct, access to data and samples, and dissemination and publication of research results.[133]

Therefore, having analysed the gaps in research guidelines in respect of the protection of communities, he concluded that the existing protections are incomplete, but failed to provide an effective alternative recommendation.

---

133 Weijer, C., Goldsan, G. and Emanuel, E. J. (1999), 'Protecting Communities in Research: Current Guidelines and Limits of Extrapolation', *Nature Genetics*, vol. 23, pp. 275–80 at 277.

Community review

Another attempt to revise current ethical framework to protect a community or group in HPGR was put forward by Sharp and Foster. They suggested that the target group or community of HPGR is similar to other vulnerable populations, such as children, pregnant women and prisoners, which have already been singled out for special protection. Their approach stresses the need for members of study populations to be directly involved in the review process, particularly when the research aims to identify genetic variations that may be unique to, or more prevalent among, members of those populations. This requirement they encapsulated in the principle of 'community review'.[134]

Sharp and Foster proposed that the term 'community review' was 'a general category describing various approaches to involving populations in the evaluation of genetic research'.[135] They argued that the goals of community review are: reviewing research protocols considering the cultural sensitivities of specific target group; identifying and minimising the risks of harm that may be caused by research to all the involved parties, including individual participants, participating communities and others community members; promoting collaborations and longer partnerships between researchers and target groups, through communicating interests and concerns with each other; establishing trust between researchers and target groups through researchers' respect for the social and cultural structure in place within those communities; and helping provide additional protection for individual participants by assisting them in assessing the risks and benefits of the research.[136]

Community review takes four forms; each one attempts to achieve the different goals described above. Sharp and Foster described them as follows:

> Community dialogue: this form of review includes both formal and informal discussion of a proposed study and its potential implications for a socially identifiable group. These discussions may be initiated by researchers or arise independently within a community after contact with researchers. Community dialogue is meant to identify collective concerns and consider ways of minimizing research-related risks, but does not provide a comprehensive review of the research in question and often will not engage a representative sample of community members.
> Community consultation: in contrast to community dialogue, this type of review is more structured. Community consultation documents and records the concerns of a socially identifiable group by consulting a representative subset of its individual members and organizations. Other reviewers can then incorporate these perspectives in their assessments of

134 Sharp, R. R. and Foster, M. W. (2000) 'Involving Study Populations in the Review of Genetic Research', *Journal of Law, Medicine & Ethics*, vol. 28, pp. 41–51 at 41.
135 ibid at 42.
136 ibid.

the research. How these perspectives are documented will vary, ranging from structured community forums to the creation of an independent community review panel. These forums and review panels may choose to endorse or oppose the research in an explicit way, but with community consultation, these evaluations are not binding on researchers.

Formal community approval (disapproval): an even more structured type of community review is the negotiation of a formal contractual agreement between researchers and a study population. This arrangement can be thought of as roughly analogous to obtaining informed consent from individual research participant. In this form of review, members of a study population (or recognized political representatives) are asked to give their collective permission for a research study. That collective decision, however, is not binding on individual community members, who still may choose to participate in the research (or not to participate).

Community partnership: the most structured way to involve members of a study population in the review process is to make them partners in the research. As partners, members of the study population are involved early in the design of the research project and 'review' the study by helping to define its goals and methodology, and implement its experimental design.[137]

It is argued that these different forms of community review could be used at various stages of a HPGR, as there are subtle differences in emphasis between them. For example, community consultation could be a way to identify community concerns in the initial design of a HPGR proposal; while 'subsequent consideration of these concerns could prompt researchers to seek community approval at a later stage in the research, perhaps in connection with the publication of research findings'.[138] In addition, these four forms of community review are highly dependent on each other. For instance, community dialogue and consultation both help to 'convey respect for members of study populations, seeking formal community approval demonstrates respect for the decision-making authority of the constituent communities'.[139] Similarly, community partnership 'goes further and suggests a deeper sense of respect for study populations by taking note of the unique social and cultural arrangements that exist within participating communities'.[140]

Sharp and Foster also argued that the form of community review adopted should be tailored to be appropriate to a given community, or a particular study, and depend on the following factors: (i) the frequency of social interaction among members of the study population; and (ii) the extent of shared

137 See note 134 at 43.
138 ibid.
139 ibid.
140 ibid.

socio-cultural belief and values that are distinctive to the study population.[141] The determination of the most appropriate community review form for a particular HPGR for a given community should take these two features into account. According to them, and as noted above, the risks that may be caused by HPGR are of two distinct types: 'external risks', which refer to the possible discrimination and stigmatisation of members of the study population; and 'internal risks', which result from the disruption of interactions among members of the study population. For instance, in a population where interactions between members are infrequent, and their distinctive beliefs few, the main risks of HPGR involve potential misuse of genetic information by others outside the community, possibly resulting in discrimination and stigmatisation. These risks are not unique to any particular group and can often be identified by individuals who are not themselves members of the population placed at risk. Nevertheless, community dialogue or consultation can still be helpful in identifying research-related risks and assessing how members of the study population view the significance of these risks.[142] In contrast, where the frequency of social interaction between members of a population is high, and the distinctive shared socio-cultural beliefs help to distinguish members of the population from other communities, HPGR can cause additional risks, such as that genetic findings could reveal that their shared socio-cultural belief is mistaken. Therefore, in these communities, the full range of community review is essential to identify the risks that may be caused by HPGR.[143] In addition, they also offered a model agreement for genetic research in socially identifiable populations, which 'defined the scope of research, provided options for naming the population in publications (including anonymity), and addressed the distribution of royalties from intellectual property, the future use of archival samples, and specific cultural concerns'.[144]

There are several advantages to Sharp's and Foster's 'community review' approach to protecting target groups or communities in HPGR. First, they address the unique risks that groups or communities may face in HPGR, especially 'internal risks', which can probably only be recognised within the group; and suggested that these implications should be factored into the risk-benefit evaluation of proposed research.[145] Although IRBs and other review measures could be instructed to pay special attention to possible intra-community risks, including the disruption of existing social arrangements and relationships between members of a study population, the active

---

141 ibid at 44–45.
142 ibid at 45.
143 ibid.
144 Foster, M. W., Bernsten, D. and Carter, T. H. (1998) 'A Model Agreement for Genetic Research in Socially Identifiable Populations', *American Journal of Human Genetics*, vol. 63, pp. 696–702 at 696.
145 See note 134 at 46.

involvement of the target group in community review can help identify internal risks in populations whose socio-cultural traditions and structures differ from those of IRB members. Secondly, they illustrated four distinctive forms of community review and their main features, and proposed a means to choose the most appropriate forms of community review for the target group in a specific HPGR. Thirdly, they established a model agreement for obtaining community consensus for HPGR in an Apache tribe in Oklahoma. The essence of the model is that research should be preceded by careful efforts to understand how decisions are made in the particular community. This process of reaching communal consensus provides a feasible approach to generating a general model which may be suitable as a standard for evaluation of the collective risks for target groups in HPGR.

There are, however, also disadvantages to community review. Its feasibility is problematic for two reasons. First, with regard to the nesting of community there are difficulties resulting from the fact that individuals are members of multiple communities, many of which are nested within each other. The complexity of human population structure poses more than practical difficulties for the notion of community review. For example, as has been discussed, Juengst has argued that the nesting problem results from the concerns of local communities that may fail to correspond with those of communities at broader levels of inclusiveness; hence, consulting with larger communities may fail to identify the unique cultural concerns of local communities and, correspondingly, the concerns of local communities may fail to reflect those of larger communities.[146] The second reason concerns the extent of dispersion within communities. It has been argued that the dispersion of individual members and the lack of frequent social interactions between members of a study population combine to limit the effectiveness of community review.[147] In widely dispersed populations, individuals may be viewed by outsiders as members of the same community, although they rarely interact with each other socially.

In addition, community review is only one element of protecting members of a community or group if an individualistic approach is taken to consent in research. The community collective interests would be considered by researchers and ethical review committees through group involvement. Nevertheless, the final decision of an individual on HPGR participation might still be based on the information on potential effects on him or her, rather than taking into account the need for information disclosure to include potential group harms.

Finally, the inappropriate use of community review may harm the target group or community in HPGR. As Juengst noted:

---

146 See note 59 at 196.
147 Reilly, P. R. (1998) 'Rethinking Risks to Human Subjects in Genetic Research', *American Journal of Human Genetics*, vol. 63, pp. 682–85.

... acting as if social groups were the groups under study suggests that they are reducible to the demes we construct around them, setting the stage for new forms of scientific racism and providing new tools for discrimination; moreover, geneticists expect that the biological populations they pick out will ultimately 'correct', rather than respect, the indigenous beliefs that they were ostensibly commissioned to celebrate.[148]

Hence, researchers implementing a community review approach to socially identified groups without fully cultural sensitivity consultation might harm them by reifying race, ethnicity and other socially constructed categories, since it might reinforce the idea that biological differences underlie social differences between communities.

Therefore, although the application of both 'respect for community' and 'community review' would offer some help for group protection in HPGR, since both of them have some weaknesses, neither of them alone would provide sufficient protection to the interests of target groups in HPGR.

Michael Parker's work

Through the direct practical experience from the ethics programme of the Malaria Genomic Epidemiology Network (MalariaGEN),[149] Parker and his team suggested that the ethical issues in HPGR in developing countries 'can best be identified, analysed and addressed where ethics is embedded in the design and implementation of such research projects'.[150]

In their view, valid consent was considered as a process rather than a simple one-off matter of signing a form in HPGR. On seeking valid consent, although there may also be tension between individual and community consent in HPGR, they realised that, in most developing countries, consent should not be seen as valid without a familial or communal dimension. Therefore, they pointed out that community consent is no substitute for individual informed consent, but could be considered a precondition.[151] They identified community engagement as a crucial part of protecting the interests of research participants and a key element of ethical best practice in HPGR. They indicated that community engagement activities may also contribute to

---

148 See note 59 at 196.
149 More information of the programme can be seen on the official website of MalariaGEN, available at http://www.malariagen.net/ (last visited 4 July 2013).
150 De Vries, J. Bull, S., Doumbo, O., Ibrahim, M., Mercarau-Puijalon, O. and Parker, M., (2011) 'Ethical Issues in Human Genomics Research in Developing Countries', *BMC Medical Ethics*, vol. 12, no. 5.
151 Chokshi, D.A., Thera, M.A., Parker, M., Diakite, M., Makani, J., et al (2007) 'Valid Consent for Genomic Epidemiology in Developing Countries', *PLoS Medicine*, vol. 4, no. 4, e95, pp. 0636–41.

minimising inducement influence in the process of decision-making in participating in HPGR in developing countries.[152]

In order to deal with the ethical challenge in the context of conducting research in rural areas of lower income countries, they realised that additional protections for participants need to be considered in such research. Through a qualitative study on consent seeking to genomic research in a rural Ghanaian community, they concluded as follows:

> Capacity building for local ethics committees to enable appropriate consideration of ethical issues raised by genomic research is likely to be necessary in many contexts with limited experience of this form of research. Care will also be needed to determine the roles and responsibilities of local ethics committees and community representatives in contributing to the ongoing governance of genomic resources derived from their populations.
> An additional important measure may be to ensure that community engagement activities are routinely conducted before, during and after, genomic research … Even where the communities to be enrolled in research cannot be identified in advance, community engagement activities may provide a chance for researchers to consult about important aspects of genomic studies, including topics such as potential future uses of genomic data. Such activities can provide insights into community views on more complex and abstract aspects of research that, if appropriately documented, can inform both the design of consent processes and the decisions of community representatives and local ethics committees involved in ongoing governance of genomic resources. Further research is needed to determine how to appropriately engage with communities to elicit informed opinions of the acceptability of downstream uses of genome wide association data and other potential ethical issues.[153]

One advantage of Parker's work is that it identified and analysed research participant protection as the main ethical concern in conducting HPGR and highlights the importance of community in seeking valid consent for HPGR in developing countries. Based on their projects experience, they also provided some practical suggestions on how to achieve a successful and appropriate community engagement, including how the relevant community is to be identified and represented, the identification and establishment of procedures, principles and mechanisms of engagement, how to explain to communities what the study involves in ways that are accessible and make

---

152 ibid at 0638.
153 Tindana et al (2012) 'Seeking Consent to Genetic and Genomic Research in a Rural Ghanaian Setting: A Qualitative Study of the MalariaGEN Experience', *BMC Medical Ethics*, vol. 13, no. 15.

understanding and engagement possible.[154] At the same time, they also admitted that owing to the complexity of community engagement, they did not resolve ways of addressing these challenges within their projects and there may not be a one-size-fits-all solution. Another advantage of their work is that they provided insights into specific issues when conducting HPGR in a low-income context and rural setting. They indicated the importance of ensuring that resources are available for the design, conduct and evaluation of such education.[155]

However, there are also disadvantages to Parker's work. Although his work pays much attention to community engagement in HPGR, it does not consider the interests of group as a whole or how to provide appropriate group protection in HPGR in developing countries.

In summary, a target group may be vulnerable in the context of HPGR, especially where the HPGR is conducted in developing countries. Target groups are vulnerable to all three types of vulnerability: consent-based, risk-based and justice-based because of low education levels, difficulties in correct understanding of the risks of HPGR or undue inducement. These common characteristics of target groups all make them more likely to accept risks that are either not understood or appreciated, or that are unfair. Target groups of HPGR are thought to be vulnerable to exploitation, because the researchers or research institutions of HPGR, who are mostly research institutions or companies from developed countries, may be more likely to take unfair advantage of their inadequate economic and social resources by offering target groups unfair 'benefits' in exchange for their participation. If HPGR relies on individual consent to enrol participants who are vulnerable, target groups may not be able to protect their own interests properly. Furthermore, the absence of effective and adequate legal regulations and ethical guidelines in most developing countries, as well as poor law enforcement, also exacerbate the vulnerability of target groups in HPGR. Therefore, the target group and its members need to be protected as vulnerable groups in HPGR by specific legal and ethical regulations, regarding the specific situations and cultural sensitivities of target groups. In addition to information disclosure on group harms to potential participants to enable individuals to consider such issues as part of their own risk-benefit assessment before they are asked to consent, the collective ideas of target groups on issues relevant to group collective interests should also be considered. It can be suggested that target group involvement in HPGR is needed. An alternative model of group protection in HPGR, with the consideration of both appropriate information disclosure and group involvement, will be offered in Chapter 7 in the context of developing countries. In order to explain the particular context of HPGR in developing countries, the next chapter will consider the social and legal factors relevant to such research.

154 See note 150.
155 See note 153.

6 Developing countries: the mother lode of genes?

HPGR in developing countries: the case of the PRC

It has been indicated that, in this chapter, the People's Republic of China (PRC) will be used as a model to demonstrate the difficulties associated with human population genetic research (HPGR) in developing countries.

A brief introduction of HPGR in the PRC

Facing the new era of genetics, the PRC has its own ambitions and problems. HPGR projects in the PRC, especially those conducted by foreign researchers, are highly controversial.

On the one hand, the PRC's active participation in the Human Genome Project and its completion of the sequencing of the rice genome indicated that China is seeking an advanced place in genetics and genomics.[1] In the area of human population genetics, HPGR has also been encouraged and supported by the government. China began its own HPGR, the Chinese Human Genome Diversity Project (CHGDP) in November 1993, which still continues on a large scale. It was designed to 'collect the cell lines of the 56 official ethnic groups in China in the National Cell Line Repository in the Kunming Institute of Medical Biology [part of the Chinese Academic of Medical Sciences] and Beijing Institute of Genetics [part of the Chinese Academic of Sciences]'.[2] According to a paper by Chu et al,[3] CHGDP has collected genetic information and cell-lines from the official ethnic groups and has tested their

---

1 See Doring, O. (2003) 'China's Struggle for Practical Regulations in Medical Ethics', *Nature Reviews: Genetics*, vol. 4, pp. 233–39 at 234.

2 Chu, J. (2000) 'Chinese Human Genome Diversity Project: A synopsis' in *Genetic, Linguistic and Archaeological Perspectives on Human Diversity in Southeast Asia*, J. Li, M. Seielstad and C. Xiao, eds. (Singapore: World Scientific Publishing) pp. 95–105.

3 Chu, J. Y., Huang, W., Kuang, Q., Wang, J. M., Xu, J. J., Chu, Z. T., Yang, Z. Q., Lin, K. Q., Li, P., Wu, M., Geng, Z. C., Tan, C. C., Du, R. F. and Jin, L. (1998) 'Genetic Relationship of Populations in China', *The National Academy of Sciences*, vol. 95, pp. 11763–68.

DNA.[4] The project was also concerned with determining the types and incidences of genetic diseases and preserving each ethnic group's genetic information.[5] Along with the rapid development of the Chinese economy, transport between different areas in the PRC became easier and faster, which has led to an increase in intermarriage between different people from different areas, and it may also lead to the dilution of the unique population genetic information of China's minority ethnic groups. The Chinese HPGR proposed to collect the DNA samples of ethnic minorities and store the collections in gene banks, especially those of some of the rural populations and ethnic groups of Central and Southwest China. For example, a large gene bank for ethnic minorities in Yunnan Province, which aims to study the diversification of inheritance and inherited diseases of the ethnic minorities, has stored 1250 men's DNA from 25 ethnic groups.[6] Given that the participants in this project live in isolated rural areas in Yunnan, they are thought to have 'no history of marrying other ethnic peoples, and every man has the same ethnic origin for at least three generations in succession',[7] so their genetic information is deemed to have high purity. So far this is the largest data bank of its kind in the world.[8] This type of HPGR project is thought to be helpful to 'reconstruct the history of populations by studying genetic variation to determine patterns of human migration'.[9] Hence, some scholars have even noted that: 'the leaders of the People's Republic hope that the biotech revolution — now shaking the formerly isolated communist nation — will have similar effects to those induced by the Soviet Union's legendary Sputnik space programme, bringing the country to the world's attention'.[10]

The encouraging attitude of the Chinese government toward genetic research, arguably combined with a considerable lower level of standards in biomedical regulation, or a weakness in enforcing the related guidelines, has promoted a number of foreign researchers to conduct HPGR in China. For example, a French company, Genset, sent a letter to the Chinese Academy of Medical Science (CAMS) seeking research cooperation. The plan was to employ some of CAMS's researchers to collect DNA and diagnose genetic conditions. Genset and its partner, the French trading company Tang Frère International, would then analyse these DNA samples in France, using gene-sequencing machines, to develop new diagnostic methods and new drugs. In this letter, they declared that: '[w]e view gene research as

4   ibid at 11763.
5   ibid.
6   Sleeboom, M. (2005) 'The Harvard Case of Xu Xiping: Exploitation of the People, Scientific Advance, or Genetic Theft?', *New Genetics and Society*, vol. 24, no. 1, pp. 57–78 at 59.
7   ibid.
8   ibid.
9   ibid.
10   See Doring, O. (2003) 'China's Struggle for Practical Regulations in Medical Ethics', *Nature Reviews: Genetics*, vol. 4, pp. 233–39 at 233.

extremely important for Chinese health care in the 21st century and we are convinced that our joint effort will lead to fundamental discoveries which will benefit not just China but the rest of the world'.[11] The Harvard study is also a typical HPGR project. A newspaper report described the Harvard case as following:

> The China project was hatched in the office of Geoffrey Duyk, a Harvard geneticist who had one foot out the door to industry. At the time, 1994, genetics seemed the next big thing in American medicine. Among those enamored was Scott Weiss, a prominent Harvard respiratory epidemiologist. Weiss had come to Duyk for help in launching a study into genetic causes of asthma and similar illnesses. Duyk perked up when Weiss said he had a line on an unusually homogeneous population of 62 million people in Anhui province, a region isolated by geography and poverty for 2,000 years ... The research required thousands of volunteers, nearly impossible to obtain in such a remote place without an experienced guide. Weiss had just the person – he had mentored a post-doctoral fellow, Xu Xiping, who came from Anhui and had conducted several public health studies there. Xu was an epidemiologist with no real expertise in genetics, but he had hometown connections and a proven aptitude for getting things done in China.[12]

Therefore, the appeal of the PRC as a HPGR sample lode has been widely acknowledged.

On the other hand, along with the breakout of scandals associated with HPGR, such as the Harvard study, a sensitive debate on HPGR has also been raised in the PRC.[13] Advocates have argued that HPGR in China could help to discover more about the diversity of human genetic information and the causes of some diseases, which could benefit the progress of medical research both in China and elsewhere.[14] Opponents have argued that HPGR conducted by foreign research institutions in the PRC could result in risks of harm to both the interests of the target groups and the national security of the PRC. According to Yang, HPGR conducted by foreign countries in the PRC could lead to the collection of Chinese genetic information by foreign organisations

11 Sleeboom, M. (2005) 'The Harvard Case of Xu Xiping: Exploitation of the People, Scientific Advance, or Genetic Theft?', *New Genetics and Society*, vol. 24, no. 1, pp. 57–78 at 60.

12 ibid.

13 Most of the dominant media in China have reported this research project and reviewed it, including *Guangming Daily* (in Chinese) (16 April 2001), available at http://www.people.com.cn/GB/kejiao/42/155/20010416/443413.html and *Liaowang Magazine* (in Chinese) (26 March 2001), available at http://xys.org/xys/ebooks/others/science/jiyinhezuo.txt (both last visited 4 July 2013).

14 Yang, H. 'We Will Start to Research the Characteristics of the National/ethnic Disease Gene' (in Chinese) *Beijing Youth* (28 October 2000).

to produce medicine which could then be sold to the PRC at a high cost,[15] as well as potentially being used to create genetic weapons targeted at Chinese people.[16] Furthermore, some bioethical scholars, such as Sleeboom, are concerned that it could also be used to 'make claims on disputed territory, resources, and self-determination'.[17] Meanwhile, given the absence of relevant ethical and legal regulations on HPGR in the PRC, HPGR may also lead to the violation of the interests of both target groups and individual participants.[18] In the Harvard study, the blood and genetic samples of 200 million Chinese people were taken to the US. If there are no effective legal regulations or policies, these samples will be analysed in foreign counties and potentially be developed into new diagnostic methods and new drugs, without ensuring the interests of the Chinese target groups and individual participants who provided their population's genetic information.

Attractions of conducting HPGR in the PRC

Although some points have been outlined above and in Chapter 1, the special advantages of the PRC as a research target of HPGR should be reinforced and explored in more detail.

First, owing to size, geographic diversity, and social traditions and customs, there are a great many isolated populations within the PRC. The population size makes it possible to recruit a large number of participants for HPGR.[19] To be accurate, according to the China Statistical Yearbook (2008) of the National Bureau of Statistics of China, by the end of 2007, the total population of the PRC was 1,321,290,000 persons; what is more, the rural population consists of 727,500,000 persons.[20]

In addition, the Chinese people have remained relatively isolated in the past, which has preserved the relative genetic homogeneity of the population in many regions, especially in the areas where the minorities are living, for reasons such as that little modern transportation exists in rural PRC, or that there is a tradition for most members of Chinese families to live together. Therefore, the PRC contains rich genetic resources and several isolated areas

15 ibid.
16 Yang, H. 'For the Sake of Our National Security: Carefully Preserve Our Genetic Code' (in Chinese) *China Production Daily* (4 December 2002).
17 ibid at 59.
18 Xue, D. and Lin, Z. 'A Focus Topic of Bioethics' (in Chinese) *Guangming Daily* (16 April 2001).
19 Cavalli-Sforza, L. (1998) 'The Chinese Human Genome Diversity Project', *The National Academy of Sciences*, vol. 95, p. 11501.
20 China Statistical Yearbook 2008 of National Bureau of Statistics of China, available on the official website of National Bureau of Statistics of China at http://www.stats.gov.cn/tjsj/ndsj/2008/indexeh.htm (last visited 4 July 2013). This data does not include the population of Hong Kong SAR, Macao SAR and Taiwan Province.

which have idiographic cultures. The tradition of Chinese populations, which are relatively stable, with relatives tending to live in the same area, makes it easier to study certain groups/communities and carry out long-term follow-up. Furthermore, divorce is rare in rural PRC; thus, the households are stable. This facilitates the collection of comparative data.

Secondly, it is very cost-beneficial to conduct HPGR in the PRC. The current per capita income of rural PRC is still very low. According to data from the National Bureau of Statistics of China, by the end of 2007, the per capita annual income of rural household was 4140.4[21] yuan.[22] Medical services in rural PRC do not work well; a large number of people there cannot be provided with basic medical care. Hence, research institutions and researchers can recruit large numbers of participants by providing simple free physical examinations or providing some cheap standing drugs, such as vitamins and hypotensors. The story of poor farmer Chu in the Harvard case,[23] which has been mentioned previously, illustrates this well. His family provided several blood samples, but only received a token amount of money and some simple food.[24] The difficulties in ensuring that participants are not exploited but at the same time are not subjected to undue influence have been discussed in Chapter 5.

Thirdly, conducting collaborative HPGR in the PRC seems to be relatively easy. The PRC's ambitions in genetics and Chinese genetic researchers' desire to collaborate HPGR projects with foreign research institutions with advanced technology and wide experience also contribute to it. Before the Harvard case, there were few legal regulations or government policies on conducting HPGR, even HPGR conducted by foreign researchers or institutions. For example, according to Xiong et al's reports, in 1996, a new cooperative medical centre was set up in Yuexi district sponsored by Xu Xiping, from which more than 1400 genetic samples were taken.[25] After this case, since 1998, researchers or research institutions need state permission for HPGR and also permission to take samples abroad. However, researchers or research institutions can conduct HPGR by running their own laboratories or through jointly operated laboratories with Chinese researchers in the PRC. Some Chinese researchers prefer to conduct these kinds of cooperative projects in HPGR. For example, Fang Zhi-an, head of the committee for health and education of the Anqing City's Peoples' Congress' Standing Committee, was satisfied with his cooperation with Xu Xiping, who is an associate professor

---

21 The yuan is the basic unit of money in China. The current exchange rate of pound and yuan is about 1:10.8.
22 *China Statistical Yearbook 2008 of National Bureau of Statistics of China*, available on the official website of National Bureau of Statistics of China at http://www.stats.gov.cn/tjsj/ndsj/2008/indexeh.htm (last visited 4 July 2013).
23 See Chapter 1.
24 ibid.
25 ibid.

at Harvard University, and the Harvard project. He believes that it has initiated the development of local hygiene work and has trained both Chinese talents locally, in Anqing, and nationally. What is more, Fang and Xu have co-authored more than 10 articles in international academic journals.[26] However, some foreign researchers' Chinese partners felt that the collaborations were not balanced and that Chinese academic interests have been frustrated. For example, Liu Jianhui, the vice-director of science research management of Anhui Medical University, who is the other partner of Xu Xiping in the Harvard studies, complained that the Chinese should receive more information on the outcome of the research.[27]

According to the Human Development Report, 85.4 per cent (5,727,771,964) of the world's population lives in developing countries.[28] In the context of HPGR, most of these countries have similar situations to that of the PRC. Owing to the large size of the population, the unique genetic history, geographical diversity, high participation rates, low cost and stable social traditions and customs, target groups in developing countries are ideal research targets of HPGR. Hence, not only domestic, but also foreign, researchers and research institutions are enthusiastic about conducting HPGR which targets certain groups or communities there.

Cultural sensitivity of target groups in HPGR in the PRC

As has been demonstrated in previous chapters, conducting HPGR without understanding the cultural sensitivities of the target group may lead to harms to target groups. In most developing countries, ethnic minorities and isolated groups, which are target groups in HPGR, have their own cultural sensitivities, which are distinct from Western ones.

A brief introduction to bioethics in the PRC

Although bioethics as a discipline does not formally exist within traditional Chinese culture, undoubtedly the PRC has its own unique bioethical traditions which are distinct from Western bioethics. For example, Bowman and Hui have explained that in traditional Chinese medicine the view of illness is entirely different from Western views. They note that in Chinese traditional medicine, the body, soul and spirit are viewed as an integrated whole.

26　See note 6 at 65.
27　Xiong, L. and Wang, Y. 'Lingren shengyi de guoji jiyin hezuo yanjiu xiangmu' ['The Suspicious International Collaborate Genetic Research Project'] (in Chinese) *Outlook Weekly* (26 March 2001).
28　2013 Human Development Report, it can be seen on the official website of United Nations Development Programme at http://www.undp.org/content/dam/undp/library/corporate/HDR/2013GlobalHDR/English/HDR2013%20Report%20English.pdf (last visited 4 July 2013).

Furthermore, because human beings are considered products of nature, humankind and the natural environment are seen to be inseparably and interdependently related; protecting the integrity of the human-nature dyad is thus fundamental to health.[29]

In the context of ethical discussion, in the traditional Chinese medical view it is commonly acknowledged that Confucianism dominated medical ethics in pre-modern PRC. Generally speaking, Confucianism is an ethic that teaches people how to be human. Different from Western individual-oriented political and social philosophy, Confucianism focuses on the collective interests of family, community, society, and even nation. It is interesting to note that the word 'ethics' in Chinese is made up of two characters: *lun* and *li*.[30] The *lun* means human relationship, and *li* means reason or logic. It indicates that ethics is the reasonable relationship of the individual's transactions with his fellow human beings. The make-up of 'ethics' in the Chinese character itself discloses that traditional Chinese understanding of ethics simply directs one towards the ideal interpersonal relationship. It reflects the idea of relational personhood. Qiu, who is currently a leading bioethical scholar in the PRC, describes Confucian teaching and its basis as follows:

> For Confucians, demarcation between a human and an animal lies in whether you care for others or you care only yourself. The basic concept of Confucianism is ren, which means 'loving people'. The golden rules of Confucianism are: 'you should not do to others what you don't want to do to yourself', and 'after establishing yourself, you should help others to establish themselves; after you develop yourself, you should help others to develop' ... One reason is that Chinese hold a different concept of the 'person' from the Westerners. For the Chinese, a person is not as independent as some Westerners presume. No person can survive without support from others; so a person is a relational person or a person in relation. Metaphorically, a person is an atom in the West, but a person is a drop of sea water in China. For some Westerners, if an individual person does not exist, the whole world becomes meaningless. But for Chinese a drop of water evaporates, but the sea will still exist. So the collective is more important than the individual in China. If there is any conflict of interest between the individual and the collective, the former should be subordinated to the latter.[31]

29 Bowman, K. W. and Hui, E. C. (2008) 'Chinese Bioethics' in *The Cambridge Textbook of Bioethics*, P. A. Singer and A. M. Viens, eds. (Cambridge University Press) pp. 397–402 at 398.

30 In Chinese, 伦理.

31 Qiu, R. (2004) 'China: Views of a Bioethicist' in *Genetic and Ethics in Global Perspective*, D. C. Wertz and J. C. Fletcher, eds. (Kluwer Academic Publisher) at 192.

Therefore, some scholars rightly concluded that 'a Confucian person is socially situated, defined, and shaped in a relational context where he must achieve humaneness (*jen*) through interaction with other particular individuals'.[32]

However, in order fully to understand traditional Chinese medical morality, one must take into account the influence of Taoism and Buddhism, as well as Confucianism. In Confucian teaching, death is seen as a type of accomplishment in this world, such as the fulfilment of *ren*. *Ren* denotes 'the cultivation of positive human attributes such as humaneness, charity and beneficence'.[33] Hence, one's death can be a 'good' one, which is to say worthy and acceptable, for the person has fulfilled his or her moral duties in life. If a patient has been cured, it means that he or she has unfinished business, which is worth the *Tian*[34] extending his or her life to complete unfinished tasks or fulfil moral duties. Another significant position is based in Taoism, which insists that: 'Tao signifies the supreme metaphysical force that exists everywhere in everything and dominates the exercise and functioning of all things in the universe'.[35] Under Taoism, a human being is bred and activated by Tao, so human beings inherit the infinite potential of Tao. It means that Tao is not only embodied in every person's selfhood, but also exists in every other being. The boundary between personhood and others is not always clear. As Fu pointed out:

> The self, as the centre of relations, is not merely 'a privatised self, the small self and a self that is a closed system'. Instead, it can be and should be broadened to become a public-spirited, great self and a self that is an open system, and deepen in self transformation through genuine communication with others'.[36]

Hence, Taoism teaches people to pursue maintaining youth and attaining longevity and immortality. However, philosophical Taoism has a radically different perspective, which is reflected in the phrase 'Man comes into life and goes out to death'.[37] Thus, one should view death calmly. Buddhism provides a more unpredictable response to the suffering of dying and the event of death. This philosophy claims that 'if the person maintains his or her belief in the impermanence and cyclical nature of life, he or she may be easily resigned to death; but if the person sees the suffering of the dying event as

32 Fu, D. and Tsai, C., (2001) 'How Should Doctors Approach Patients: A Confucian Reflection on Personhood', *Journal of Medical Ethics*, vol. 27, no. 1, pp. 44–50 at 47.
33 ibid at 399–400.
34 In traditional Chinese Culture, everything was mastered by *Tian* (in Chinese, 天). *Tian* is not an Elohim, such as Heaven. *Tian* is a kind of power that cannot be denied, like destiny.
35 See note 32.
36 ibid.
37 ibid.

an occasion to "work out" his or her karma (which may include suffering from one's bad deeds) in this lifetime, then the person may not welcome death quite so readily'.[38] The tenets of traditional Chinese medicine were deeply influenced by each of these three philosophical traditions. However, all these three traditions are quite relational. Some other scholars, such as Liang Shumin (who is one of the most well known Chinese traditional cultural scholars of the last century), made this argument clearer that: '... in Chinese thinking, individuals are never recognised as separate entities; they are always regarded as part of a network, each with a specific role in relation to others'.[39] He even concluded that the traditional Chinese ethic is neither individual-based nor society based, but relational-based.[40] Family, community, country and the world, from the traditional Chinese viewpoint, are different aspects of selfhood where one engages in promoting them and transforming oneself.

In addition, Chinese bioethical perception is not influenced by a single theoretical perspective. From 1949, when the PRC was established, communitarian ethics gradually became the dominant paradigm, especially during the Cultural Revolution.[41] Traditional Chinese moral norms were officially attacked as the 'pernicious influence of feudalism', and ideas from the West, except Marxism, were censured as the 'bourgeois fallacy'.[42] However, traditional Chinese values never completely disappeared; along with the new policies of openness and reform, traditional medical ethics started to revive. Thus, as Fox and Swazey[43] have pointed out, contemporary Chinese medical morality is an unbalanced combination of Maoism-Marxism-Leninism,

---

38 ibid.
39 Liang, S.M. (1974) 'Zhong Guo Wen Hua Yao Yi' ['The essential features of Chinese culture'] (in Chinese, 中国文化要义) (Hong Kong: Chi-cheng T'u-Shu Kung Hsu).
40 ibid.
41 The Cultural Revolution is 'The Great Proletarian Cultural Revolution'. It was a violent mass movement that resulted in social, political and economic upheaval in the People's Republic of China starting in 1966 and ending officially with Mao's death in 1976. It was launched by Mao Zedong, the chairman of the Communist Party of China, on 16 May 1966; he alleged that 'liberal bourgeois' elements were permeating the party and society at large and that they wanted to restore capitalism. Mao insisted, in accordance with his theory of permanent revolution, that these elements should be removed through revolutionary violent class struggle by mobilising China's youth who, responding to his appeal, then formed Red Guard groups around the country.
42 Nie, J. B. (2005) 'Cultural Values Embodying Universal Norms: A Critique of A Popular Assumption About Cultures and Human Rights', *Developing World Bioethics*, vol. 5, no. 3, pp. 251–57 at 253.
43 In 1981, Renée Fox and Judith Swazey conducted six weeks of fieldwork primarily at a Western-style urban hospital in Tianjin, a Northern industrial city. Unlike the scholars at the Kennedy Institute of Ethics, they had no plan to explore ethical issues in medicine when leaving for the PRC. However, when they returned, the two sociologists brought back a 'medical morality' – the peculiar 'form currently taken by medical ethical interest and activity' in the PRC. See Fox, R. C. and Swazey, J. P. (1984) 'Medical Morality is

Confucianism, Taoism and Chinese Buddhism.[44] Despite this, many Chinese scholars also hold that there exists a characteristic Chinese way of thinking about and acting in public and private life, interpersonal interactions and moral issues in medical practice. For example, Qiu argued that there is an 'awakening of the rights sense, especially in intellectuals, university students, and the young, along with the advance of modernization';[45] however, he summarised the common Chinese view of Chinese medical ethics as follows:

> A quasi-holistic socio-political philosophy has been developed from Chinese cultural tradition. It is based on two thousand years of power-centralized, autocratic monarchy—one that has lacked any rights-oriented, individualistic, liberal democratic tradition. In recent decades, Marxism—rather, a mixture of Russian and Chinese versions of Marxism—has become the dominant ideology. The historicism and social holism of this system, inter woven with traditional ideas, puts the greatest emphasis on nation, society, and country rather than on individuals.[46]

Along with the PRC's Economic Reform and Open Policy published in 1978,[47] a significant number of Western ideas flooded into the PRC. Some Chinese scholars who favour Western bioethics have used this to illustrate the theoretical blind-spots and practical deficiency of Chinese medical ethics and to stress the importance of learning from the developed Western countries.[48] Currently, most of the medical institutes in the PRC have set up bioethics courses and conduct educational bioethics activities based on internationally acknowledged ethical norms such as the Nuremberg Code,[49] the Declaration of Helsinki[50] and the International Standards of Ethical

Not Bioethics: Medical Ethics in China and the United States', *Perspectives in Biology and Medicine*, vol. 27, pp. 336–60.

44 Fox, R. C. and Swazey, J. P. (1984) 'Medical Morality is Not Bioethics: Medical Ethics in China and the United States', *Perspectives in Biology and Medicine*, vol. 27, pp. 336–60.

45 Qiu, R. (1987) *Bioethics* (in Chinese) (Shanghai: Shanghai People's Press).

46 Qiu, R. (1992) 'Medical Ethics and Chinese Culture' in *Transcultural Dimensions in Medical Ethics*, E. Pellegrino, P. Mazzerella and P. Corsi, eds. (Frederick, MD: University Publishing Group) at 170–72.

47 It refers to the programme of economic reforms called 'Socialism with Chinese characteristics' in the PRC that were started in December 1978 by reformists within the Communist Party of China (CPC) led by Deng Xiaoping. The goal of Chinese economic reform was to transform China's stagnant, impoverished planned economy into a market economy capable of generating strong economic growth and increasing the wellbeing of Chinese citizens.

48 See note 42 at 253.

49 Trials of War Criminals before the Nuremberg Military Tribunals under Control Council Law No. 10, vol. 2 (Washington, D.C.: US Government Printing Office, 1949) at 181–82.

50 The WMA Declaration of Helsinki Ethical Principles for Medical Research Involving Human Subjects was adopted by the 18th WMA General Assembly, Helsinki, Finland, June 1964, and amended by the 29th WMA General Assembly, Tokyo, Japan, October

Examination of Biomedical Research Involving Human Subjects.[51] [52] Meanwhile, ethics committees have been established in most large-scale hospitals in the PRC, with responsibilities for ethics education and ethical review consultation for medical professionals on how to implement the principles of bioethics.[53] Hence, medical professionals and the highly-educated populations in the PRC are mostly influenced by, and accept, Western bioethics.

Therefore, Nie has argued that: '[I]n today's China, one can easily find in the way people actually live, and even in official State publications, the co-existence of traditional Confucianism, Taoism, and Buddhism along with sinonized Western Marxism and communism; the conceptions of filial piety and loyalty to the country along with the ideals of individual happiness, self-fulfilment, and self-perfection'.[54] For example, Chinese people's unique view on truth-telling in health care can illustrate that although almost all Chinese people believe in the combined ideology of Maoism-Marxism-Leninism, Confucianism, Buddhism and Western bioethics, their moral experience and practices, when ill, are very unlikely to reach the same answer.[55]

With regard to truth-telling in health care, there is not a single distinctive Chinese approach – eg. toward either disclosing or concealing the diagnosis of terminal disease. For the sake of patients' wellbeing, many contemporary Mainland Chinese physicians, along with family members and friends, do not directly tell the whole truth to patients who are suffering terminal diseases. But this is far from standard practice in traditional PRC. Partly (and only partly) owing to Western influence, more and more physicians prefer to discuss frankly and openly all the related medical issues with their patients. Many patients know the nature of their disease from other sources as well, including the ward in which they are hospitalised, the department in which

1975, 35th WMA General Assembly, Venice, Italy, October 1983, 41st WMA General Assembly, Hong Kong, September 1989, 48th WMA General Assembly, Somerset West, Republic of South Africa, October 1996 and the 52nd WMA General Assembly, Edinburgh, Scotland, October 2000, 53rd WMA General Assembly, Washington 2002 (Note of Clarification on paragraph 29 added), 55th WMA General Assembly, Tokyo 2004 (Note of Clarification on paragraph 30 added), 59th WMA General Assembly, Seoul, October 2008. The full text of the Helsinki Declaration can be seen on the official website of World Medical Association (WMA) at http://www.wma.net/en/30publications/10policies/b3/index.html (last visited 4 July 2013).

51 The International Ethical Guidelines for Biomedical Research Involving Human Subjects were prepared by the Council for International Organizations of Medical Sciences (CIOMS) in collaboration with the WHO, Geneva, 2002. The full text of the CIOMS Guidelines can be seen on the official website of the World Health Organization (WHO) at http://whqlibdoc.who.int/emro/2004/9290213639_annex2.pdf (last visited 4 July 2013).

52 Li, E. (2008) 'Bioethics in China', *Bioethics*, vol. 22, no. 8, pp. 448–54 at 450.

53 ibid at 450–51.

54 See note 42 at 249.

55 ibid at 249–50.

the doctor works, and the gestures of people in and around their family. It is not uncommon, however, for a patient who knows the truth to pretend otherwise to his or her loved ones in order to reduce their suffering. For the physician to speak directly to the patient is just one way of telling the truth.[56]

As a result, in general, contemporary Chinese bioethics is indeed a mixture of a great number of values and beliefs – ancient and modern, Western and Eastern.

Cultural sensitivity of target groups of HPGR in the PRC

Given that the target groups in HPGR are ethnic minorities and isolated groups in rural areas in the PRC, their bioethical conceptions, decision-making processes and cultural sensitivities are more likely to be influenced by traditional Confucianism and Marxism. Therefore, the bioethical background of the most likely target groups of HPGR in the PRC needs to be explored in more detail.

Almost every scholar who is interested in Chinese bioethics would notice the specific view of Chinese people on autonomy or informed consent. For example, Bowman and Hui described this issue as follows:

> The concept of autonomy best highlights the contrast between Western and Chinese cultures. In the West, the principle of autonomy implies that every person has the right to self-determination. In the context of healthcare, this means that the patient is the best person to make healthcare decisions. Within Chinese culture, however, the person is viewed as a 'relational self' – a self for whom social relationships, rather than rationality and individualism, provide the basis for moral judgement. From this perspective, an insistence on self-determination erodes the value placed on personal interconnectedness and the social and moral meaning of such relationships. In traditional Chinese society, the influences of which still endure, the family is based on an extended or clan structure and plays a central role in an individual's life ... All major decisions made by the family are thus informed by these hierarchical structures ... In Chinese culture, the family functions as collective decision maker and also as a powerful conduit for moral, religious, and social norms. The family's role in self-determination is, therefore, integral to any notion of Chinese bioethics.[57]

What is more, they also argued that respect for an individual's right to self-determination is not prominent in traditional Chinese culture, because 'the Confucian concept of relational personhood challenges the assumption that

56 ibid at 250.
57 See note 29 at 397–98.

the patient should be given the diagnosis and prognosis and the opportunity to make his or her own medical decisions', as well as the fact that 'social and moral meaning rests in interdependence, which overrides self-determination'.[58] Consequently, before making a decision, many Chinese patients, by contrast to Western ones, would consider not only the influence on him or her, but also disclose relevant information to those who are important to him or her and consult their opinion. When making such a decision, an individual would also take into account the potential effects on his or her family or community as well as potential influence on him or her. Under this culture, the decision of each individual should be for the greater common good, for the greater good of the community of many different individuals. Thus, sometimes, it may mean that they would also like to regard family or community ideas as their decision, even when they themselves are competent.

Currently, Chinese culture is characterised by strong communal values and an emphasis on social harmony. As Fan has pointed out: '[s]ince, compared to Western societies, East Asian states are still homogeneous in their conceptions of the good, a set of values relating to clinical decision making is generally accepted by various communities, families and individuals, thus serving as an objective or impersonal conception of the good'.[59] For example, in the clinical context, this feature can be reflected by the following example: if a patient refuses treatment because he judges his life is no longer worth living, when the relevant others do not agree in terms of the objective conception of the good, the patient's wishes would not be followed, whether or not the patient is competent.[60]

Another example is provided by Fan, a bioethics scholar who labelled the East Asian principle of autonomy as 'a family-determination-oriented principle'.[61] She offered a description of the principle of autonomy in East Asia, which is that '[p]ositively: every agent should be able to make his or her decisions and actions harmoniously in cooperation with other relevant persons; and negatively: no harmoniously made decisions and actions should be subjected to controlling constraints by others'.[62] She also provided a clinical care decision-making process in East Asia to illustrate the distinction between the understanding of Western and East Asia on autonomy as following:

> For instance, when a patient requests or refuses a treatment while a relevant family member holds an opposite opinion, the physician generally should not simply follow the patient's wish as in the West, even if

---

58 ibid at 400.
59 See note 61 at 317.
60 ibid at 318.
61 Fan, R. (1997) 'Self-Determination vs. Family-Determination: Two Incommensurable Principles of Autonomy', *Bioethics*, vol. 11, nos 3–4, pp. 309–22 at 315.
62 ibid at 316.

the patient is evidently competent. Instead, the physician should tell the patient and the family members to negotiate and provide an agreement to him before he can undertake a medical act. Indeed, on the one hand, East Asian people make a clear distinction between intra-familial and extra-familial authority. On the other hand, it is not a sick family member him/herself but the entire family that has real authority in clinical decision making. Western people might be concerned about this claim of the family-sovereignty. But the family under this notion can be viewed as an autonomous social unit from the physician and the state, analogous to the autonomous individual in the West.[63]

She also pointed out that the basis for this distinction is the Confucian understanding of the nature of the family and individuals. In Confucianism, it is the arrangement of Heaven (*tian*) that every individual is born to a family; hence, there are special relations that exist between family members and one's life is lived inseparably from the family. Familial relationships are three of the five basic human relations in Confucianism. Thus, Confucian morality requires that one should consider one's family as an autonomous unit from the rest of society, flourishing or suffering as a whole.[64] Although her argument emphasised only one of the Chinese traditional moral ideologies – Confucianism – which centred on the family, Fan has pointed out an essential characteristic of Chinese ethical understanding on autonomy; which is a decision should not be taken in isolation based on the individual's own interests. In Western countries, some groups also have similar relational perspectives.[65] However, in the West, in most cases, if possible, a competent patient generally has the final word regarding medical decisions about his or her care, while in the PRC both the patient and family members tend to reach an agreement before a clinical decision can be made. This tendency makes the PRC in a better position to adopt a relational autonomy model in HPGR.

Therefore, the major value advocated by Chinese culture can be described as 'harmonious dependence'.[66] According to Chinese people's understanding, individuals are not only independent persons, but also members of certain families, groups or communities; thus, their decisions, especially medical decisions, require a full range consideration of the interests of all relevant parties who would be affected by this decision. This feature means that, whatever the relevant guidelines say, the Chinese may not apply the individualised

63 ibid at 316–17.
64 ibid at 317.
65 See Keller, J. (1997) 'Autonomy, Relationality and Feminist Ethics', *Hypatia*, vol. 12, pp. 152–64. See also Ells, C. (2001) 'Shifting the Autonomy Debate to Theory as Ideology', *Journal of Medicine and Philosophy*, vol. 26, no. 4, pp. 417–30.
66 See note 61 at 318.

Western bioethical standard directly. For example, Engelhardt, through analysis of difficult cases on medical consent, concluded that when making a medical decision on a patient, even if the patient is competent, the family would play an important role in securing patient consent and others, such as community and fellow-workers would also be involved, rather than the patient making the decision independently.[67] Hence, it is reasonable to agree with some Chinese scholars who consider that transplanting Western medical morality would be practically impossible and also dangerous in theory.[68] It needs to be clarified that this assertion does not mean that it is useless to seek informed consent from participants of HPGR in the PRC, but is intended to highlight the significance of seeking informed consent through a mechanism which is suitable to the specific situation and is sensitive to cultural values.

There may also be difficulties posed by the background and experience of potential research participants. For example, a study on informed consent strategies, which was conducted in three areas south-west of Shanghai, in an epidemiological project approved by the regional research ethics committees in Sweden and China,[69] found that although informed consent was adopted in the epidemiological project, even where the informed consent procedures in the PRC were sought to be conducted to the same standard enforced in the Western countries, it was not always easy to convey information and obtain real consent, since the educational level and background knowledge of these subjects of biomedical research were not the same as those in the West. Furthermore, the study was conducted in Shanghai, which is the most modernised city in the PRC, where the average educational level is higher than the average level of the PRC. Owing to the generally low level of education of large populations in the rural areas of mainland China, and the influence of traditional cultural sensitivities, more problems could emerge in the practice of informed consent in HPGR. For example, in 2005, the well known scientific journal *Nature* published a story of the unethical conduct of a clinical trial for a drug called VGV-1 on HIV-positive farmers from Henan province by a collaborate research project of Beijing's Ditan Hospital and Viral Genetics of Azusa, which is a US drug company.[70] In this research project, participants said that they had been told that they would be injected with a new drug which would keep them in good health for 20 years without further treatment and were not notified that there were also associated risks.[71]

67 Engelhardt, H. T. (1980) 'Bioethics in the People's Republic of China', *Hastings Centre Report*, vol. 10, no. 2, pp. 7–10 at 8.
68 Qiu, Qiangxin (1999) *Medical Ethics* (Beijing: People's Health Press).
69 Lynoe, N., Sandlund, M., Jacobsson, L., Nordberg, G. and Jin, T. (2004) 'Informed Consent in China: Quality of Information Provided to Participants in a Research Project', *Scandinavian Journal of Public Health*, vol. 32, no. 6, pp. 472–75 at 472.
70 Cyranoski, D. (2005) 'Chinese Clinical Trials: Consenting adults? Not necessarily…', *Nature*, vol. 435, no. 7039, pp. 138–39.
71 ibid at 139.

The known risks of harm of this drug trial were not disclosed to the participants, but participants then 'signed informed-consent forms that they could not understand and that doctors made no effort to explain'.[72] The other inappropriate issues in the trial included that 'copies of the forms had to be paid for; expenses were not covered as agreed; participants weren't informed of the trial's results, despite asking'.[73] The potential participants in HPGR are more vulnerable to failing to understand the relevant information and making poor decisions even than the participants in the study above. The use of language with adequate accuracy and articulation, easily understood by people with a low level of education, and with respect for cultural sensitivities is crucially important for appropriate information disclosure and consent; it is particularly important when the researchers come from other countries.

Therefore, in the context of HPGR in the PRC, rather than applying Western frameworks slavishly, in order to protect the interests of a target group it would be better to consider and give respect to the specific needs and cultural sensitivities of target groups in the PRC, which are highly influenced by the traditional Chinese Confucian moral order. The need for cultural sensitivity makes Chinese target groups in HPGR more appropriately considered under a relational autonomy model, rather than a purely individualistic model. The following three examples can illustrate this viewpoint.

First, possible risks of harm that may be posed by HPGR to both individual participants and target groups should be disclosed to the potential participants. In some communities or groups, according to traditional customs, individuals would be likely to wish to consider both the interests of their group or community as well as their own private interests. Evaluating the interests and preferences of the group or community before decision-making is their cultural approach.

Secondly, where decisions may be relevant to the interests of a group or community, individuals may seek or rely on group or community leaders' opinions in forming their own decisions. Again, this may be part of the cultural norms of members of a group, so that seeking or accepting such views cannot be regarded as being undue influence. This suggests that community and group leaders should be consulted where HPGR is proposed.

Thirdly, in some Chinese groups and communities, if issues are relevant to the interests of the group or community as a whole, there is a cultural tradition and expectation of group consultation and involvement. This custom would suggest the involvement of members of target groups in research design and at the ethical review stage to help correctly to identify and avoid potential risks of harm. This might take the form of the involvement of

---

72 ibid.
73 ibid.

community leaders or a wider range of people from the target group, depending on the scope of the study and cultural norms within the target group.

In this vein, target groups in HPGR from the PRC are quite suitable to be considered in terms of relational autonomy.

Current regulation of group protection on HPGR in developing countries

For the reasons stated above, the increase in HPGR in developing countries leads to the question about what steps have been taken by developing countries to protect their citizens and groups who may participate in HPGR. This section, with the PRC as its example, will provide a critical evaluation on the relevant law and guidelines currently in place in respect of human subject research, with particular consideration of their relevance and adequacy in respect of HPGR.

Critical evaluation of existing legal regulations and ethical guidelines on HPGR in the PRC

The principal legal regulations and ethical guidelines on biomedical research in the PRC include Measures for the Ethical Review of Biomedical Research Involving Human Subjects[74] and Interim Measures for the Administration of Human Genetic Resources.[75] Both of these documents are formulated by various ministries of the State Council, so they are administrative rules in the hierarchy of the Chinese legal system.

Measures for the ethical review of biomedical research involving human subjects (Measures 2007)

Measures 2007 is the most substantial legal regulation on biomedical research involving human subjects in the PRC. It was promulgated by the Ministry of Public Health of the PRC on 11 January 2007.

The targets of Measures 2007 are regulating biomedical research involving human subjects, protecting human life and human health, safeguarding human dignity, as well as respecting and protecting the legal rights and

---

74 'She Ji Ren de Sheng Wu Yi Xue Yan Jiu Lun Li Shen Cha Ban Fa (Shi Xing)' ['Measures for the Ethical Review of Biomedical Research Involving Human Subjects'] (in Chinese), available on the official website of the Ministry of Health of the PRC at http://www.moh. gov.cn/qjjys/s3581/200804/b9f1bfee4ab344ec892e68097296e2a8.shtml (last visited 5 July 2013).

75 'Ren Lei Yi Chuan Zi Yuan Guan Li Zhan Xing Ban Fa' ['Interim Measures for the Administration of Human Genetic Resources'] (in Chinese), available on the official website of the Ministry of Science and Technology of the PRC at http://www.most.gov. cn/fggw/xzfg/200811/t20081106_64877.htm (last visited 4 July 2013).

interests of human subjects of biomedical research.[76] Measures 2007 contains 30 articles and is divided into five sections. In respect of biomedical research involving human subjects, it essentially sets regulations for the principles of ethical review including the establishment of ethics committees, measures and procedures for ethical review, as well as the administration and supervision of such review. In Measures 2007, 'biomedical research involving human subjects and the application of its relevant techniques' are defined as research activities on human subjects, adopting modern physical, chemical and medical methods, which focus on human physiological and pathological phenomena, as well as the diagnosis, prevention and treatment of diseases and trial application activities of medical health techniques or products on human subjects through biomedical research.[77] From the perspective of protecting human subjects' interests and dignity, Measures 2007 highlights that ethical review shall abide by state laws, regulations, relevant rules and well known bioethical principles. Furthermore, the process of ethical review should be independent, objective, fair and transparent.[78]

In Measures 2007, the ethical review principles include:

(1) respect for and protection of a human subject's self-determination and right to decide whether or not to participate in certain research, strict requirements for informed consent, avoiding any improper approach, such as deception, coercion or bribery, to gain a human subject's consent and allowing a human subject's withdrawal from any process of research[79]
(2) the security, health and interests of human subjects are absolutely superior to the consideration of scientific and social interests; to endeavour to enable the human subject to be benefited to the greatest degree and to avoid harm as much as possible[80]
(3) to reduce or exempt the human subjects' financial losses to enable him or her to benefit from research[81]
(4) to respect and protect the privacy of the human subject, inform the human subject about the storage and use of his or her private data and the security measures to protect such data[82]
(5) to ensure timely treatment and appropriate compensation for the human subject, if he or she is injured in research[83]

76 See note 74 Article 1.
77 ibid Article 3.
78 ibid Article 4.
79 ibid Article 14.
80 ibid.
81 ibid.
82 ibid.
83 ibid.

(6) to provide special protection to vulnerable groups, such as children, pregnant women, persons with learning disabilities, mental patients, prisoners and persons in poor and less-educated positions.[84]

Measures 2007 clarifies the role and responsibilities of institutional ethics committees, as well as their establishment, membership composition and powers of examination and approval.[85] Meanwhile, Measures 2007 also proposes that, according to need, the Ministry of Health and the provincial administrative departments of public health should establish an ethical review guidance and counselling organisation, which will discuss significant ethical issues, offer consultations for the drafting of regulations, provisions and policy measures, organise ethical review on some major research projects, and guide and supervise the ethical review by institutional ethical committees.[86]

In addition, Measures 2007 stresses the role of government in ethical review of biomedical research involving human subjects. In order to ensure the quality of ethical review, the Ministry of Health and the provincial administrative departments of public health will supervise the multiple levels of ethical review committees, including the establishment of institutional ethical committees, ensure compliance with principles for ethical review and monitor results.[87] Foreign researchers or research institutions who conduct biomedical research involving human subjects inside the PRC should obtain approval from the relevant Chinese ethical committees and review their research projects according to Measures 2007, regardless of whether or not their research projects have been reviewed in their own countries.[88]

Interim measures for the administration of human genetic resources (HGR Measures 1998)

HGR Measure 1998 was drafted by the Ministry of Health and the Ministry of Science and Technology, and promulgated by the general office of the State Council upon the approval of the State Council of the PRC on 10 June 1998.

The primary targets of HGR Measures 1998 are efficiently protecting and rationally utilising human genetic resources (HGR) in the PRC, strengthening the research and development of human gene technology and promoting international cooperation and exchange on the basis of equality and mutual benefits.[89] In HGR Measures 1998, 'human genetic resources' are defined as materials such as human organs, tissues, cells, blood specimens, preparations of

84 ibid.
85 ibid Articles 6–13.
86 ibid Article 5.
87 ibid Article 24.
88 ibid Article 26.
89 See note 75 Article 1.

any types or recombinant DNA constructs which contain the human genome, genes or gene products. They also include information related to such genetic material.[90] HGR Measures 1998 mainly regulates such activities in the PRC as sampling, collecting, researching, developing, trading or exporting HGR outside the territory of the PRC.[91] It has six sections and 26 articles and contains detailed regulations on the administration of HGR and also the examination and approval of research on HGR in the PRC. It includes provisions concerning benefit-sharing of intellectual property rights, as well as rewards and penalties in respect of such research.

In general, in accordance with HGR Measures 1998, the PRC adopts a reporting and registration system. Any institution or individual who discovers or holds important pedigrees and genetic resources in specified regions shall immediately report to the Human Genetic Resources Administration of China (HGRAC). No institution or individual may sample, collect, trade or export HGR, including both physical samples and relevant genetic information, or take them outside the territory of the PRC, or provide them to other countries in any form without permission.[92] The state adopts a unified review and approval system, regulated at different levels, over HGR. The Administrative Department of Science and Technology and the Administrative Department of Public Health under the State Council are jointly in charge of the administration of the HGR of the PRC at the national level and had responsibility for establishing the HGRAC to carry out routine duties.[93]

The HGRAC has the following responsibilities:

(1) to draft the relevant rules and implementing documents; to promulgate such rules for entering into force upon approval and to ensure the enforcement of the Measures through coordination and supervision[94]
(2) to be in charge of the registration and administration of the important pedigrees and genetic resources in the specified regions[95]
(3) to review and examine international collaborative projects involving human genetic resources in China[96]
(4) to review and approve applications for export of human genetic resources, and thereafter to issue export permits for human genetic materials and[97]
(5) other duties related to the administration of human genetic resources in China.[98]

90 ibid Article 2.
91 ibid Article 3.
92 ibid Article 4.
93 ibid Articles 6 and 7.
94 ibid Article 8.
95 ibid.
96 ibid.
97 ibid.
98 ibid.

Where HGR from the PRC are involved in any international collaborative project, the Chinese collaborating party is responsible for going through the appropriate formalities of application for approval. Institutions directly under the Central Government must apply to the relevant administrative department under the State Council and local institutions or institutions without a specific supervisory department must apply to the local administrative departments. Upon receiving the approval of the relevant departments, the Chinese collaborating party must apply to the HGRAC for examination and approval prior to entering into an official contract.[99] In addition, relevant departments under the State Council and local administrative departments, in reviewing any application for international collaborative projects, will consult the relevant local administrative departments of the region where human genetic materials are to be collected.

In terms of the intellectual property rights of HGR, HGR Measures 1998 provides that the Chinese research and development institution shall have priority in accessing information about the HGR within the territory of the PRC, particularly the important pedigrees and genetic resources in the specified regions and the relevant data. Providing information and specimens and any transfer of such HGR to other institutions are prohibited without permission. No foreign collaborating institution or individual who has access to the above-mentioned information may publicise, publish, apply for patent rights or disclose it by any other means without permission.[100] What is more, international collaborative projects involving HGR must follow the principles of mutual benefits, credit and trust, joint participation and sharing of achievements. All of the rights and obligations of each party should be set out in advance, in order fully and effectively to protect their own respective intellectual property rights.[101]

According to HGR Measures 1998, if any Chinese institution or individual, in violation of the provisions stipulated in HGR Measures 1998, exports human genetic materials without authorisation by any means, the human genetic materials will be confiscated by Chinese Customs and the institution or individual will be punished. Punishment ranges from administrative sanctions to prosecution by the judicial department, according to the seriousness of the circumstances.[102] If anyone, in violation of the provisions stipulated in the Measures, provides human genetic materials to foreign institutions or individuals without permission, the human genetic materials will be confiscated and the institution or individual will be fined. If the circumstances are serious, he or she will be investigated for liability according to Chinese law.[103]

---

99   See note 75 Article 11.
100 ibid Article 17.
101 ibid Article 18.
102 ibid Article 21.
103 ibid Article 22.

While it might seem that the PRC has confronted the issues involved in human subject research and particularly genetic research in a serious manner, on reflection these regulations are not well suited to HPGR and do not provide adequate protection for participants in such research. The deficiencies can be described as follows.

First, the current rules are still essentially reactive. This means that when certain cases cause risks or harms to certain individuals or groups, legislation or ethical guidelines will be promulgated, designed to avoid the recurrence of similar cases. For example, HGR Measures 1998 was the reactive legislation to a number of scandals,[104] such as the Harvard case, which has been described above. At that time, China realised the benefits relevant to genetic resource and the urgency of avoiding similar genetic resource loss cases. Reserving claims for all benefits derived from international biomedical research using Chinese biological sources is the main and the most crucial intent of HGR Measures 1998. Hence, it becomes understandable that HGR Measures 1998, as a reactive legislation to genetic resource loss cases, focuses mostly on the interests of the state in genetic research, but lacks protection for human subjects and target groups. Accordingly, these reactive legal regulations lack the full anticipation of possible scenarios and are not reviewed in the light of the development of biomedical technology. Furthermore, they are not at the highest level of the hierarchy of the Chinese legal system. In fact, as measures which have been legislated by the ministries of the State Council, Measures 2007 and HGR Measures 1998 only have the lowest legal effect in national legislation. If conflicted with other higher level legislation, those higher levels of legislation shall prevail. Thus, Measures 2007 and HGR Measures 1998 are not powerful enough.

Secondly, the starting points of these legal regulations and ethical guidelines are the state administrative system; hence, they concern the interests of the state more than the interests of the individuals or groups who are the targets of biomedical research. Thus, the core regulations of HGR Measures 1998 provide for reporting and registration systems for important pedigrees and genetic resource, as well as the regulations of export and intellectual property of HGR in the PRC. Nevertheless, Measures 2007 made some positive efforts toward human subject protection. For example, it clearly confirmed that informed consent should be an essential requirement which needs to be strictly reviewed by ethical committees. It also stipulates that information disclosure when seeking consent should be expressed by simple words; in minority areas, it can be expressed in local languages to seek to ensure that the potential participants have a proper understanding of what is

---

104 Doring, O. (2003) 'China's Struggle for Practical Regulations in Medical Ethics', *Nature Reviews: Genetics*, vol. 4, pp. 233–39 at 234–35.

involved.[105] When the research is to be conducted in minority areas, the membership of ethical review committees should consider including members from ethnic minorities in advance.[106] However, these considerations remained based on an individualistic model of autonomy, and lacked reference to protection of the interests of group or information disclosure on group risks.

Thirdly, given that these legal regulations and ethical guidelines are essentially reactive, they lack unified ethical or legislative principles and have not developed a complete set of general rules that can guide the ethical conduct of biomedical research and ensure the interests of human subjects.

For example, despite the requirement for informed consent by research subjects set out in Measures 2007, this Measure only gives limited guidance to ethics committees on how to conduct ethical review of biomedical research involving human subjects. There is little specification of the method and standards required for the conduct of the informed consent process other than the need for information to be provided in understandable language. This means that there is no legal requirement as to the scope and standard of information disclosure by researchers, nor as to other elements of seeking consent from participants in biomedical research involving human subjects in the PRC.

There are some legal requirements relevant to informed consent in the PRC in Guidelines for the Moral Principles in Human Embryonic Stem Cell Research (HESCR Guidelines 2004).[107] This was promulgated by the Ministry of Health and the Ministry of Science and Technology of the PRC on 14 January 2004, and contains 12 articles. It stipulated the principle of informed consent and the need for approval of research by ethics committees. In Article 8 of HESCR Guidelines 2004, it is noted that to protect the privacy of the subjects, research on human embryonic stem cells must be conducted in earnest pursuance of the principles of consent and agreement provided on the basis of full knowledge of all facts on the part of the subject. A letter of consent must be properly signed recording this.[108] For consent to be properly obtained, the researchers must have advised the gamete providers as to the aims and the possible consequences and risks of the research in accurate, clear and common language.[109] According to the HESCR Guidelines 2004, an ethics committee must be set up within a research unit conducting research with human embryonic stem cells, consisting of research and managerial staff from biology, medical sciences, law or sociology etc. The

105 See note 74 Article 17.
106 ibid Article 7.
107 'Ren Pei Tai Gan Xi Bao Yan Jiu Lun Li Zhi Dao Yuan Ze' ['Guidelines for the Moral Principles in Human Embryonic Stem Cell Research'] (in Chinese), available on the official website of the Ministry of Science and Technology of the PRC at http://www.most. gov.cn/fggw/zfwj/zfwj2003/200512/t20051214_54948.htm (last visited 4 July 2013).
108 ibid Article 8.
109 ibid.

duty of the ethics committee is to exercise comprehensive inspection, consultation and supervision as to the underlying principles and scientific aims and conduct of human embryonic stem cell research.[110] However, the applicable scope of the HESCR Guidelines 2004 is limited to human embryonic stem cell research, which does not include HPGR or any other biomedical research involving human subjects.

Apart from HESCR Guidelines 2004, there are some other laws in the PRC which contain articles that may be relevant to informed consent, including the Law of Licensed Doctors of the People's Republic of China[111] and Managerial Regulation of the Medical Institutions of the People's Republic of China.[112] Article 26 of the Law of Licensed Doctors of the PRC stipulates that doctors who wish to conduct any experimental clinical treatment shall obtain the approval of the hospital authorities and the consent of the patient himself or his relatives.[113] Although this law is at the level of other national laws, and was promulgated by the Standing Committee of the NPC, it only stipulates some simple regulations on patients' consent, not concerns specifically relating to the interests of human subjects in biomedical research. Article 33 of the Managerial Regulation of the Medical Institutions of the PRC also stipulates that the medical institution shall obtain the consent of the patient himself, and shall also obtain written consent from his family members or other relatives, before conducting any operation, special testing or special treatment, although this does not provide a clear mechanism to deal with the possible conflicts between patient and his or her family.[114] However, the applicable scope of this regulation is innovative treatment rather than biomedical research involving human subjects.

Therefore, although the Measures 2007 has clearly established general principles for biomedical research involving human subjects, such as the need to obtain informed consent, which are widely accepted by both international guidelines and most Western countries, the legislative framework of the PRC only provides broad principles, not more specific regulation to protect the interests of individuals and groups who may be asked to participate in HPGR.

110 ibid Article 9.
111 Zhong Hua Ren Min Gong He Guo Zhi Ye Yi Shi Fa ['Law of Licensed Doctors of the People's Republic of China'] (in Chinese), available on the official website of the Ministry of Health of the PRC at http://www.gov.cn/banshi/2005-08/01/content_18970.htm (last visited 5 July 2013).
112 'Yi Liao Ji Gou Guan Li Tiao Li' ['Managerial Regulation of the Medical Institutions of the People's Republic of China'] (in Chinese), available on the official website of the Ministry of Health of the PRC at http://www.moh.gov.cn/uploadfile/200591152042127.doc (last visited 4 July 2013).
113 See note 111 Article 26.
114 See note 112 Article 33.

Finally, these legal regulations, such as they are, are not designed to fit the particular position of the PRC. They are based on Western principles that focus on individual autonomy and in many cases are copied word for word from Western regulations. For example, the rules of Measures 2007 on informed consent are almost directly transplanted from the relevant rules of the CIOMS Guidelines and the Helsinki Declaration. As discussed above the cultural tradition of bioethics in the PRC is not entirely the same as in Western countries. Thus, it is reasonable to suppose that these transplanted regulations may not work effectively or be culturally appropriate in the PRC, where the traditional ethics emphasise social harmony over individual interests.

Critical evaluation of existing legal regulations and public policies on ethnic minorities in the PRC

Developing legal regulation and public policies concerning ethnic minorities is one of the basic principles of the legal system in the PRC. The government white paper China's Ethnic Policy and Common Prosperity and Development of All Ethnic Groups[115] noted in its preface that:

> China is a unified multi-ethnic country jointly created by the people of all its ethnic groups. In the long course of historical evolution people of all ethnic groups in China have maintained close contacts, developed interdependently, communicated and fused with one another, and stood together through weal and woe, forming today's unified multi-ethnic Chinese nation, and promoting the development of the nation and social progress.[116]

It also describes the current make-up of ethnic minorities in the PRC as follows:

> Over the past 60 years, the total population of the ethnic minorities has been on a constant increase, comprising a rising proportion in China's total population. The five national censuses that have been conducted show that the total population of ethnic minorities was 35.32 million in 1953, 6.06 percent of the total population; 40.02 million in 1964, 5.76 percent of the total; 67.30 million in 1982, 6.68 percent of the total; 91.20 million in 1990, 8.04 percent of the total; and 106.43 million in 2000, 8.41 percent of the total. The populations of the ethnic groups vary greatly from one to another. For example, the Zhuang has a population of 17 million, far more than that of the Hezhe, numbering only some 4,000.[117]

---

115 This government white paper in English was available on the official website of Information Office of the State Council of the People's Republic of China at http://www.china.org.cn/government/whitepaper/node_7078073.htm (last visited 5 July 2013).
116 ibid.
117 ibid.

The Constitution provides that China practises a certain degree of regional autonomy, which may have an ethnic basis. Regional autonomy is exercised and organs of self-government are established in areas where various ethnic minorities live in compact communities. National autonomous areas are classified into autonomous regions, autonomous prefectures and autonomous counties. There are in total five autonomous regions (the Inner Mongolia Autonomous Region, the Xinjiang Uygur Autonomous Region, the Guangxi Zhuang Autonomous Region, the Ningxia Hui Autonomous Region and the Tibet Autonomous Region), 30 autonomous prefectures, 116 autonomous counties and three autonomous banners in the whole country.[118] All national autonomous areas are integral parts of the PRC. According to statistics revealed in the fifth national census, conducted in 2000, of the country's 55 ethnic minorities, 44 had their own autonomous areas. The population of ethnic minorities practising regional autonomy accounted for 71 per cent of the total population of ethnic minorities, and the area where such regional autonomy was practised accounted for 64 per cent of the entire territory of the PRC. In addition, the PRC has established 1100 ethnic townships, as a supplement to the system of regional ethnic autonomy.[119]

The PRC has its unique regional national autonomy system; and regional national autonomy policy is also a basic policy, which the PRC adopts to handle problems among its ethnic groups, as well as a fundamental political system. The establishment of the regional national autonomy system is determined by the relationships among its local ethnic groups, the economic development of the locality, and its historical background. First, as far as history and traditions are concerned, the long-term existence of a unified multi-ethnic country is the historical background for implementing regional ethnic autonomy.[120] The white paper on Chinese ethnic minorities noted that '[a]s early as in the pre-Qin Dynasty times before 221 BC the concepts of "country" and "unification" had taken shape in the minds of the Chinese people'.[121] Secondly, as far as ethnic relationships are concerned, the Chinese people consist of multi-ethnic groups, and the close and extensive ties among

---

118 An introduction to the Chinese regional national autonomy system is provided by the official website of the Ministry of Justice of the PRC, available at http://www.legalinfo.gov.cn/ (in Chinese) (last visited 4 July 2013).

119 See note 115 Chapter 4.

120 About 4000–5000 years ago, five major ethnic groups – the Huaxia, Dongyi, Nanman, Xirong and Beidi – emerged in what is now the Chinese territory. Through continuous migration, living together, intermarriage and communication, the five ethnic groups became assimilated to each other in the course of their development, and gradually became integrated into one people, but within it new ethnic groups continually sprang up. Some of the latter remain distinct to this day, while others, including the once-renowned Xiongnu (Hun), Yuezhi (or Rouzhi), Xianbei, Rouran, Tuyuhun, Tujue, Dangxiang, Khitan and Saka peoples, have disappeared in the course of history owing to wars, deterioration of the eco-environment or loss of identity. See note 115 Chapter 4.

121 ibid.

them are the economic and cultural base for the implementation of regional ethnic autonomy.[122] Thirdly, the distribution of ethnic groups plays a large part in determining the scope of regional autonomy. Some of the PRC's ethnic groups inhabit vast areas, while others live in individual compact communities in small areas or live in a mixture of each.[123] Fourthly, as far as economic developments are concerned, the previous and current economic conditions of ethnic minorities led to the policy of regional ethnic autonomy to deal with poverty, which is still the key issue in ethnic minority areas.[124] Hence, ethnic minorities are believed to need special policies and support from the state.

Therefore, in 2001, in consideration of the actual conditions when the socialist market economy was established, the Standing Committee of the NPC made revisions to the Law on Regional Ethnic Autonomy.[125] Subsequently, the Provisions of the State Council on Implementation of the Law of the People's Republic of China on Regional Ethnic Autonomy,[126]

---

122 Traditionally, the Han people, accounting for the majority of the PRC's total population, have lived mainly in the Central Plains on the middle and lower reaches of the Yellow and Yangtze rivers, where the climate is mild and the flat, fertile land is suitable for farming. The minority peoples mostly lived in peripheral areas, where the abundant grasslands, deserts, forests, plateaus, mountains, hills and lakes are favourable for stock raising, hunting and fishing. The 'tea-horse' and 'silk-horse' trade between the Han people in the Central Plains and the surrounding minority peoples satisfied the demand of the Han people for horses for use in agriculture, transportation and military affairs while catering to the needs of minority peoples for daily necessities, thereby boosting economic complementarities and common development. In addition, the Liao (916–1125), Jin (1115–1234), Western Xia (1038–1227), and Dali (937–1253) states, established by minority peoples in various parts of the PRC, quite clearly influenced by the Han rulers of various dynasties in government systems and territorial control, and absorbed many elements of the Central Plains culture. See note 115 Chapter 1.

123 The PRC's northwest and southwest are the two regions where minority peoples are most concentrated. Western PRC, consisting of nine provinces, three autonomous regions and one municipality directly under the central government, is home to 70 per cent of the PRC's minority population. The nine border provinces and autonomous regions are home to 60 per cent of the PRC's minority population. As the PRC's economy and society continue to develop, the scope of minority population distribution is growing. So far, the scattered minority population across the country has exceeded 30 million.

124 Before the founding of the PRC in 1949, most minority areas had an extremely low level of productivity, backward economic and social development and extremely poor infrastructure. At that time, some of them were on the verge of extinction, with the Hezhen numbering only some 300 people at the time of the founding of the PRC. It was on such an extremely backward basis that the social and economic construction of the ethnic minorities and minority areas began in the PRC. Thus, when the PRC was established, the Chinese government made it a basic task to rid all ethnic groups of poverty and enable them to lead a better life. See note 115 Chapter 5.

125 The Law on Regional Ethnic Autonomy of the PRC (in Chinese) is available on the official website of the Central People's Government of the PRC at http://www.gov.cn/test/2005-07/29/content_18338.htm (last visited 4 July 2013).

126 The Provisions of the State Council on Implementation of the Law of the People's Republic of China on Regional Ethnic Autonomy (in Chinese) is available on the

issued by the State Council in 2005, defined the duties of governments at higher levels to support and help the organs of self-government in ethnic autonomous areas.[127] The organs of self-government of national autonomous areas are the People's Congresses and People's Governments of autonomous regions, autonomous prefectures and autonomous counties.[128]

In addition to the functions and powers of other ordinary local organs of the state, the organs of self-government of national autonomous areas exercise the power of autonomy in accordance with the law and implement the laws and policies of the state in the light of existing local conditions.[129] The people's congresses of national autonomous areas have the power to enact regulations on the exercise of autonomy and separate regulations in light of the political, economic and cultural characteristics of the nationality or nationalities in the areas concerned.[130] The organs of self-government of the national autonomous areas independently arrange for and administer local economic development under the guidance of state plans; the organs of self-government of the national autonomous areas have the power of autonomy in administering the finances of their areas. The organs of self-government of the national autonomous areas independently administer educational, scientific, cultural, public health and physical culture affairs in their respective areas.[131]

What is more, the state is responsible for promoting the development of ethnic minorities. In exploiting natural resources and building enterprises in the national autonomous areas, the state gives due consideration to the interests of those areas; the state provides financial, material and technical assistance to the minority nationalities to accelerate their economic and cultural development; the state helps the national autonomous areas train large numbers of cadres at various levels and specialised personnel and skilled workers of various professions and trades from among the nationality or nationalities in those areas.[132]

Although these specific regional powers and laws may provide some protection to ethnic minorities in the PRC, it cannot be said that there is

official website of the Central People's Government of the PRC at http://www.gov.cn/zwgk/2005-05/27/content_1518.htm (last visited 13 May 2010).

127 ibid Article 2.

128 According to this law, among the chairmen and vice chairmen of the standing committee of these governing bodies should be one or more citizens of the nationality exercising regional autonomy in the area. The chairman of an autonomous region, the prefect of an autonomous prefecture or the head of an autonomous county should be a citizen of the nationality exercising regional autonomy in the area concerned.

129 See note 125 Article 19.

130 If a resolution, decision, order or instruction of a state organ at a higher level does not suit the conditions in a national autonomous area, the organ of self-government of the area may either implement it with certain alterations or cease implementing it after reporting to and receiving the approval of the state organ at the higher level.

131 See note 125 Articles 20–45.

132 ibid Articles 54–72

adequate protection for the target groups in HPGR in the PRC for the following reasons:

First, all such laws are focused on the interests of official ethnic minorities, which cannot include all the target groups of HPGR. HPGR researchers hope that identifying differences in genetic sequences between peoples will help to determine what makes certain groups of people different from others. In fact, there are a number of factors that are relevant to the delineation of populations for HPGR. These criteria need a balance between linguistic and genetic development, or environmental isolation and genetic development. Hence, Cavalli-Sforza states that the methods used by HPGR researchers to identify target populations include genealogical records and linguistics.

The use of these methods, however, leads to research problems closely related to history and culture, which do not assume languages to be static: languages migrate and change, and are not necessarily aligned with the biological make-up of genetic groups.[133] This means that the target subjects that the Chinese legislation and policies on ethnic minority intend to protect are not necessarily the same as the target groups in HPGR.

In the PRC, the official definition of 'ethnic minorities' was created in the 1950s by a political decision.[134] The specific standards for the division of ethnic minorities include not only the genetic make-up of peoples, but also other factors, such as their living environment and traditional customs. Thus, Sleeboom-Faulkner claims that: '[i]deas about genetic particularity in the PRC have roots in ethnic and socio-biological views about national minorities and mountainous populations in remote areas'.[135] Hence, national ethnic minorities share characteristics that make them important as genetic targets to researchers; thus, some ethnic minorities could be the research target groups in HPGR. Meanwhile, excepting ethnic minorities, some genetic

---

133 Cavalli-Sforza, L. L. (2000) *Genes, Peoples and Languages* (London: Penguin Books).

134 The definition of ethnic minorities has had a tortuous history: in the 1950s, China began to adhere to the Stalinist definition of a nation, according to which a nation is an historically formed stable community of people arising on the basis of common language, common territory, common economic life and a typical cast of mind manifested in a common culture. Ironically, after 1954 and in the 1960s, the concept of nation lost its meaning through the rejection of the idea that minorities and their territories were distinctive. In its paradoxical efforts to accelerate the evolutionary process leading to a classless and nationless communist society, the Chinese Communist Party encouraged class struggle and assimilation with the Han majority. All agencies for the minorities (for instance, nationality commissions, institutes, schools, etc) were disbanded. The minorities were to be treated as the Han, and all special privileges were eliminated in this class-free society: a proletarian dictatorship in which only one form of lifestyle was recognised. After the Deng-ist reforms in 1978, however, the special nature of the national minorities was gradually recognised. See note 135 at 407.

135 Sleeboom-Faulkner, M. (2006) 'How to Define a Population: Cultural Politics and Population Genetics in the People's Republic of China and the Republic of China', *BioSocieties*, vol. 1, pp. 399–419 at 404.

populations from remote, mountainous and isolated areas also have those characteristics and could be excellent research targets of HPGR. Unfortunately, those isolated groups are not protected by the legislation on ethnic minorities. For example, the Harvard study involved HPGR conducted on the people of Anhui rural areas, who are Han people, not an ethnic minority.

As suggested above, the research subjects of HPGR are not only official ethnic minorities, but also other rural and isolated groups in the PRC: thus, the special legislation on ethnic minorities cannot provide protection for all the research subjects of the HPGR in the PRC.

Secondly, the majority of the regulations or legislation on ethnic minority protection in the PRC are on a macro level, and most of them focus on political rights. This means that they do not pay any attention to ethnic minorities' interests and rights as groups concerning issues such as participation in biomedical research.

The legislative purpose of the Law of the People's Republic of China on Regional Ethnic Autonomy, clearly stated in its Preface, is 'critical to enhancing the relationship of equality, unity and mutual assistance among different ethnic groups, to upholding national unification, and to accelerating the development of places where regional autonomy is practiced and promoting their progress'.[136] Therefore, it can be seen as a law which is used to construct an essential part of the basic political system of the PRC. It is not difficult to understand why it concentrated on regulations on how to build a regional autonomous government and its functions. However, there was a lack of regulation on how to provide adequate protection to ethnic minorities and their interests in other aspects of their lives. Thus, in the context of HPGR in the PRC, although some ethnic minorities would likely be involved as target groups, their interests, which might be harmed in HPGR, cannot be protected by the legal regulations on ethnic minorities.

In summary, as an example of developing countries, the situation of the PRC represents most of the developing countries which have already adopted legal regulations and ethical guidelines on human subject protection, such as Uganda,[137] Malawi,[138] Kenya,[139] Nigeria[140] and South Africa.[141] Similar to

---

136 See note 125 Preface.
137 Guidelines for the Conduct of Health Research Involving Human Subjects in Uganda (Uganda: National Consensus Conference 1997).
138 National Research Council of Malawi, Procedures and Guidelines for the Conduct of Research in Malawi (2002).
139 National Council for Science and Technology, Guidelines for Ethical Conduct of Biomedical Research Involving Human Subjects in Kenya (2004).
140 National Code for Health Research Ethics (Nigeria: 2006).
141 The National Health Act 2003 (Act No. 61 of 2003), which establishes the National Health Research Ethics Council; the Guidelines for Good Practice in the Conduct of Clinical Trials in Human Participants in South Africa; see also 12(2)(c) of the Constitution of the Republic of South Africa (Act No. 108 of 1996), which makes informed consent in research a constitutional requirement.

the analysis above, although there are special laws and rules which aim to provide protections to ethnic minorities and regulate the ethical conduct of biomedical research involving human subjects, they are all created in line with the international guidelines and have some deficiencies and therefore fail to provide adequate protections to research subjects of HPGR. The legal regulation and ethical guidelines on biomedical research involving human subjects in developing countries are almost directly transplanted from Western ones and international guidelines, without localisation concerning their own cultural sensitivities and vulnerabilities. It is important to stress once again that current dominant Western legal regulations and ethical guidelines, which are still grounded in an individualistic autonomy model, are also ill-suited to take account of the particular concerns surrounding group or community collective genetic information and the vulnerability of target groups in HPGR. Effective regulation of HPGR in developing countries will need to consider these matters.

At the same time, given the practical situation and the distinctive cultural sensitivities of target groups in developing countries including the PRC, the values of Western bioethical principles and guidelines may not all work well in developing countries. Nonetheless, developing countries, which have rich HGR, seem to be ideal mother lodes of human genes for HPGR.

There are some other developing countries, however, that do not have either legislation or national ethical guidelines specifically covering research involving humans in any significant manner, such as Sudan and Ghana. The protection of target groups and human subjects in these developing countries can only rely on the guidelines and self-regulation by researchers, including external researchers whose primary goals are to further their own professional interests, which include obtaining grants, publishing research results, fulfilling promotion criteria, developing new modes of disease prevention, diagnosis and treatment, and securing patent rights. The situation these countries face may be more intensified in the context of HPGR, owing to cultural sensitivities and group interests which could not be protected adequately under current Western legal regulation and international ethical guidelines.

Therefore, to further the goals of the ethical conduct of HPGR and enhance the protection of target groups and individual participants in developing countries, it is essential to continue to clarify how legal and ethical frameworks can be amended to adapt to the specific situation of developing countries.

7   Conclusion

This discussion has concentrated on two main issues. First, it has evaluated the specific concerns raised by genetic research, which become even more prominent in human population genetic research (HPGR). Secondly, by analysing the characteristics of target groups in HPGR, the vulnerability and cultural sensitivity of target groups in HPGR in developing countries has been considered. Behind these discussions has been the fundamental question as to whether or not the interests of target groups in HPGR in developing countries could be adequately protected by the current Western legal and ethical framework on human subject research. It has also been proposed that there should be a new ethical autonomy model and relevant regulations on group interest protection in HPGR in developing countries.

The need for group protection in HPGR in developing countries

Research ethics and the understanding of adequate protections for research participants are evolving all the time, following the trends of biomedical research development as well as evolvement of social values. Scholars have summarised that, since World War II, there have been four major paradigms of research ethics.[1] These paradigms highlighted distinctive values and provided different approaches on research participant protection. First, from the 1940s to the early 1970s, researcher paternalism was the dominant paradigm. It emphasised the social value of research and trust in investigators, and the main protections for research participants were based on researchers' judgments about whether or not risk-benefit ratios of certain research projects were reasonable. Research participants' informed consent was not highlighted. This paradigm has a basic hypothesis that researchers were concerned about the wellbeing of participants and wanted to protect them from unreasonable risks

1   Emanuel, E. J. and Grady, C. (2006) 'Four Paradigms of Clinical Research and Research Oversight', *Cambridge Quarterly of Healthcare Ethics*, vol. 16, pp. 82–96.

of harm. Secondly, from the early 1970s to the mid-1980s, because of a series of human research scandals such as the Tuskegee Syphilis Study, regulatory protectionism was gradually taking the centre stage. This paradigm required strict protections of research participants from the dangers posed by researchers and research itself, institutional review board (IRB) review and individual informed consent were taken as the principal mechanisms to protect research participants from the risks and burdens of research. Thirdly, from the mid-1980s to the mid-1990s, the high demand for more biomedical research on fatal diseases such as HIV and breast cancer promoted the paradigm move to the participant access stage. It was based on the argument that 'more efficient and equitable studies could be done with better patient compliance if community physicians participated in clinical trials'.[2] Under this paradigm, the judgment of the participants about what was in their own best interests was seen as the best protection for participants, not 'government regulations or bureaucrats deciding what risks were excessive'.[3] The individual's autonomy and benefits of biomedical research was highlighted. Finally, beginning in the mid-1990s, along with the development of genetic research, the new paradigm, collaborative partnership, began to emerge. There were two main reasons for the movement to this paradigm. First, the limitation of the participant access type research regulations only focused on individuals but not on communities, which led to the vulnerability of communities. Secondly, there was also the need to protect developing country communities from exploitation during the conduct of biomedical research. This paradigm emphasised 'the importance of the community in ensuring the relevance and integrity of research practices'[4] and 'more focused on community participation in the entire research process, from funding priorities to protocol development to dissemination of results'.[5] Although this paradigm may only apply to some types of biomedical research, such as HPGR, epidemiology and intervention studies, it provided a new perspective for the entire research ethics. It was a relational-based paradigm, with a clear recognition that biomedical research does not occur in isolation, and it might influence other relevant individuals, even groups as a whole, both during and after the research. The interests of relevant individuals and groups should also be considered and protected adequately.

These shifts of paradigms are evolvements, rather than radical substitution. This discussion has followed the trends of paradigm evolvement to emphasise protection of group interests in HPGR in developing countries, and intended to make the specific argument more convincing. It needs to be highlighted here that the argument in this book does not intend to reject individual

2 ibid at 90.
3 ibid at 91.
4 ibid at 92.
5 ibid at 93.

autonomy and the informed consent model in research regulations radically, but places them in a wider context of protections that need to be satisfied prior to seeking the consent of individuals, which is protection for group interests in biomedical research such as HPGR in developing countries. The book has provided some suggestions on how to establish a more relational model with consideration of cultural sensitivity.

With regard to genetic information, it has been argued that it has some unique qualities when compared with other health information, in the sense that certain types of genetic information, such as group collective genetic information', can be gained from any individual, but may reveal the collective information of a certain family; even a group or community. Hence, the main risks of harm in genetic research are primarily related to the disclosure of information and research results that could lead to discrimination, social stigmatisation, familial disruption, or psychological distress to the human subject and his or her family or community members.[6] For example, genetic research might lead to risks of harm including 'inadvertent disclosure of painful facts about family relationships (such as non-paternity); stigmatization associated with having a genetic abnormality; and intra-familial discord'.[7] The inappropriate publication or misuse of an individual's genetic information would violate not only his or her interests but also the interests of his or her family members, even group or community members. In the context of HPGR, the concerns or interests of groups become important. Since HPGR focuses on the collective genetic information of specific target groups/communities rather than individual human subjects, the information collected by HPGR is group or community collective genetic information. Hence, this discussion then turned to a discussion of potential harms to target groups in HPGR.

It needs to be highlighted that there really are potential risks of harm that the target group as a whole might be exposed to upon the disclosure of information or research results of HPGR. Such harms might be external harms, such as genetic discrimination and stigmatisation of the whole target group, as well as threats to national security and the survival of certain groups and communities. There might also be internal harms, which may occur inside the target group of HPGR, such as harm to the constitution of the group itself, and challenges to or disparagement of target groups' spiritual traditions, historical narratives or traditional beliefs. However, the application of

6 Beskow, L. M., Burke, W., Merz, J. F., Barr, P. A., Terry, S., Penchaszadeh, V. B., Gostin, L. O., Gwinn, M. and Khoury, M. J. (2001) 'Informed Consent for Population-Based Research Involving Genetics', *Journal of the American Medical Association*, vol. 286, no. 18, pp. 2315–21 at 2318.

7 Green, R. M. and Thomas, A. M. (1998) 'DNA: Five Distinguishing Features for Policy Analysis', *Harvard Journal of Law and Technology*, vol. 11, pp. 571–91 at 573.

current Western legal regulations and ethical guidelines is problematic, since they do not provide protections against these types of risk of harms.

The target groups in HPGR are frequently ethnic minorities and isolated groups in rural areas of developing countries. Given the common features of target groups, such as poverty, low-educational levels and lack of social and medical resources, this discussion argued that they have three different kinds of vulnerabilities in HPGR – consent-based, risk-based and justice-based vulnerability.[8] In addition, in developing countries, it is common that there is a lack of effective legislation and regulations on the biomedical research governance and human subject protection. This situation, together with poor law enforcement in most developing countries, makes target groups of HPGR more vulnerable. Hence, target groups in HPGR should be treated as vulnerable groups and they need specific protection to eliminate or reduce their vulnerabilities.

However, through the analysis, it has been concluded that the vulnerability of target groups in HPGR cannot be eliminated or reduced by current ethical frameworks. Currently, most guidelines for the protection of groups in research have been drafted for research involving specific indigenous peoples, such as American Indians. Although almost all of the guidelines require that researchers respect the culture of the community, none of these guidelines provides guidance on how to cope with circumstances when it may be unclear who represents a particular group. There is no guideline that provides for a specific, clear guidance and standard for group involvement. It is also rare to see any requirement that group representatives be involved in the conduct and ethical review of research. Therefore, it is concluded that these guidelines are inadequate to protect the special vulnerabilities of the target groups in HPGR.

There are a great many arguments and supporting evidence to provide a justification for group collective rights in international law, human rights law and even medical law itself. For example, as has been illustrated in Chapter 5, in the context of medical law, there are arguments concerning collective human rights to public health in order to advance health rights in a globalised world. While, this discussion then argued that although viewing target groups as holders of legally enforceable rights in respect of HPGR is not feasible under current dominant (Western) legal and ethical regulations, it can surely be agreed that their interests should and could be protected in other ways.

The specific situation of HPGR conduct and relevant regulation in developing countries has also been analysed and critiqued in the case of the People's Republic of China (PRC). In the PRC, target groups in HPGR are more likely to be influenced by traditional Confucianism and Marxism.

---

8 Coleman, C. H. (2009) 'Vulnerability as a Regulatory Category in Human Subject Research', *Journal of Law, Medicine and Ethics*, vol. 37, no. 1, pp. 12–18 at 15.

According to these traditions, individuals would not only take their own interests into account when making decisions about issues relevant to the interests of their group or community, but would also probably wish to consider these wider interests. In some groups, individuals would also wish to rely on the views of group or community leaders. It is part of their cultural traditions which ought to be respected and should not be seen as undue influence. However, under current Chinese regulations, which are almost outright adapted from Western ethical guidelines and legal regulation, group interests would not be considered and protected. Meanwhile, under current ethical guidelines, researchers and IRBs or research ethics committees (RECs) from Western countries also may not appreciate these facets of decision-making. Therefore, although individual informed consent has its own justification in bioethics, even if the informed consent procedures in developing countries were conducted to the same standards that are enforced in Western countries, the simple application of individualised informed consent may not fit into the cultural context of decision-making in developing countries, particularly in the context of HPGR.

An argument for domestic legislation on group protection in HPGR in developing countries

Although it is beyond the scope of this book to enter into a discussion of the relationship between legal regulations and ethical guidelines, it is necessary to promote a movement of legalisation of research ethics in the field of group interest protection in HPGR in developing countries. In the context of developing countries, the governance of HPGR should transfer from the pattern of relying on research ethics only to the pattern of ruling by research ethics as well as law.

Both research ethics and legislation on research involving human subjects intend to define acceptable and unacceptable research conduct. They also mutually connect and may influence each other. Research ethics contain moral obligations in relation to biomedical research conduct on human subjects; thus, it involves an interaction between ethics and research. Law on research involving human subjects is based on moral obligations and is interconnected with research ethics. What is more, there may be some overlap in their regulatory scopes. For example, some kinds of research would be prohibited and punished by legal regulation. Meanwhile, these types of research methods would also be condemned by research ethics. In parallel, some other kinds of research required by law are also encouraged and promoted by research ethics. Moreover, during the process of regulating research involving human subjects, their functions are complementary to each other. Research ethics could help relevant researchers establish correct inner concepts and standards of research conduct to avoid illegal actions from their thinking.

While, when the regulation of research ethics failed, legal regulation could punish that unacceptable action or misconduct by virtue of national enforcement power.

However, goals and mechanisms of law and research ethics are clearly different from each other. The main difference is that research ethics may only be instructional, which would bring ethical criticism if breached but law sets mandatory minimum standards, which would bring about legal liability if infringed. The legal liability is formulated or approved by the state and put into implementation with force. Therefore, as some scholars have rightly noted:

> Law is usually considered the product of authoritative law-making institutions associated with the nation state. Ethical principles, on the other hand, may be grounded in a wider range of sources with no necessary connection to the state. So law and ethics can be distinguished, on the basis of their different sources, and on occasions, they point to different conclusions in the same case.[9]

Law and research ethics are two entirely different normative systems.

To provide adequate protections for target groups in HPGR, this discussion suggests that domestic law and legal frameworks need to play an active role in the protection of target groups and that both the basic protections on research participants offered by the international guidelines and specific rules for group protection need to be included in national laws in developing countries, with specific concern on vulnerability and cultural sensitivity. Creating basic legal requirements would seem to be one of the best options for developing countries. These legal requirements may be added to existing legislation or embodied in new legal regulations.

One of the most significant reasons for employing legal regulation for target group protection in HPGR in developing countries is that formal legal regulation is particularly effective where the interests of the vulnerable are under potential risks of harm. Owing to the vulnerability of target groups in HPGR, governments of developing countries need to play an active role in protecting target groups. In order to ensure governments undertake their responsibilities, it is important for there to be a legislative requirement obliging government to supervise the conduct of HPGR in developing countries to protect the interests of target groups and individual participants. In addition, in developing countries RECs also need a firm foundation in legal regulation to fulfil their responsibilities effectively; if the absence of such regulation, they would operate from a weak and dependent position. As some scholars have argued:

---

9 Dawson, J. (2003) 'An Introduction to the Law of Research' in J. Dawson and N. Peart eds., *The Law of Research* (University of Otago Press) 14–25 at 25.

However hard they work, however thorough their examination of research protocols on a case-by-case basis, however much better constituted and trained, and however well supported they may be administratively, unless they have the power to ensure that all research is submitted to them and to stop research that they regard as unethical, they will not be taken sufficiently seriously. For these reasons and others ... there should be proper legislation.[10]

The importance of RECs with members from target groups and local government in HPGR has been discussed above, while ensuring the independence and legitimacy of RECs requires that they operate within the legal framework, not merely ethical guidelines.

Moreover, one prospective function of law is norm-setting, which should play a vital role in the context of group protection in HPGR in developing countries. Legal regulation on research involving human subjects, in theory, should provide protection to citizens and prevent potential harm as well as creating an enabling environment for acceptable conduct in research. In developing countries, where regulating HPGR involving human subjects is still a relatively new endeavour, there is a need to address how HPGR should be governed in such a way as to create an enabling environment for HPGR and to clarify the responsibilities of relevant parties in HPGR. Group interest in HPGR, which is important to target groups in HPGR but not widely accepted or recognised by international guidelines on research involving human subjects, should be clarified and protected explicitly by law in developing countries. Employing appropriate legal frameworks could be useful to achieve this goal, by addressing group interest protection in HPGR, the line of authority and the responsibilities of stakeholders in HPGR process, including researchers, local government and RECs. It would also provide clear guidance on what should be done to prevent potential harm to target groups in HPGR. In other words, the potential group harms and risks connected with HPGR emphasise the need to be backed by law, which creates room for legal accountability and is likely to be the best approach to regulating research in developing countries.

Furthermore, the goals and priority of researchers from developed countries may not necessarily be in the interest of target groups in HPGR in developing countries. The power of researchers over research participants caused by lack of resources, as well as the inherent tension in producing scientific benefits and protecting interests of target groups calls for an authoritative independent framework for the protection of target groups in HPGR in developing countries. In view of the sovereignty of each nation and the

10 Verdun-Jones, S. and Weisstub, D.N. (1996) 'The Regulation of Biomedical Research Experimentation in Canada: Developing An Effective Apparatus for the Implementation of Ethical Principles in a Scientific Milieu', *Ottawa Law Review*, vol. 297, p. 316.

resulting problems for sponsoring developed countries in protecting target groups of host developing countries, domestic legal regulation would be the best way to protect target groups in HPGR. It has been argued that:

> It is rare for countries to have laws directly preventing their nationals doing research overseas that would not be permitted at home, or even bringing back the products of such research, unless they pose a safety risk, such as importing genetically manipulated organisms created overseas.[11]

There are no ethical reasons or motives for developed countries to prevent researchers from doing research abroad or using the research results at home, even if the research does not comply with the laws of the host country. As some authors rightly observed:

> [L]egislation is debated openly, its provisions are publicized, and the legislative process provides accountability ... legislators are subject to the electoral process and parliamentary debates on legislative proposals are subject to public scrutiny. Legislation promotes uniformity and enforceability and can contain clarifications about the conditions under which vulnerable persons can legally be participants in research. In short, 'legislation has all the advantages that have been claimed for guidelines, and none of the disadvantages'.[12]

Therefore, a domestic legal framework, including formal legal mechanisms, would be an appropriate instrument for the protection of target groups.

However, there are some opposing views on employing legislation to regulate biomedical research. One main argument is that since biomedical research is changing constantly, and the rules of law require stability, incompatible contradictions between the two are unavoidable. It has to be admitted that legislation may not necessarily foresee all the future problems and issues relevant to biomedical research. As some scholars have rightly pointed out: 'changing values, advances in science, and unanticipated situations combine to create the possibility that prospective, comprehensive law-making will be fundamentally flawed'.[13] It needs to be highlighted again, however, that

---

11 Skene, L. (2007) 'Undertaking Research in Other Countries: National Ethico-Legal Barometers and International Ethical Consensus Statements', *PLoS Med* 4(2) e10.

12 Starkman, B. (1998) 'Models for Regulating Research: The Council of Europe and International Trends' in D. N. Weisstub ed., *Research On Human Subjects: Ethics, Law and Social Policy* (Elsevier Science) 264 at 274.

13 Dworkin, B. R. (1996) *Limits: The Role of Law in Bioethical Decision-Making* (Indiana University Press) at 2.

target groups in this discussion are vulnerable groups in developing countries. Although it may be flawed, since it does not anticipate all future events, legislation, as a crucial tool for protecting vulnerable groups and research participants, is much better than a legal vacuum with no guarantee of legal protections for target groups and individual participants. In developing countries the lack of experience of ethical governance of biomedical research, the advantages of legally enforceable protections for target groups and individual participants, explicit clarity and comprehensiveness of responsibilities, and a healthy environment within which researchers can conduct HPGR all outweigh the possible disadvantages.

Legislation alone could not ensure ethical conduct in biomedical research. The establishment of a culture of ethical conduct in biomedical research is a necessity. However, research, especially that targeted on vulnerable groups in developing countries, without legislation also does not make ethical conduct, but may lead to exploitation and unethical practices. Legislation would be the best approach to regulate HPGR in developing countries.

In summary, as Western developed countries gain economic and technological ascendance, they need human population genetic resources which some developing countries have in abundance; accordingly, most HPGR is likely to be conducted by researchers from developed countries in developing countries. Some developing countries, such as the PRC, which is both engaged in HPGR and contains groups and communities with specific cultural sensitivities, have realised the need for specific protection in HPGR and made some legislative attempts to do so. However, after a critical analysis of these documents, it became clear that such regulations as do exist have borrowed their terminology and conceptual basis directly from Western ideologies, despite different cultural and philosophical traditions. Yet, as has been argued above, Western ethical and legal frameworks, which focus on individual autonomy and the welfare of individual participants, do not provide adequate protection for target groups in HPGR. Therefore, these legal regulations, copied word for word from Western frameworks, may not be culturally appropriate in developing countries, where the traditional ethic emphasises social harmony over individual interests. Although there are special legislation and ethical rules which aim to provide protections for ethnic minorities and regulate the ethical conduct of biomedical research involving human subjects, such as in the PRC, they may also have some deficiencies and therefore fail to provide adequate protections to research subjects of HPGR. In addition, of the laws and regulations related to human subject protection, most turn out not to be promulgated by the highest level of the legislature. The concept of vulnerable group protection should also be introduced in high level legislation on human subject protection. Therefore, this discussion suggests that the developing countries should establish comprehensive legislation relating specifically to HPGR, which highlights vulnerable population protection. This legislation should be formulated by the highest level of legislature; for example, in the PRC, it should be Chinese Country Legislature – the Chinese Congress and Its Standing Committee.

Possible contents of legislation on group protection in HPGR in developing countries

Following the above discussion, it is necessary to propose some recommendations on how to reconstruct a legal and ethical framework in HPGR in developing countries.

The first issue to clarify is whether Western research ethical principles and guidelines should be included in our new ethical and legal framework. There has always been a scholarly dispute whether Western principles of biomedical research could be 'universalisable'.[14] The opponents insisted that attempts to ground international bioethics in fundamental principles cannot withstand the challenges posed by multiculturalism and post-modernism.[15] The advocates argued that the multiculturalist premise should be rejected for fundamental moral principles to be valid and accepted by all cultures, since 'the validity of moral principles does not require their universal acceptance, but rather, their universal applicability'.[16] Some scholars even argued that:

> To say that there are ethical universals—that is, norms and values having cross cultural validity—is to make an understatement. It would be more accurate to say that all ethical norms or rules are cultural universals, because a rule or norm cannot properly be described as 'ethical' unless it is understood as having cross cultural validity, in the sense of being perceived as applying in all similar circumstances, irrespective of place and time.[17]

Meanwhile, these advocates also admitted there were still some concerns relevant to cultural differences. Macklin pointed out that during the process of updating international research ethical guidelines, while general agreement could be reached on several highly controversial aspects of international research ethics, deeper intractable disagreements between different cultures would persist within each agreement category.[18]

---

14 See Macklin, R. (1999) 'International Research: Ethical Imperialism or Ethical Pluralism?', *Accountability in Research*, vol. 7, pp. 59–83. Also see Benatar, S. R. (2010) 'Responsibilities in International Research: A New Look Revisited', *Journal of Medical Ethics*, vol. 36, no. 4, pp. 194–97.

15 Baker, R. (1998) 'A Theory of International Bioethics: Multiculturalism, Postmodernism, and the Bankruptcy of Fundamentalism', *Kennedy Institute of Ethics Journal*, vol. 8, pp. 201–31.

16 Macklin, R. (1998) 'A Defence of Fundamental Universal Principles: A Response to Robert Baker', *Kennedy Institute of Ethics Journal*, vol. 8, no. 4, pp. 403–22 at 420.

17 Tangwa, G. B. (2004) 'Between Universalism and Relativism: A Conceptual Exploration of Problems in Formulating and Applying International Biomedical Ethical Guidelines', *Journal of Medical Ethics*, vol. 30, pp. 63–67 at 63–64.

18 Macklin, R. (2001) 'After Helsinki: Unresolved Issues in International Research', *Kennedy Institute of Ethics Journal*, vol. 11, pp. 17–36.

This discussion holds the idea that these fundamental ethical rules on biomedical research, such as individual informed consent and risk-benefit assessment, should be accepted by, or in other words be universal to, legal and ethical frameworks in developing countries; but this acceptance should be culturally relevant, with more nuanced considerations of specific social relations. It means that, in applying biomedical ethical principles the factual situations such as HPGR in developing countries, cultural elements should be considered. Therefore, on the basis of the rules of Western research ethics, developing cultural relevant ethical principles and legal regulations on biomedical research has become a major task for developing countries.

For the legislative concept, it would be appropriate to adopt the relational autonomy model in HPGR in developing countries. As discussed above, the adoption of this model does not mean that obtaining group consent instead of individual consent from participants should be a legal obligation in HPGR. The general rules of individual consent in biomedical research, as discussed in detail in Chapter 3, should be a crucial and fundamental part of the legislation. Rather, relational autonomy requires that the interests of all relevant parties need also to be considered during the design of research, ethical review, the consent process and the conduct and monitoring of research. The protection on interests of target groups should be noted by legislation. In order to protect the interests of target groups in HPGR, both researchers and IRBs or RECs need to take responsibility for ensuring adequate target group protection.

To provide adequate protections for human subjects in HPGR, this discussion suggests that high level legislation needs to play an active role in the protection of participants and that the basic protections offered by the international guidelines need to be reconstructed into a form which is appropriate to the specific situation in any developing country in which this kind of research is undertaken or proposed. While this discussion has specifically focused on HPGR in the context of the PRC, it is evident from examples provided of HPGR conducted in other developing countries that the same kinds of concerns would arise more widely; it is therefore proposed that the following approaches should be adopted by both international ethical guidelines and domestic legal regulations on target group protection in all HPGR.

Enhancing researchers' responsibilities for group protection

The general legal requirements of researchers in HPGR in developing countries should include the following.

First, researchers in HPGR should undertake consultation with target groups about relevant cultural issues at the research design. There are several obstacles that can interfere with HPGR being conducted in an ethical way by researchers from developed countries. These are caused by distinctions between researchers and target groups in HPGR, such as marked inequality of bargaining power and resources and a lack of cultural sensitivity regarding decision-making. In the context of HPGR, target groups should be involved in the development, design and conduct of the research, since the process of consultation could offer a potential mechanism to protect communities against exploitation. Consultation on research design should be a necessary prerequisite to ensuring that the HPGR is undertaken in a way that respects the cultural norms of the target group or community and alerts the group to the possibility of harms arising from the research questions or findings. The content of the researchers' consultation in all HPGR projects should include the following three main aspects:

(a) In order to establish a proper research protocol, researchers should investigate the basic social, economic and average educational background of the target group.
(b) To identify the possible external and internal harms relevant to HPGR, social and cultural concerns should also be investigated by researchers intending to conduct HPGR. These may include harms including discrimination and stigmatisation and disruption of the group's common beliefs, traditions or narratives. The bioethical background of the target group, which may be very different from the Western standard of research ethics, should be investigated and taken into account by researchers.
(c) Researchers in HPGR also have an obligation to investigate the culturally appropriate form of decision-making. In addition, in order to ensure the quality of group consultation, researchers in HPGR ought to collaborate with the group to define how the research problem might be approached and explained to participants and, where relevant, oral traditions and other sources of group collective beliefs or common culture ought to be used in a respectful manner.

Secondly, researchers should obtain a collective permission from a target group leader or recognised authority for HPGR, if the target group has the cultural tradition of collective decision-making. The mechanism of group approval in HPGR should respect the cultural sensitivities or customs in collective decision-making, which should be based on the results of group consultation. Target groups in HPGR may have their own specific means of collective decision-making. If there is a community authority or community leader who can represent the target group to give collective formal and explicit approval or disapproval, such as in the case of the Apache Business Committee which represents the Apache Tribe of Oklahoma when making fundamental collective decisions,[19] group approval or disapproval should be sought from these community authorities or community leaders. Similarly, in developing countries such

19 Foster, M. W., Bernsten, D. and Carter, T. H. (1998) 'A Model Agreement for Genetic Research in Socially Identifiable Populations', *American Journal of Human Genetics*, vol. 63, pp. 696–702 at 701.

as the PRC, most of the target groups have their own group leaders or authorities which should be the agent to provide group approval or disapproval. While such collective approval or disapproval would not obviate the need to obtain consent from individual participants, it would be a highly relevant factor in determining whether the study should proceed – and if there is collective disapproval, this should be regarded as determinative. Potential participants may wish to rely upon the views of community leaders in making their own decisions and information about them should be made available to them.

Thirdly, in order to eliminate or reduce the vulnerabilities of members of target groups in HPGR, at the stage of individual information disclosure, researchers should consider the potential participants' cultural traditions and educational level. Researchers should pay careful attention to the method of communication with individuals. Researchers should use communication measures which are appropriate giving adequate time to potential participants to ask questions about the HPGR, and providing adequate time for consideration of their decisions. Information should be provided in languages and concepts that are understandable to them and which enable meaningful consent to be given.

Considering the interests of groups in ethical review

In the context of developing countries, ethical review should be a legal requirement for HPGR. In addition, the legal regulation should also require ethical review committees to have additional responsibilities to ensure that the interests of target groups are safeguarded and avoid the risk of exploitation. The ethical review should be conducted by an independent ethical review committee including members from target groups, rather than simply an institutional ethical review committee.

In order to consider the interests of the group, the following measures should be included in domestic legislation on ethical review for all HPGR projects.

First, ethical review committees in HPGR should include members from the target group with varying genders, age groups and educational levels. The number of representatives should be decided by the population size of the target group. If there are group leaders or recognised authorities in target groups, they must be included in ethical review committees. If there is no group leader or group recognised authority, the representatives should include the most affected members, the most educated members and some other random members. Some would argue that it can never be certain that the representatives will really voice the real opinion of the target group they represent. However, these selective representatives are members of the target group and may be expected to share common traditions and beliefs. It is reasonable to expect that their opinions could reflect the views of the target group members and their participation would also help to examine whether or not certain HPGR may lead to potential risks of harm that research participants and other members of the target group view as important.

Secondly, those responsible for administering RECs should provide proper training to members from target groups to assure the competence and quality of their ethical review participation. The training for review of HPGR should emphasise the development of the ability of members from target groups to evaluate scientific issues in HPGR and to make complex risk-benefit assessments. The training should include at least the following elements: background scientific knowledge of HPGR; potential risks of harm of HPGR; appropriate harm minimisation measures; general research ethical principles; and standard ethical review procedures in a way that is understandable to target group members.

Thirdly, in addition to risk-benefit assessments concerning individual human subjects, risk-benefit evaluations of the interests of target groups of the proposed HPGR should also be conducted, with emphasis on the assessment of potential collective risks of harm related to HPGR and awareness of the specific cultural sensitivities of target groups. It should identify how various social, religious, economic, cultural and political groups view the risks related to the proposed HPGR. The standard of ethical review of group risks of harm in HPGR should include the following factors: (i) the group risks of harm related to HPGR must be minimised, to the extent that doing so is consistent with sound scientific design; (b) the group risks of harm posed by HPGR must be reasonable in relation to the knowledge that is expected to be gained from the study; and (c) the group risks of harm from HPGR must be no more than a minor increase over the minimal group risks of daily life for the identified group.

Fourthly, ethical review committees should be responsible for determining any proposed compensation or payment based on the degree of risk and other burdens of HPGR in developing countries. Given the different levels of economic development between researchers from developed countries and target groups in HPGR from developing countries, there may be a dilemma for researchers in offering compensation or payment to target groups: offer too little and the participants are exploited; offer too much and their participation may be unduly influenced. Independent ethical review committees with members from target groups are more capable of identifying the appropriate level of compensation or payment which fits into the specific economic development levels of the target groups.

Highlighting the involvement of target groups at all stages of the research

In addition to representatives from target groups being included in ethical review committees, the involvement of target groups in other stages of HPGR should also be a legal requirement for HPGR, as follows:

(a) At the research design stage in HPGR, how to deal with the research data and samples should also be discussed by the researchers and target groups, including where data or samples will be stored, whether or not any will be destroyed and who ultimately controls them after the completion of the research.

(b) At the publication stage of the HPGR results, the opinion of target groups should be respected. Before publication, group representatives should be carefully informed of the potential contents' relevance to the target group and their potential implications and any objections noted. A consultation to avoid harms caused by publication should be made between researchers and the target group.

(c) The mechanism of choosing group representatives to consider such issues should follow the rules of group representatives involved in the ethical review committees.

According to the analysis presented in this discussion, in order to provide adequate protections for target groups in HPGR, it has been argued that developing countries need to play an active role in the protection of the target group. It is suggested that the following two aspects of legal regulation should be developed in the proposed domestic legislation on human subject protection in developing countries. However, as noted, it can be further proposed that in order to eliminate or reduce the vulnerabilities of target groups in other developing countries where similar concerns are likely to arise, these two aspects of regulation should also be adopted by all developing countries.

Double review in international collaborative HPGR

In order to ensure the welfare and interests of vulnerable target groups in HPGR, international collaborative HPGR must be regulated by both Western frameworks and legislation of host developing countries. This proposed legislation would, for example, require that foreign researchers or research institutions who conduct HPGR in developing countries, no matter whether or not it has been reviewed according to the legal regulations or ethical guidelines of their own countries, also obtain approval from ethical review committees which are in conformity with the standard required by relevant laws on biomedical research of the host country, which would be more aware of the cultural sensitivities of target groups in HPGR and be able to take account of their vulnerabilities. This double review principle would play the role of preventing researchers from developed countries from taking advantage of loopholes in their own countries' regulations to exploit target groups in the host country. Significantly, if the approach to ethical review advocated here is adopted, such double review would in fact provide additional protections for participants and target groups to those currently existing in the Western research ethics framework.

Supervision of HPGR by developing countries

In consideration of the vulnerability of target groups in HPGR, it is reasonable to question whether representatives from vulnerable target groups in HPGR in ethical review committees established by researchers have appropriate knowledge of regulations governing biomedical research involving human subjects. Therefore, local government should play a supervisory role in the whole process of HPGR. The best way to achieve the supervision is to require that the ethical review committees of HPGR should be established by local government. Since the ethical review committees would be set up by local government, it would be helpful to deal with the issues relevant to group consideration, such as correctly identify the extent of dispersion within communities and avoid the inappropriate use of ethical review which may harm the target group. These committees need a firm foundation in law specific to biomedical research. Ensuring the independence and legitimacy of these committees requires that they operate within the proposed high level legislation on human subject protection, not merely national ethical guidelines, although the latter has the advantage of ease of amendment. These committees would supervise the whole process of HPGR, including the selection of target groups, group consultation, information disclosure, group approval, research results publication and further use of research samples.

As proposed earlier, their supervision should include consideration of the wide range of issues which ethics review committees may have to consider in the context of the socio-economic factors operating in specific situations and certain areas. These committees should also consider the issues specific to the particular target groups and the particular research; for instance, determining whether HPGR will be harmful to a target group given the specific needs of that community. If these committees find that the intended HPGR fails to meet any legal requirement stipulated in the proposed special law on biomedical research relevant to HPGR, they should report this to the local government. The local government should then require the researchers to stop the project immediately.

The proposed general model for additional legal protections for groups in HPGR in developing countries is summarised in Figure 7.1.

Conclusion

HPGR seeks to identify the diversity and variation of the human genome and how human group and individual genetic diversity has developed. Since HPGR targets specific groups to discover variation, it also raises many pressing ethical and legal concerns. The discussion here has focused on concerns raised by the application of the current dominant Western ethical and legal frameworks on human research subject protection in HPGR. It has discussed target group protection in HPGR and examines it in the context of developing countries, specifically in the PRC. It has argued that the current understanding of universal values on human research subject protection needs to be modified to take account of the particular challenges presented by HPGR in developing countries.

The growth of international research has given rise to increasing concern that international researchers may benefit excessively from conducting biomedical research in the developing world, and thus exploit the vulnerability of potential participants and their communities.[20] Thus, attention has now turned to the question of how to provide adequate protection to vulnerable populations in developing countries with respect to their specific cultural sensitivities. This change makes studies of the legal and ethical protection in biomedical research involving human subjects in developing countries more significant than before.

Although this discussion was intended to examine the need for an alternative model for group protection in HPGR in the specific situation of the PRC, it has a broader application, which could be expanded to all the developing countries, for the following reasons.

First, this discussion throws some light on general issues of group protection in HPGR by examining the existing Western ethical and legal frameworks on biomedical research. It has illustrated that in addition to risks of harm to individual participants, HPGR may expose target groups and other members of certain groups who are not directly involved to additional risks of harm. Current Western ethical and legal frameworks on biomedical research cannot provide adequate protection of the interests of target groups in HPGR. Although there are some studies that highlight concerns about the interests of third parties in biomedical research,[21] they are mostly still based on individualised autonomy or only consider the issues of indigenous people in developed countries. One of the reasons why there is a lack of study in this area could be the influence of Western individualism that dominates in biomedical research; namely, respect for (individual) persons. This can lead to the interests of groups being ignored. Therefore, there is a need for additional protections which can take specific account of the special interests of target groups in HPGR. This discussion has sought to help legislators and policymakers to understand in a precise way the inadequacies of current Western ethical and legal frameworks on biomedical research in group protection in HPGR, with specific consideration of the vulnerabilities of target groups in developing countries.

---

20 Ballantyne, A. (2008) 'Fair Benefits' Accounts of Exploitation Require A Normative Principle of Fairness: Response to Gbadegesin and Wendler, and Emanuel et al.', *Bioethics*, vol. 22, no. 4, pp. 239–44 at 240.

21 See Resnik, D. B. and Sharp, R. R. (2006) 'Protecting Third Parties in Human Subjects Research', *IRB: Ethics and Human Research*, vol. 28, no. 4, pp. 1–7. Also see Kimmelman, J. (2005) 'Medical Research, Risk, and Bystanders', *IRB: Ethics and Human Research*, vol. 27, no. 4, pp. 1–6.

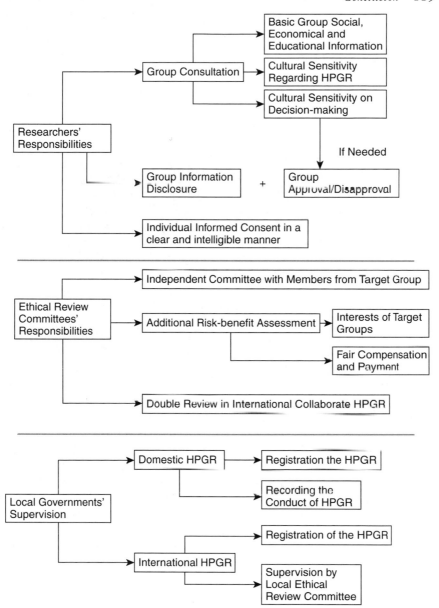

Figure 7.1 General model for additional legal protections to groups in HPGR

Secondly, this discussion pays attention to vulnerable target group protection in HPGR by examining their vulnerabilities from all three different types – consent-based, risk-based and justice-based vulnerability. Given the common situations of poverty, isolation, low-educational level and lack of social and economic resources in developing countries, target groups in HPGR from developing countries other than the PRC can also be recognised as vulnerable groups. Thus, those suggestions provided by this discussion to reduce or eliminate the vulnerability of target groups in HPGR could also be applied by other developing countries.

Thirdly, this discussion highlights the significance of cultural sensitivity in HPGR, although the community collective decision-making tradition of target groups in rural areas of the PRC has been used as an example. In developing countries, target groups in HPGR may have their own traditions of decision-making, although these may differ from the Chinese one, which may also not fit into the Western pattern. There are few scholars with awareness of cultural distinctions between different cultures. Thus, it is far from easy for researchers in developed countries to discuss vulnerable group protection in biomedical research conducted in developing countries. Despite this difficulty, this discussion has demonstrated that studies in this area can be carried out by examining vulnerable target group protection in HPGR. The mechanisms which aim to protect the cultural sensitivity, group approval and community review conducted by target groups and ethical review committees involving target group representatives could also be referenced by other developing countries.

Finally, this discussion also proposes an argument that domestic legislation or legal regulations on target group protection in HPGR in developing countries are necessary. The PRC, as an example of a developing country, is rich in genetic resources which lend themselves to the conduct of HPGR. This discussion has provided recommendations on how to reconstruct a legal framework for HPGR in the PRC to ensure protection of the interests of target groups and eliminate or reduce their vulnerabilities, with specific awareness of the cultural sensitivity of target groups in the PRC. For developing countries which have not adopted legal regulations or ethical guidelines on human subject protection, or are in the process of formulating national regulations, although they may not have the same legal system or cultural sensitivity as the PRC, this discussion could raise the awareness of the need for target group protection with due consideration of their special vulnerabilities and group interests. In addition, the detailed discussion on general rules of medical consent provided in Chapter 3 could also be absorbed by their future legislation and ethical guidelines. For those developing countries which have already adopted legal regulations and ethical guidelines on human subject protection, this discussion can also serve to remind regulators that the existing regulations and guidelines may need to be amended to provide adequate protection for target groups. Lastly, this discussion could raise the awareness of group protection in biomedical research conducted in developing countries, which could contribute to the amendment of international declarations and ethical guidelines, with specific consideration of the vulnerability and cultural sensitivities of target groups.

Appendix 1 A brief introduction to the Chinese legal system

The People's Republic of China (PRC) is a socialist state. Since the Third Plenary Session of the Eleventh Central Committee of the Communist Party of China (CPC) in 1978, the PRC has attached more importance to the role of law in state administration and social life by strengthening the legislative framework. It has sought steadily to improve legislative procedures, laying stress on legislative techniques and the quality of legislation. At present, 'ruling the country by law' is the fundamental guideline to administer the state and manage society under the leadership of the CPC, and this was written into the Constitution of the PRC[1] in 1999. The PRC has been actively building and seeking to improve its legal system since its foundation. As a result, a socialist legal system, with the Constitution as its core and with Chinese characteristics, has taken shape.[2]

The Chinese legal system is similar to the civil law systems of Japan, France and Germany.[3] The primary sources of law in PRC are written legislation. The PRC's legal system contains branches as follows: constitutional and related law, civil and commercial law, economic law, administrative law, social law, criminal law and litigation and non-litigation procedural law.[4] Cases cannot be cited as legal sources in Chinese courts.

According to the Constitution, the PRC implements a unified legislative system, which is to say that there is only one legislative system, albeit of multiple levels, in the country. The Constitution stipulates that the National

1 Constitution of the People's Republic of China (the Constitution). The full text of the Constitution can be seen on the official website of the Chinese government (in Chinese), available at http://www.gov.cn/ziliao/flfg/2005-06/14/content_6310_4.htm (last visited 5 July 2013).
2 The introduction of China's legal system and legal structure is based on the information provided by the official website of the Ministry of Justice of the PRC, available at http://www.legalinfo.gov.cn/ (last visited 5 July 2013).
3 For China's legal system, see Chow, D. (2003) *The Legal System of the People's Republic of China in a Nutshell* (St. Paul, MN: West Group). See also, Hsu, C. (2003) *Understanding China's Legal System* (New York: New York University Press).
4 These branches are divided by the Ministry of Justice of the PRC; see note 2.

People's Congress (NPC) and its Standing Committees exercise the legislative power of the state to enact laws. The State Council formulates administrative regulations according to the Constitution and laws. The NPC and its Standing Committees of each province, autonomous region or municipality directly under the Central Government formulate local regulations, which must not contravene the Constitution, laws or administrative regulations. The People's Congress of each national autonomous area has the power to enact regulations on the exercise of autonomy[5] and separate regulations in the light of the political, economic and cultural characteristics of the nationality or nationalities in the area concerned. Departments of, and agencies with, administrative functions directly under the State Council formulate rules according to the laws and administrative regulations of the State Council. In addition, the people's government of each province, autonomous region or municipality, as well as the people's government of the city where a province or autonomous region is located, and of the city where a special economic zone is located or larger cities designated by the State Council, may formulate rules. As to a special administrative region, it refers to Hong Kong and Macao, according to the principle of 'one country, two systems'. The Constitution stipulates that the state may, when necessary, establish special administrative regions and the systems to be instituted in special administrative regions shall be provided by law enacted by the NPC in the light of specific conditions. This is the embodiment of the concept of 'one country, two systems' in the Constitution. While upholding the sovereignty, unity and integrity of the country and that a special administrative region is an inalienable part of the PRC, such a region is allowed to implement economic, social, political and legal systems different from those for other regions of the country, that is, its current capitalist system and way of life may remain unchanged for years. The provisions of Article 31 of the Constitution, the system (including the legislative system) in a special administrative region shall be stipulated by law enacted by the NPC. The Basic Laws of Special Administrative Regions are adopted by the NPC. According to the basic laws of special administrative regions, the special administrative regions exercise a high degree of autonomy and, except that the foreign affairs and defence remain under the power of the Central People's Government, enjoy executive, legislative and independent judicial power including that of final adjudication, with their existing legal system remaining basically unchanged as do their existing social and economic systems and ways of life. The sources of Chinese law include the Constitution, laws, administrative regulations, local regulations, regulations of national autonomous areas, regulations of special

---

5 The detailed practical system and functions of ethnic minority autonomy are addressed in Chapter 6.

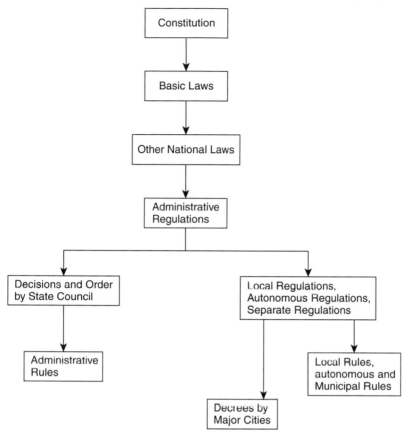

Figure 1 The hierarchy of the Chinese legal system

economic zones, rules and basic laws of special administrative regions, international treaties and practices.[6]

The Legislation Law of the People's Republic of China (the Legislation Law 2000) lays down the general rules of the hierarchy of Chinese law.[7] Under the Legislation Law 2000, legislation can be divided into at least seven different categories: the Chinese Constitution 1982; basic laws and national law; administrative regulations; local regulations; autonomy regulations; separate regulations; administrative rules and local rules (including provincial, autonomous and municipal rules, and decrees by major cities). Figure 1 above

---

6 The introduction of the Chinese legislative system is also based on the information provided by the Ministry of Justice of the PRC; see note 2.

7 See Chapter 5 'Scope of Application and Filing' of the Legislation Law of People's Republic of China, which was adopted by the 3rd Session of the 9th NPC in 2000. An English translation is available at http://www.novexcn.com/legislat_law_00.html (last visited 5 July 2013).

shows the hierarchy of the Chinese legal system. The Chinese Constitution 1982 has the highest legal authority.[8] National law is enacted by NPC or its Standing Committee. It can be divided into two sub-categories: basic laws and others. There is no clear definition of what laws can be basic laws. The Legislation Law 2000 does not clearly provide that basic laws are higher than other national laws. In practice, however, basic laws are generally considered more important than other national laws. Administrative rules are issued by the 'various ministries, commissions, the People's Bank of China, the Auditing Agency, and a body directly under the State Council exercising a regulatory function'.[9]

8 The Legislation Law 2000 Article 78.
9 See note 7.

Appendix 2 Amendments to Chinese provisions on human subject protection

Better Chinese high level legislation on human subject protection

Of the laws and regulations related to human subject protection analysed in detail in Chapter 6, most turn out not to be promulgated by the highest level of the legislature, which in the People's Republic of China (PRC) is the Chinese Congress and its Standing Committee. They are, therefore, not powerful enough. To provide adequate protections for human subjects in biomedical research, this book suggests that high level legislation needs to play an active role in the protection of participants and that the basic protections offered by the international guidelines need to be reconstructed into a form which is appropriate to the specific situation in that country. In the context of the PRC, human subject and target group protection need a firm foundation in high level legislation if it is to be effective and sensitive to cultural practices and norms. In addition, the concept of vulnerable group protection should also be introduced in Chinese high level legislation on human subject protection. It is suggested that the legislation on human subject protection, which highlights vulnerable population protection in the PRC should be formulated by the Chinese Country Legislature – the Chinese Congress and its Standing Committee.

There is evidence that vulnerable groups, such as ethnic minorities and isolated groups in rural areas, tend to be underrepresented in biomedical research.[1] However, some international declarations and ethical guidelines on human subject protection do pay specific attention to the issues raised by the participation of minorities in research. For example, the CIOMS guidelines make reference to this issue as follows:

> Members of vulnerable groups also have the same entitlement to access to the benefits of investigational interventions that show promise of

---

1 For discussion, see Sheikh, A. (2006) 'Are Racial and Ethnic Minorities Less Willing to Participate in Health Research?', *PLoS Medicine*, vol. 3, no. 2, pp. 0166–67.

therapeutic benefit as persons not considered vulnerable, particularly when no superior or equivalent approaches to therapy are available.[2]

This statement acknowledges the dilemma that, on the one hand, it is unjust selectively to recruit vulnerable populations to serve as research subjects simply because they may be more easily induced to participate in exchange for small payments; on the other hand, such vulnerable populations should not be categorically excluded from research protocols. The concerns of vulnerable population protection and the benefits of participation should be considered together to seek an appropriate balance. In the clinical trial setting, this dilemma also exists. Some countries have realised this situation and introduced relevant policies to promote the participation of minorities in potentially beneficial clinical research. For example, Noah illustrated this situation in the US as follows:

> Evidence suggests ... that racial and ethnic minorities have less opportunity to participate in potentially beneficial clinical research. For reasons of scientific and practical convenience, minority groups were commonly excluded from clinical trials until the mid-1990s. More recently, in recognition of the fact that minority participation in medical research enhances scientific understanding of variations in disease and treatment response among races and out of concern for healthcare justice, the government has instituted policies designed to encourage the inclusion of minorities in clinical trials. Even so, the research community must proceed with caution in any efforts to equalize participation, both because of the inherent risks of medical research to individual participants and because some efforts at racial inclusion may have unintended negative consequences.[3]

Therefore, special protections for vulnerable populations in biomedical research involving human subjects in the PRC should not deliberately prohibit vulnerable populations from being the subject of those research projects.

However, it needs to be noted that the situation of human population genetic research (HPGR) should be treated as a special case. Most HPGR projects are designed simply to improve scientific understanding and are unlikely to offer direct benefits to participating groups. Thus, since the target groups of HPGR

2 The International Ethical Guidelines for Biomedical Research Involving Human Subjects were prepared by the Council for International Organizations of Medical Sciences (CIOMS) in collaboration with the WHO, Geneva (2002). The full text of the CIOMS Guidelines can be seen on the official website of the World Health Organization (WHO) at http://whqlibdoc.who.int/emro/2004/9290213639_annex2.pdf (last visited 5 July 2013). See Commentary and reference to Guideline 12.

3 Noah, B. A. (2003) 'The Participation of Underrepresented Minorities in Clinical Research', *American Journal of Law and Medicine*, vol. 29, nos 2–3, pp. 221–45 at 224.

are vulnerable groups, and some HPGR protocols pose potential risks to those groups, participation in HPGR should not be promoted. Meanwhile, if target groups have decided to participate in certain HPGR, their interests should be ensured by the provision of systematic and effective protection to vulnerable target groups and their members, while guarding against the imposition of unfair burdens or risks for any one group of participants.

Amendment to provisions of researchers' responsibilities

As discussed in Chapter 6, most HPGR projects are conducted by researchers from developed countries, while the target groups in HPGR are almost always isolated groups or ethnic minorities in rural areas of developing countries, such as the PRC; thus, the vast majority of target groups in HPGR are vulnerable groups with their own cultural sensitivities and who require additional protections. Researchers, who have advantages in terms of power and resources, must accept a series of obligations to mitigate the vulnerabilities of target groups in the whole process of HPGR.

Group consultation

There are several obstacles that can interfere with HPGR being conducted in an ethical way by researchers from developed countries. These are caused by distinctions between researchers and target groups in HPGR, such as marked inequality of power and resources and a lack of cultural sensitivity regarding decision-making. In the context of HPGR, target groups should be involved in the development, design and conduct of the research, since the process of consultation could offer a potential mechanism to protect communities against exploitation. Consultation on research design should be a necessary prerequisite to ensuring that the HPGR is undertaken in a way that respects the cultural sensitivity of target group and alerts the group to the possibility of harms arising from the research questions or findings.

The content of the researchers' consultation in HPGR in the PRC should include the following three main aspects'

First, in order to establish a proper research protocol, researchers should investigate the basic social, economic and average education background of the target group. Since target groups in HPGR are usually impoverished people, who are highly susceptible to the prospect of financial rewards, even small financial payments can act as a coercive force, compelling the poor to do what the rich would be reluctant to consider. They may be unable to give unqualified consent to HPGR, when confronted with compensation for research participation. What is more, non-financial incentives that could improve the living standards of target groups may also be overly coercive. These offers might include food, clothing, basic medical treatment and drugs. The limits of the economic and social resources in developing countries can transform these simple rewards or basic resources into forceful incentives for target groups in HPGR. Researchers conducting HPGR must not assume that the incentive level should be based on their own standards. Any incentive level researchers offer should be tailored to the level of social and economic development of the target group. It is the obligation of researchers to identify the proper way of providing compensation or rewards to ensure that the human subjects make their own decisions on whether or not to participate without the pressure of undue incentives. In addition, the average educational background of the target group should be related to the expression of information disclosure, which should be clear and understandable.

Secondly, in order to identify the possible internal harms relevant to certain HPGR, cultural sensitivity that may be harmed by certain HPGR, such as a group's common belief, specific group traditions or group narratives, should also be investigated by researchers of HPGR. The cultural sensitivity such as bioethical background, which would be opposite to the application of Western standard of research ethics, should be investigated by researchers in HPGR. For example, for individuals in non-Western societies, perspectives on the nature of disease, the subject-investigator relationship and the doctor-patient relationship may be entirely different from those in Western societies.[4] The meaning of 'person' may also be different between Western and non-Western societies. It has been argued that: 'the majority viewpoint manifest in most other societies, both technologically developing (e.g., Central Africa) and technologically developed (e.g., Japan), does not reflect the American perspective of radical individualism'.[5] As De Craemer puts it:

> The American notion of person has still other characteristic features. It is markedly rational, and also legalistic-prototypically expressed in the language of rights, and central not only to our Declaration of Independence and Constitution, but to a very wide range of issues that find their way into our courts and our legislatures.
>
> In turn, these rational-legal aspects of our cultural outlook on personhood are associated with the voluntary, functionally specific, contractual model of social relations that has a predominant place in our society, particularly in economic and political spheres ...
>
> The American view of the human person is pervaded by logical-rational dichotomies. This view sharply opposes body and mind, thought and feeling, the conscious and unconscious, self and other, reality and nonreality (imagining, dreaming, and hearing voices, for example, are not 'real;).[6]

4 Clinton, R. N. 1990, 'Rights of Indigenous Peoples as Collective Group Rights', *Arizona Law Review*, vol. 32, no. 4, pp. 739–48
5 Levine, R. J. (1991) 'Informed Consent: Some Challenges to the Universal Validity of the Western Model', *Journal of Law, Medicine and Ethics*, vol. 19, pp. 207–13 at 209.
6 De Craemer, W. (1983) 'A Cross-Cultural Perspective on Personhood', *The Milbank Memorial Fund Quarterly: Health and Society*, vol. 61, no. 1, pp. 19–34 at 21.

He further argues in his summary statement that the 'American way of think-ing about the person represents the way men and women of all societies and cultures should and do think about personhood when they are being supremely rational and moral'.[7] In the PRC, as was discussed in Chapter 6, however, the culture of isolated groups in rural areas is characterised by communal values and highlights social harmony. In both Confucianism and Marxism, people cannot be seen in isolation. Instead, they are at the centre of relationships. A person exists in a social context in order to fulfil his or her social responsibilities, and a person's nature manifests itself only through human relatedness. As has been said: '[t]he Chinese believe in the importance of individual autonomy, but they also believe that this right of autonomy is guided by social needs'.[8] These bioethical backgrounds should be considered by researchers ethically to conduct certain HPGR, with acknowledgement of, and respect for, target groups' cultural sensitivities.

Thirdly, researchers in HPGR also have an obligation to investigate the cultural sensitivity regarding decision-making. According to the result of group consultation on cultural sensitivity regarding decision-making, researchers could decide whether or not group approval or disapproval is needed. If the cultural sensitivity on decision-making is individual as final decision-maker, the process of group approval or disapproval does not need to be conducted. If certain target group have the cultural sensitivity on group decision-making or used to follow the decision of the group leader, then, group approval or disapproval should be conducted. It needs to be high-lighted that the requirement on group approval or disapproval does not mean the complete abandonment of individual informed consent. It means that the result of this group approval or disapproval should be the precondition of whether or not certain HPGR could be conducted. If group approved, the individual informed consent should also be conducted before collecting samples from individual participants. Rather, when conducting individual informed consent, the group approval should be provided to individual participants. For example, according to Confucianism, which is a traditional and influential culture in the PRC, especially in isolated rural areas, the family is not only a means for human flourishing, but also has its own status in decision-making. One's family members sustain an element of one's own being. This leads to the belief that one's choices have a profound effect on both the individual and the family as a whole. This understanding of the family is reflected in the Confucian approach to making medical decisions, assessing medical technology and financing health care. Medical decision-making involves the whole family, since the whole family's interests as well as the individuals' are at stake. The interests of the family must also be taken

---

7 ibid at 34.
8 Doring, O. (2003) 'China's Struggle for Practical Regulations in Medical Ethics', *Nature Reviews: Genetics*, vol. 4, pp. 233–39 at 236.

into account when assessing medical technology. This does not mean that individual interests should always give way to family interests when conflicts occur. However, in most cases of target groups in HPGR in the PRC, the opinion of community leaders or senior family members would be a significant reference for members of target groups. This opinion from a community leader or senior family member, which would be likely to influence the decision of potential participants, is a part of the social context of an individual's decision-making; thus, it is not undue influence, at least in this culture. Accordingly, in most cases of HPGR in the PRC, group approval or disapproval should be considered. Therefore, the cultural sensitivities of target groups, which will influence their decision-making, should be identified and understood by the researcher in HPGR before the research design stage.

In recognition of these issues, there should be a basic legal requirement on researchers in HPGR to conduct precise consultation about relevant cultural sensitivity issues at the stage of research design in the PRC.

In order to ensure the quality of group consultation, researchers in HPGR ought to collaborate with the group to define how the research problem might be approached and, where relevant, oral tradition and other sources of group collective beliefs or common culture ought to be used in a respectful manner. The consultation process should include: (i) researchers' survey and communication with group representatives on the cultural sensitivity of certain groups, for example, asking group leaders, affected and unaffected persons a series of questions about how they recognise and make decisions about illness; and (ii) dialogue or communication between researchers and group members. The contents of consultation should include questions regarding who they ask for advice in medical decision-making, who may have assisted them in seeking care, who may have provided care for them and their social relationships to those persons, whether there is any group common belief or cultural sensitivity concerning disease, health and life. If necessary, social scientists with working experience of the target groups, as well as prominent community members, could be consulted to interpret these answers.

In addition, the final consultation should also be submitted to both supervision authorities of local government in the PRC and institutional review boards (IRBs) or research ethics committees (RECs), for the purposes of scrutiny.

Group approval or disapproval

The term 'group approval or disapproval' is ambiguous. Proponents of group approval do not always make clear what precisely they mean by it. In group approval, as it is understood here, researchers should obtain a collective permission from a target group leader or recognised authority for HPGR, only if the target group has the cultural tradition of collective decision-making. It needs to be highlighted that the collective decision, group approval or disapproval, is not binding on individual members who may choose to consent or refuse to participate in HPGR. The results of group approval or disapproval here would be one piece of necessary relevant information which would be provided to potential individual participants as a reference to help them to make their own decision on whether or not to participate in certain HPGR, according to their decision-making patterns.

Since the main criticisms of group approval focused on giving a target group the authority to veto proposed HPGR involving their members,[9] it is important to stress that the group approval or disapproval discussed here is not intended to extend a 'veto power' to the target group in HPGR. Rather, in the context of the PRC, as has been discussed above, likely target groups have a culture of group decision-making, or acceptance that the group leader has the right to decide. If researchers intend to achieve genuine consent from individual members of such target groups with cultural sensitivity regarding group decision-making, researchers in HPGR should obtain and provide the opinions of their group leaders or recognised authorities on the proposed research in order to help individual members to make their own decisions.

The mechanism of group approval in HPGR should respect the cultural sensitivities or customs in collective decision-making, which should be based on the results of group consultation. Target groups in HPGR may have their own specific means of collective decision-making. If there is a community authority or community leader who can represent the target group to make collective formal and explicit approval or disapproval, such as in the case of the Apache Business Committee which represents the Apache Tribe of Oklahoma when making fundamental collective decisions,[10] group approval or disapproval should be sought from these community authorities or community leaders. Similarly, in the PRC, most of the target groups have their own group leaders or authorities, which should be the agent to provide group approval or disapproval.

Therefore, if researchers obtain group approval for a particular HPGR, it implies that researchers can conduct this HPGR only when it is based on informed consent from individual group members. If the target group considers that HPGR might lead to harms and does not approve it, in the context of the PRC, certain HPGR would not be conducted, since researchers would be unlikely to be able to recruit sufficient numbers of participants from target groups where the decision of community leaders is

9   Juengst, E. T. (1998) 'Groups as Gatekeepers to Genomic Research: Conceptually Confusing, Morally Hazardous, and Practically Useless', *Kennedy Institute of Ethics Journal*, vol. 8, no. 2, pp. 183–200 at 183.

10 Foster, M. W., Bernsten, D. and Carter, T. H. (1998) 'A Model Agreement for Genetic Research in Socially Identifiable Populations', *American Journal of Human Genetics*, vol. 63, pp. 696–702 at 701.

generally accepted as definitive. Meanwhile, group disapproval is also likely to lead to the project not being approved at ethical review and hence not proceeding.

The legal requirement of group approval or disapproval needs to respect changes to or withdrawal of group approval by target groups in HPGR. If group approval is required for the research study to proceed, then major changes in the agreed-upon protocol should also be examined by the target group.

In addition to being provided to potential individual participants in HPGR as necessary information for decision-making, the written result of group decisions should also be submitted to both supervision authorities of local government in the PRC and IRBs or RECs.

Individual informed consent

The information that must be disclosed to a potential human subject who is considering participating in biomedical research, which he or she in turn must have the opportunity to evaluate (a process that includes having access to a member of the research team), is listed in various research guidelines and legal regulations. In general, this information includes a broad description of the nature of the study (including what part is experimental and how long the study will last), a description of reasonably foreseeable risks, a description of any potential benefits to the subject, a statement of how the confidentiality of records will be maintained, a statement of whether there will be compensation for injury, a designation of a contact person who is a member of the research team, and a declaration that participation is voluntary and that there is no penalty for withdrawal. In addition to information that has been listed in current research guidelines, given there are additional risks of harm that may be caused by HPGR to the target group as a whole as discussed in Chapter 4, the special rules on HPGR in the PRC should require the following two additional contents: (i) potential benefits and risks of harm to the interests of target groups in HPGR, which is similar to the list of information concerning disclosure with potential participants about anticipated benefits and potential risks to individual participants; (ii) if has the cultural sensitivity on group decision-making, group decisions made by the group leader or group recognised authority should also be disclosed to potential individual participants as a reference to make their own decisions.

The disclosure standard applied in HPGR in the PRC should require disclosure of whatever it can reasonably be concluded potential participants would consider significant in their decision-making. Since target groups in HPGR may be vulnerable, the standard would require researchers to disclose to potential participants all of the relevant information that any qualified individual of a target group would reasonably need to know in order to make a decision on whether or not participate in the HPGR. This standard is similar to the reasonable patient rule which has been used as a standard of disclosure in legal cases about medical treatment decisions in some countries.[11]

In order to eliminate or reduce the vulnerabilities of target groups in HPGR, the new legal requirement in the PRC should be stipulated in a more appropriate way which could fit into the specific situations of target groups. The detailed measures include the following.

First, the conduct of information disclosure needs to be undertaken in a clear and intelligible manner, such as using local languages where necessary. As O'Neill pointed out, a normal person 'may find that being confronted with the full detail of research protocols provides excess, inassimilable information, to which they can hardly hope to give genuinely informed consent'.[12] Given that the target groups in HPGR in the PRC are vulnerable groups with low educational levels, the situation of confusing with a thick stack of papers which lists complex questions described by difficult medical terms would be even worse. Therefore, in order to ensure the quality of information disclosure, the new legal requirement should also require that researchers should provide information in the language of the potential participants and at a level appropriate to their reading level, where providing written information is likely to be of practical value. It should also provide an emphasis on process rather than mere agreement or signing a consent form.

Secondly, considering the cultural sensitivity and educational level of the members of target groups in HPGR, during the process of information disclosure, researchers should pay attention to the method of communication with group members. In order to ensure the fullest possible understanding of relevant information, the new guideline should suggest that researchers use specific group communication measures which are appropriate to certain target groups, such as face to-face meetings between communities and researchers, giving adequate time to potential participants to ask questions about the HPGR, and providing adequate time for consideration of their decision.

Thirdly, the new legal requirement should require researchers clearly to inform potential participants of the right to refuse to take part in HPGR or to withdraw consent to participate at any time without reprisal, as well as provide easy procedures to exercise the decision of refusal or withdrawal. As O'Neill suggested, ethically acceptable consent should meet the standard that 'the possibility of refusal should be made as clear and as easy to exercise as the possibility of consent'.[13]

The written informed consent forms from individual participants in HPGR should be submitted to both supervision authorities of local government in the PRC and ethical review committees. The process of individual

11 The discussion on 'reasonable patient standard' can be seen in Chapter 3.
12 O'Neill, O. (2002) *Autonomy and Trust in Bioethics* (Cambridge University Press) at 157.
13 ibid at 159.

informed consent should be fully reviewed by ethical review committees, and be supervised by supervision authorities of local government in the PRC.

Amendment to provisions of ethical review

In order to ensure the welfare and wellbeing of human subjects, all international declarations and conventions, research guidelines and some national regulations propose that RECs or IRBs[14] should undertake a risk-benefit assessment and risk management of biomedical research involving human subjects. Without the approval of RECs or IRBs, no biomedical research can be ethically conducted, no matter whether or not a person consents to participate in it. RECs or IRBs allow biomedical researchers and bioethical experts with varying backgrounds to promote adequate review of research activities and weigh the merits of proposed biomedical research and its potential impact on the rights, safety and welfare of human subjects from their own viewpoints. In general, ethical review committees provide ethical advice to researchers so as to assist decision-making on the adequacy of proposed research projects, with respect to the protection of potential and actual human subjects. Ethical review committees may function at the institutional, local, regional or national level, and in some cases at the international level. For example, ethical review committees play a major part in the Declaration of Helsinki.[15] Article 15 of the Declaration highlights the requirements of ethical review in the whole process of the design and performance of each experimental procedure involving human subjects.[16]

In the context of HPGR in developing countries such as the PRC, owing to the vulnerabilities of target groups caused by poverty, low educational levels and lack of social and medical resources, ethical review committees should accept additional responsibilities to ensure the interests of target groups and avoid the risk of exploitation. Therefore, this type of ethical

14 RECs or IRBs are also known as independent ethics committees (IECs) in the Declaration of Helsinki, and as ethical review boards (ERBs) in the UK.

15 The WMA Declaration of Helsinki Ethical Principles for Medical Research Involving Human Subjects was adopted by the 18th WMA General Assembly, Helsinki, Finland, June 1964, and amended by the 29th WMA General Assembly, Tokyo, Japan, October 1975, 35th WMA General Assembly, Venice, Italy, October 1983, 41st WMA General Assembly, Hong Kong, September 1989, 48th WMA General Assembly, Somerset West, Republic of South Africa, October 1996 and the 52nd WMA General Assembly, Edinburgh, Scotland, October 2000, 53rd WMA General Assembly, Washington 2002 (Note of Clarification on paragraph 29 added), 55th WMA General Assembly, Tokyo 2004 (Note of Clarification on paragraph 30 added), 59th WMA General Assembly, Seoul, October 2008. The full text of the Helsinki Declaration can be seen on the official website of the World Medical Association (WMA) at http://www.wma.net/en/30publications/10policies/b3/index.html) (last visited 5 July 2013).

16 ibid Article 15.

review should be conducted without the researcher, the sponsor or any kind of undue influence. The Chinese provision in HPGR should require the ethical review in HPGR must be conducted by an independent ethical review committee, including members from target groups rather than institutional ethical review committees.

Membership and composition of ethical review committees in HPGR

As discussed in Chapter 4, in HPGR, in addition to the potential risks of harm to individual human subjects, there are potential risks of harm to the target group as a whole. However, one important difficulty for ethical review committees is that members who are outsiders often struggle to identify intra-community risks, such as the disruption of existing social arrangements and relationships between members of a target group. Therefore, in the PRC, it is proposed that ethical review committees including members from the target group with varying genders, age groups and educational backgrounds should be an essential requirement of ethical review of IRBs or RECs in HPGR. The number of representatives should be decided by the population size of target group. If there are group leaders or group recognised authorities of target groups, they must be included in ethical review committees. If there is no group leader or group recognised authority, the representatives should include the most affected members, the most educated members and some other random members.

Some would argue that it can never be certain that the representatives will really voice the real opinion of the target group they represent. However, these selective representatives are members of the target group and have common traditions and beliefs with members of the target group. They should therefore be capable of making reasonable decisions on the basis of understanding the information relevant to the HPGR; their opinions could partly reflect the views of the target group members and would also help to examine whether or not certain HPGR may lead to potential risks of harm that research participants and other members of the target group view as important. If they are concerned that HPGR could potentially harm their internal or external interests, such as disrupting existing social arrangements or harming their common beliefs, then these risks of harm are something that ought to be taken into consideration in the ethical review process of the research.

Additional assessment contents in HPGR

In order to provide adequate protection to target groups and reduce their vulnerabilities, in addition to risk-benefit assessment on individual and group-based human subjects, the provisions on ethical review should include the following two additional factors.

First, it should require risk-benefit evaluations on the interests of target groups of the proposed HPGR. It should highlight the assessment of potential group collective risks of harm related to certain HPGR, with the awareness of the specific cultural sensitivities of target groups. As Sharp and Forster have pointed out:

> Presently, little is known about how members of various underserved or marginalized communities weigh individual research risks against group risks, how salient collective risks are in relation to other risks encountered in daily life, or how individuals attempt to reconcile potential conflicts that may exist between personal interests in research participation and collective opposition to proposed research. Because not all collective harms carry the same weight—that is, some group harms are more significant than others—it is important to assess how members of historically underserved communities evaluate collective research-related harms. Moreover, without such information it will be difficult, if not impossible, to tailor oversight processes to specific communities.[17]

Thus, in order to identify how various social, religious, economic, cultural and political groups view risks related to certain HPGR, in the PRC, the special rules on HPGR should require an additional risk-benefit assessment of the interests of the target group as a whole.

The standard of ethical review of group risks of harm in HPGR should fit the three ethical requirements which are required in all ethical reviews of non-therapeutic procedures,[18] namely (i) the group risks of harm related to HPGR must be minimised, to the extent that doing so is consistent with sound scientific design. This can involve avoiding unnecessary procedures, identifying less risky ways of testing a study hypothesis or excluding participants who are at increased risk of being harmed; (ii) the group risks of harm posed by HPGR must be reasonable in relation to the knowledge that is expected to be gained from the study; and (iii) since target groups in HPGR may be vulnerable populations, the group risks of harms of HPGR must be no more than a minor increase over the minimal group risks of daily life for the identified group in question.

Secondly, ethical review committees should also be responsible for determining the proposed compensation or payment based on the degree of risk and other burdens in HPGR. In some literature on ethical conduct of biomedical research in developing countries, it has been argued that there

17 Sharp, R. R. and Foster, M. W. (2002) 'Community Involvement in the Ethical Review of Genetic Research: Lessons from American Indian and Alaska Native Populations', *Environmental Health Perspectives*, vol. 110, pp. 145–48 at 147.
18 Weijer, C. (2000) 'The Ethical Analysis of Risk', *Journal of Law, Medicine and Ethics*, vol. 28, pp. 344–61.

was a tendency to exaggerate the risk of undue inducement, which would lead to restricting payments to participants on the grounds of potential undue inducement.[19] This situation would provide decreasing costs of researchers, while reducing the financial welfare of the participants. Therefore, it has been suggested that ethical review committees should undertake assessment of compensation, such as required infrastructure charges, as part of their general assessment of the acceptable standard of the research protocol.[20] Given the different levels of economic development between researchers from developed countries and target groups in HPGR from developing countries, there would be a dilemma for researchers in offering compensation or payment to target groups: offer too little and they are exploited, offer too much and their participation may be unduly influenced. Independent ethical review committees with members from target groups are more capable of identifying the appropriate level of compensation or payment which fits into the specific economic development levels of target groups. Therefore, an additional review of proposed compensation or payment by researchers would be helpful to eliminate or reduce the vulnerabilities of target groups in HPGR in the PRC.

Double review in international collaborate HPGR

As Western developed countries gain economic and technological ascendance, they need human population genetic resources which some developing countries such as the PRC have in abundance; accordingly, most HPGR will be conducted by researchers from developed countries in developing countries. Owing to the conflict of interests between developed and developing countries in HPGR, the legal regulations and ethical guidelines on biomedical research would have some differentiated standards on ethical review. Therefore, the Declaration of Helsinki emphasised that independent committees should act in conformity with the laws and regulations of the country in which the research is performed.[21] Article 15 also stipulated that the committee has the right to monitor ongoing trials. According to these provisions, the researcher has the obligation to provide information to the committee, especially about any serious adverse events. The ethical committee is still there for consideration, comment and guidance, but it has to be told about conflicts of interests. If there is any serious adverse event, the ethical committee must be notified.[22]

---

19 Ballantyne, A. (2008) 'Benefits to Research Subjects in International Trials: Do They Reduce Exploitation or Increase Undue Inducement?', *Developing World Bioethics*, vol. 8, no. 3, pp. 178–91.
20 ibid at 190.
21 See note 15 Article 15.
22 ibid.

Therefore, in order to ensure the welfare and interests of vulnerable target groups in HPGR and decrease the practical burden of ethical review committees, the provision of ethical review in the PRC must require double review of HPGR. It should require that foreign researchers or research institutions who conduct HPGR inside the PRC, no matter whether or not it has been reviewed according to the legal regulations or ethical guidelines of their own countries, should obtain approval from ethical review committees, which are in conformity with the provisions of relevant Chinese laws, regulations and rules on biomedical research. This double review principle would play the role of preventing researchers from developing countries taking advantage of the legitimate loophole of their own countries to exploit target groups in the PRC.

Amendment to provisions of supervision of local government in HPGR

At present, many developing countries, such as the PRC, lack comprehensive legal frameworks relating specifically to research involving humans in HPGR, for example in terms of adequate training or low educational standards. It is reasonable to doubt that representatives from vulnerable target groups in HPGR in ethical review committees have appropriate knowledge of regulations governing biomedical research involving human subjects. Therefore, this book suggests, in addition to independent ethical review committees, local government of the PRC should also undertake the responsibility of supervision on all HPGR conducted in the PRC. The detailed rules should include a provision that every incidence of HPGR conducted in the PRC must be registered with the local government before it is conducted, and the whole process of HPGR should be recorded and supervised by local governments.

In particular, in the context of international HPGR conducted in the PRC, local government in the PRC should play a supervisory role in the whole process of ethical review, as an additional protection to vulnerable target groups and ensure the ethical conduct of HPGR in the PRC. The approach of local government supervision in international HPGR could be to establish independent local ethical review committees. These committees need a firm foundation in special law on biomedical research to carry out their functions effectively, in the absence of which they would operate from a weak and dependent position. Ensuring the independence and legitimacy of these committees requires that they operate within a legal framework, not merely national ethical guidelines, although they have the advantage of ease of amendment. These committees would supervise the whole process of ethical review, including the selection of target groups, group consultation, information disclosure, group approval, ethical review, research results publication and further use of research samples. Their supervision should include consideration of the wide range of issues which ethics review committees may have to consider in the context of the socio-economic factors operating in specific situations and certain areas. These committees should also consider the specific issues of the target groups and the particular research; for instance, determining whether a particular HPGR will be harmful to a particular target group, given the specific needs of that community. If these committees find that certain HPGR fails to meet any legal requirement stipulated in the proposed special law on biomedical research relevant to HPGR, they should report this to the local government. The local government should then request the researchers to stop the project immediately.

Therefore, in order to protect target groups and reduce their vulnerabilities in HPGR, new approaches to legal regulation are needed in the PRC.

Bibliography

Cases

United Kingdom

Airedale NHS Trust v Bland [1993] 2 WLR 316.
Appleton and Others v Garrett [1996] PIQR P1.
Bolam v Friern Hospital Management Committee [1957] 1 WLR 582.
Bolitho Appellant v City and Hackney Health Authority Respondents [1998] AC 232.
Chatterton v Gerson [1981] QB 432.
Chester v Afshar [2005] 1 AC 134.
Hills v Potter [1984] 1 WLR 641.
R v Brown [1994] 1 AC 212.
R v Cox [1992] 12 BMLR 38.
Re MB (medical treatment) [1997] 2 FLR 426.
Re T (adult: refusal of treatment) [1992] 3 WLR 782.
Sidaway v Bethlem Royal Hospital Governors [1985] 1 AC 871.
St George's Healthcare NHS Trust v S; R v Collins ex parte S [1998] 3 WLR 936.
Tina Marie Pearce and Another v United Bristol Healthcare NHS Trust [1999] ECC 167.
Wilson v Pringle [1986] 3 WLR 1.
Wyatt v Curtis [2003] EWCA Civ 1779.

United States

Bing v Thunig, 143 N.E.2d 3 (N.Y. 1957).
Canterbury v Spence, 464 F.2d 772, 150 USApp.D.C. 263 (1972).
Cobb v Grant, 8 Cal.3d 229, 502 P.2d 1, 104 Cal.Rptr. 505 (1972).
Mohr v Williams, 59 Minn. 261; 104 N.W. 12 (1905).
Salgo v Leland Stanford Jr. Univ. Bd. of Trustees, 154 Cal.App.2d 560, 317 P.2d 170 (1957).
Schloendorff v Soc'y of N.Y. Hosp., 105 N.E. 92 (N.Y. 1914)
Tilousi v Arizona State University Board of Regents, No. 04-CV-1290-PCT-FJM (2005).
Whitlock v Duke University, 637 F.Supp.1463 (M.D.N.C. 1986).

European Commission on Human Rights

X v Denmark (1983) 32 DR 282.

Canada

Halushka v University of Sask. (1965), 52 W.W.R. 608, 53 D.L.R. (2d) 436.
Weiss v Solomon [1989] Carswell Que 72.

Australia

Rogers v Whittaker (1992) 175 CLR 479.

Books

Annas, G. J. and Grodin, M. A. (1992) *The Nazi Doctors and the Nuremberg Code: Human Rights in Human Experimentation* (Oxford University Press).

Beauchamp, T. L. and Childress, J. F. (2009) *Principles of Biomedical Ethics* (6th edn, Oxford University Press).

Berlin, I. (1969) *Two Concepts of Liberty* (Oxford: Clarendon Press).

Bernard, C. (1957) *An Introduction to the Study of Experimental Medicine* (Reprint edn, Dover Publications).

Casals, N. T. (2006) *Group Rights as Human Rights: A Liberal Approach to Mulitculturalism* (Dordrecht: Springer).

Cavalli-Sforza, L. L. (2000) *Genes, Peoples and Languages* (London: Penguin Books).

Chow, D. (2003) *The Legal System of the People's Republic of China in a Nutshell* (St. Paul, MN: West Group).

Doyal, L. and Tobias, J. S. (2001) *Informed Consent in Medical Research* (BMJ Books).

Dworkin, G. (1988) *The Theory and Practice of Autonomy* (Cambridge University Press).

Faden, R. and Beauchamp, T. L. (1986) *A History and Theory of Informed Consent* (Oxford University Press).

Foster, C. (2001) *The Ethics of Medical Research on Human* (Cambridge University Press).

Friedman, M. (1993) *What are Friends For?* (New York: Cornell University Press).

Held, V. (1993) *Feminist Morality* (Chicago: University of Chicago Press).

Hsu, C. (2003) *Understanding China's Legal System* (New York: New York University Press).

Jackson, E. (2009) *Medical Law: Text, Cases and Materials* (2nd edn, Oxford: Oxford University Press).

Laurie, G. T. (2002) *Genetic Privacy: A Challenge to Medico-Legal Norms* (Cambridge University Press).

Lee, R. and Morgan, D. (2001) *Human Fertilisation and Embryology: Regulating the Reproductive Revolution* (Blackstone Press).

Lerner, N. (2003) *Group Rights and Discrimination in International Law* (The Hague: Kluwer Law International).

Levine, R. J. (1998) *Ethics and Regulation of Clinical Research* (2nd edn, Yale University Press).

Lewin, B. (2004) *Genes 8* (Pearson Prentice Hall).

Liang, S. M. (1974) *Zhong Guo Wen Hua Yao Yi [The Essential Features of Chinese Culture]* (Hong Kong: Chi-cheng T'u-Shu Kung-Hsu).

Maclean, A. (2009) *Autonomy, Informed Consent and Medical Law* (Cambridge University Press).

Mason, J. K. and Laurie, G. T. (2011) *Mason and McCall Smith's Law and Medical Ethics* (8th edn, Oxford University Press).

McLean, S. A. M. (2010) *Autonomy, Consent and the Law* (Routledge-Cavendish).

Mehlman, M. J. and Botkin, J. R. (1998) *Access to the Genome: The Challenge to Equality* (Washington, D.C.: Georgetown University Press).

Mill, J. S. (1989) *On Liberty* (S Collini edn, Cambridge University Press).

Mill, J. S. (1998) *Utilitarianism* (Oxford University Press).

Mitnick, E. J. (2006) *Rights, Groups, and Self-invention: Group-differentiated Rights in Liberal Theory* (Ashgate).

O'Neill, O. (2002) *Autonomy and Trust in Bioethics* (Cambridge University Press).

Plomer, A. (2005) *The Law and Ethics of Medical Research: International Bioethics and Human Rights* (Cavendish Publishing Limited).

Qiu, R. (1987) *Bioethics* (in Chinese) (Shanghai: Shanghai People's Press).

Raymond, J. (1986) *A Passion for Friends* (Boston: Beacon Press).

Reverby, S. M. (2000) *Tuskegee's Truths: Rethinking the Tuskegee Syphilis Study* (The University of North Carolina Press).

Riley, J. C. (2001) *Rising Life Expectancy: A Global History* (New York: Cambridge University Press).

Sedgwick, S. (2008) *Kant's Groundwork of the Metaphysics of Morals: An Introduction* (Cambridge University Press).

Singer, P. A. and Viens, A. M. (2008) *The Cambridge Textbook of Bioethics* (Cambridge University Press).

Tong, R. (1997) *Feminist Approach to Bioethics* (West View Press).

Watson, J. D. (1968) *The Double Helix: A Personal Account of the Discovery of the Structure of DNA* (Norton Critical edn, The Hague: W. W. Norton & Company).

Wendell, S. (1996) *The Rejected Body: Feminist Philosophical Reflections on Disability* (New York: Routledge).

Wertz, D. C. and Fletcher, J. C. (2004) *Genetics and Ethics in Global Perspective* Kluwer Academic Publishers.

Wicks, E. (2007) *Human Rights and Healthcare* (Hart Publishing).

Withington, C. F. (1886) *The Relation of Hospitals to Medical Education* (Boston: Cupples Uphman).

Book chapters

Beauchamp, T. L. (2009) 'Autonomy and Consent' in *The Ethics of Consent – Theory and Practice*, F. G. Miller and A. Wertheimer, eds. (Oxford University Press, New York) pp. 55–78.

Bergelson, V. (2009) 'Consent to Harm' in *The Ethics of Consent – Theory and Practice*, F. G. Miller and A. Wertheimer, eds. (Oxford University Press, New York) pp. 163–92.

Bowman, K. W. and Hui, E. C. (2008) 'Chinese Bioethics' in *The Cambridge Textbook of Bioethics*, P. A. Singer and A. M. Viens, eds. (Cambridge University Press) pp. 397–402.

Chu, J. (2000) 'Chinese Human Genome Diversity Project: A Synopsis' in *Genetic, Linguistic and Archaeological Perspectives on Human Diversity in Southeast Asia*, J. Li, M. Seielstad, and C. Xiao, eds. (Singapore: World Scientific Publishing) pp. 95–105.

De Castro, L. D. (2007) 'Modern Biotechnology and the Postmodern Family' in *The Family, Medical Decision-Making, and Biotechnology: Critical Reflections on Asian Moral Perspectives*, S. C. Lee, ed. (Springer) pp. 113–25.

Dodds, S. (2000) 'Choice and Control in Feminist Bioethics' in *Relational Autonomy: Feminist Perspectives on Autonomy, Agency, and the Social Self*, C. Mackenzie and N. Stoljar, eds. (Oxford University Press, New York) pp. 213–35.

Engelhardt, H. T. (2007) 'The Family in Transition and in Authority: The Impact of Biotechnology' in *The Family, Medical Decision-Making, and Biotechnology: Critical Reflections on Asian Moral Perspectives*, S. C. Lee, ed. (Springer) pp. 27–45.

Erickson, S. A. (2007) 'Family Life, Bioethics and Confucianism' in *The Family, Medical Decision-Making, and Biotechnology: Critical Reflections on Asian Moral Perspectives*, S. C. Lee, ed. (Springer) pp. 47–58.

Fan, R. (2007) 'Confucian Familism and Its Bioethical Implications' in *The Family, Medical Decision-Making, and Biotechnology: Critical Reflections on Asian Moral Perspectives*, S. C. Lee, ed. (Springer) pp. 15–26.

Harris, J. (2001) 'Introduction: the Scope and Importance of Bioethics' in *Bioethics*, J. Harris, ed. (Oxford University Press).

Joffe, S. (2009) 'Consent to Medical Care: The Importance of Fiduciary Context' in *The Ethics of Consent – Theory and Practice*, F. G. Miller and A. Wertheimer, eds. (Oxford University Press, New York) pp. 347–74.

Johnston, D. (2009) 'A History of Consent in Western Thought' in *The Ethics of Consent – Theory and Practice*, F. G. Miller and A. Wertheimer, eds. (Oxford University Press, New York) pp. 25–54.

Kleinig, J. (2009) 'The Nature of Consent' in *The Ethics of Consent – Theory and Practice*, F. G. Miller and A. Wertheimer, eds. (Oxford University Press, New York) pp. 1–24.

Lee, S. C. (2007) 'On Relational Autonomy: From Feminist Critique to Confucian Model for Clinical Practice' in *The Family, Medical Decision-Making, and Biotechnology: Critical Reflections on Asian Moral Perspectives*, S. C. Lee, ed. (Springer) pp. 83–93.

Lee, S. C. and Ho, J. (2007) 'Medicine and the Biomedical Technologies in the Context of Asian Perspectives' in *The Family, Medical Decision-Making, and Biotechnology: Critical Reflections on Asian Moral Perspectives*, S. C. Lee, ed. (Springer) pp. 1–13.

Levine, R. J. (1982) 'Validity of Consent Procedures in Technologically Developing Countries' in *Human Experimentation and Medical Ethics: Proceedings of the XV CIOMS Round Table Conference*, Bankowski Z and N. Howard-Jones, eds. (Geneva: Council for International Organizations of Medical Sciences) pp. 16–30.

McCathy, C. (1993) 'A North American Perspective' in *Ethics and Research on Human Subjects: International Guidelines*, Bankowski, Z and R. J. Levine, eds. (Geneva: Council for International Organizations of Medical Sciences) pp. 208–11.

Miller, F. G. (2009) 'Consent to Clinical Research' in *The Ethics of Consent – Theory and Practice*, F. G. Miller and A. Wertheimer, eds. (Oxford University Press, New York) pp. 375–404.

Miller, F. G. and Wertheimer, A. (2009) 'Preface to a Theory of Consent Transactions: Beyond Valid Consent' in *The Ethics of Consent – Theory and Practice*, F. G. Miller and A. Wertheimer, eds. (Oxford University Press, New York) pp. 79–106.

Murray, T. H. (1997) 'Genetic Exceptionalism and "Future Diaries": Is Genetic Information Different from Other Medical Information?' in *Genetic Secrets: Protecting Privacy and Confidentiality in the Genetic Era*, M. A. Rothstein, ed. (Yale University Press) pp. 60–73.

Pogge, T. (1997) 'Group Rights and Ethnicity' in *Ethnicity and Group Rights: Nomos XXXIX*, I. Shapiro and W. Kymlicka, eds. (New York University Press, New York) pp. 187–221.

Qiu, R. (1992) 'Medical Ethics and Chinese Culture' in *Transcultural Dimensions in Medical Ethics*, E. Pellegrino, P. Mazzerella, and P. Corsi, eds. (Frederick, MD: University Publishing Group).

Qiu, R. (2004) 'China: Views of a Bioethicist' in *Genetic and Ethics in Global Perspective*, D. C. Wertz and J. C. Fletcher, eds. (Kluwer Academic Publisher).

Turner, B. S. (2006) 'Cultural Rights and Critical Recognition Theory' in *Vulnerability and Human Rights: Essays on Human Rights* (University Park, PA, Pennsylvania State University Press) pp. 45–68.

Articles

(2005) 'Universal Draft Declaration on Bioethics and Human Rights', *Developing World Bioethics*, vol. 5, no. 3, pp. 197–209.

Adalsteinsson, R. (2004) 'Human Genetic Databases and Liberty', *The Juridical Review*, no. 1, pp. 65–74.

Aerts, R. J. (2004) 'The industrial applicability and utility requirements for the patenting of genomic inventions: a comparison between European and US law', *European Intellectual Property Review*, vol. 26, no. 8, pp. 349–60.

Ahmed, F. (2010) 'Personal Autonomy and the Option of Religious Law', *International Journal of Law, Policy and the Family*, vol. 24, no. 2, pp. 222–44.

Alvarez, F. and Feinholz, D. (2006) 'Women in Developing Countries and Benefit Sharing', *Developing World Bioethics*, vol. 6, no. 3, pp. 113–21.

Amani, B. and Coombe, R. J. (2005) 'The Human Genome Diversity Project: The Politics of Patents at the Intersection of Race, Religion, and Research Ethics', *Law & Policy*, vol. 27, no. 1, pp. 152–88.

American College of Physicians (2004) 'Racial and Ethnic Disparities in Health Care', *Annals of Internal Medicine*, vol. 141, no. 3, pp. 226–32.

Andanda, P. (2005) 'Module Two: Informed Consent', *Developing World Bioethics*, vol. 5, no. 1, pp. 14–29.

Anderlik, M. R. and Rothstein, M. A. (2001) 'Privacy and Confidentiality of Genetic Information: What Rules for the New Science?', *Annual Review of Genomics and Human Genetics*, vol. 2, pp. 401–33.

Andrews, L. B. (2001) 'Legal Aspects of Genetic Information', *Yale Journal of Biology and Medicine*, vol. 64, pp. 29–40.

Andrews, L. B. (2005) 'Harnessing the Benefits of Biobanks', *The Journal of Law, Medicine & Ethics*, vol. 33, no. 1, pp. 22–30.

Angeles-Llerenas, A. R., Wirtz, V. and Lara-Alvarez, C. F. (2009) 'The Role and Responsibilities of Witnesses in the Informed Consent Process', *Developing World Bioethics*, vol. 9, no. 1, pp. 18–25.

Angell, M. (2000) 'Is Academic Medicine for Sale', *The New England Journal of Medicine*, vol. 342, pp. 1516–18.

Annas, G. J. (1993) 'Privacy Rules for DNA Databanks: Protecting Coded "Future Diaries"', *The Journal of American Medical Association*, vol. 270, no. 19, pp. 2346–50.

Annas, G. J. (1996) 'Questioning for Grails: Duplicity, Betrayal and Self-Deception Postmodern Medical Research', *Journal of Contemporary Health Law and Policy*, vol. 12, no. 297, p. 234.

Annas, G. J. (1999) 'Genetic Privacy: There Ought to be a Law', *Texas Review of Law and Politics*, vol. 4, pp. 7–15.

Annas, G. J., Glantz, L. H. and Roche, P. A. (1995) 'Drafting the Genetic Privacy Act: Science, Policy, and Practical Considerations', *Journal of Law, Medicine & Ethics*, vol. 23, no. 4, pp. 360–66.

Apel, S. B. (2001) 'Privacy in Genetic Testing: Why Women are Different', *Southern California Interdisciplinary Law Journal*, vol. 11, pp. 1–26.

Aplin, T. (2005) 'The EU database right: recent developments', *Intellectual Property Quarterly*, no. 1, pp. 52–68.

Ashcroft, R. (1999) 'Equipoise, Knowledge and Ethics in Clinical Research and Practice', *Bioethics*, vol. 13, no. 314, p. 326.

Asia, A. and Oe, S. (2005) 'A Valuable Up-to-date Compendium of Bioethical Knowledge', *Developing World Bioethics*, vol. 5, no. 3, pp. 216–19.

Askland, A. (2002) 'A Caution to Native American Institutional Review Board about Scientism and Censorship', *Jurimetrics*, vol. 42, pp. 159–63.

Athar, S. (2008) 'Enhancement Technologies and the Person: An Islamic View', *Journal of Law, Medicine & Ethics*, vol. 36, no. 1, pp. 59–64.

Baba, E. J. (2003) 'From Conflict to Confluence: Protection of Database Containing Genetic Information', *Syracuse Journal of International Law and Commerce*, vol. 30, pp. 121–50.

Baird, M. (2006) 'When and Why Does What Belong to Whom? A Proposed Model for the International Protection of Human Donors of Biological Material', *Canada-United States Law Journal*, vol. 32, pp. 331–51.

Ballantyne, A. (2008) '"Fair" Benefits' Accounts of Exploitation Require A Normative Principle of Fairness: Response to Gbadegesin and Wendler, and Emanuel et al', *Bioethics*, vol. 22, no. 4, pp. 239–44.

Ballantyne, A. (2008) 'Benefits to Research Subjects in International Trials: Do They Reduce Exploitation or Increase Undue Inducement?', *Developing World Bioethics*, vol. 8, no. 3, pp. 178–91.

Banks, T. M. (2000) 'Misusing Informed Consent: A Critique of Limitations on Research Subjects' Access to Genetic Research Results', *Saskatchewan Law Review*, no. 63, pp. 539–80.

Baker, R. (1998) 'A Theory of International Bioethics: Multiculturalism, Postmodernism, and the Bankruptcy of Fundamentalism', *Kennedy Institute of Ethics Journal*, vol. 8, pp. 201–31.

Barker, J. (2004) 'The Human Genome Diversity Project: "Peoples", "Populations", and the Cultural Politics of Identification', *Cultural Studies*, vol. 18, no. 4, pp. 571–606.

Beasley, A. D. and Graber, G. C. (1984) 'The Range of Autonomy: Informed Consent in Medicine', *Theoretical Medicine and Bioethics*, vol. 5, no. 1, pp. 31–41.

Beauchamp, T. L. (1996) 'Looking Back and Judging Our Predecessors', *Kennedy Institute of Ethics Journal*, vol. 6, no. 3, pp. 251–70.

Beauchamp, T. L. (2004) 'Does Ethical Theory Have a Future in Bioethics?', *Journal of Law, Medicine & Ethics*, vol. 32, pp. 209–17.

Beecher, H. K. (1966) 'Ethics and Clinical Research', *The New England Journal of Medicine*, vol. 274, no. 24, pp. 1354–60.

Bell, D. and Bennett, B. (2001) 'Genetic Secrets and the Family', *Medical Law Review*, vol. 9, pp. 130–61.

Benatar, D. (2005) 'The Trouble With Universal Declarations', *Developing World Bioethics*, vol. 5, no. 3, pp. 220–24.

Benatar, S. (2003) 'Bioethics, Power and Injustice: IAB Presidential Address', *Bioethics*, vol. 17, nos 5–6, pp. 387–98.

Benatar, S. R. (2004) 'Towards Progress in Resolving Dilemmas in International Research Ethics', *The Journal of Law, Medicine & Ethics*, vol. 32, no. 3, pp. 574–82.

Benatar, S. R. (2010) 'Responsibilities in International Research: A New Look Revisited', *Journal of Medical Ethics*, vol. 36, no. 4, pp. 194–97.

Benson, P. R. (1989) 'The Social Control of Human Biomedical Research: An Overview and Review of the Literature', *Social Science and Medicine*, vol. 29, pp. 1–12.

Berlin, I. and Gorelick, D. A. (2003) 'The French Law on "Protection of Persons Undergoing Biomedical Research": Implications for the US', *Journal of Law, Medicine & Ethics*, vol. 31, pp. 434–41.

Beskow, L. M., Burke, W., Merz, J. F., Barr, P. A., Terry, S., Penchaszadeh, V. B., Gostin, L. O., Gwinn, M. and Khoury, M. J. (2001) 'Informed Consent for Population-Based Research Involving Genetics', *Journal of the American Medical Association*, vol. 286, no. 18, pp. 2315–21.

Beyleveld, D. and Brownsword, R. (1998) 'Human Dignity, Human Rights, and Human Genetics', *Modern Law Review*, vol. 61, no. 5, pp. 661–80.

Bhasin, M. K. (2006) 'Genetics of Castes and Tribes of India: Indian Population Milieu', *International Journal of Human Genetics*, vol. 6, no. 3, pp. 233–74.

Bhopal, R. (2006) 'Race and Ethnicity: Responsible Use from Epidemiological and Public Health Perspectives', *Journal of Law, Medicine & Ethics*, vol. 34, no. 3, pp. 500–7.

Billing, P. R., Kohn, M. A., Cuevas, M. D., Beckwith, J., Alper, J. S. and Natowicz, M. R. (1992) 'Discrimination as a Consequence of Genetic Testing', *American Journal of Human Genetics*, vol. 50, pp. 476–82.

Black, J. (1998) 'Regulation as Facilitation: Negotiating the Genetic Revolution', *Modern Law Review*, vol. 61, no. 5, pp. 621–60.

Black, M. L., Wang, W. and Bittles, A. H. (2001) 'A Genome-Based Study of the Muslim Hui Community and the Han Population of Liaoning Province, PR China', *Human Biology*, vol. 73, no. 6, pp. 801–13.

Blackhall, L. J., Murphy, S. T., Frank, G., Michel, V. and Azen, S. (1995) 'Ethnicity and Attitudes Toward Patient Autonomy', *Journal of the American Medical Association*, vol. 274, pp. 820–25.

Bloche, M. G. (2006) 'Race, Money and Medicines', *Journal of Law, Medicine & Ethics*, vol. 34, no. 3, pp. 555–58.

Bloustein, E. J. (1964) 'Privacy as an Aspect of Human Dignity: An Answer to Dean Prosser', *New York Law Review*, vol. 39, pp. 962–1007.

Bodenheimer, T. (2000) 'Uneasy Alliance Clinical Investigators and the Pharmaceutical Industry', *The New England Journal of Medicine*, vol. 342, pp. 1539–44.

Bok, S. (1995) 'Shading the Truth in Seeking Informed Consent for Research Purposes', *Kennedy Institute of Ethics Journal*, vol. 5, no. 1, pp. 1–17.

Bonham, V. L. (2009) 'Community-based Dialogue: Engaging Communities of Color in the United States' Genetics Policy Conversation', *Journal of Health Politics, Policy and Law*, vol. 34, pp. 325–55.

Bostyn, S. J. R. (1999) 'The Patentability of Genetic Information Carriers', *Intellectual Property Quarterly*, vol. 1, pp. 1–36.

Bottis, M. C. (2000) 'Comment on a View Favoring Ignorance of Genetic Information Confidentiality, Autonomy, Beneficence and the Right Not to Know', *European Journal of Health Law*, vol. 7, pp. 173–83.

Bowcock, A. and Cavalli-Sforza, L. (1991) 'The Study of Variation in the Human Genome', *Genomics*, vol. 11, pp. 491–98.

Bowman, K. (2004) 'What are the Limits of Bioethics in a Culturally Pluralistic Society?', *The Journal of Law, Medicine & Ethics*, vol. 32, no. 3, pp. 664–69.

Bowman, K. W. and Hui, E. C. (2000) 'Bioethics for Clinicians: 20. Chinese Bioethics', *Canadian Medical Association Journal*, vol. 163, no. 11, pp. 1481–85.

Boyle, J. (1992) 'The Theory of Law and Information: Copyright, Spleens, Blackmail, and insider Trading', *California Law Review*, vol. 80, pp. 1413–540.

Brazier, M. (2006) 'Do no harm – do patients have responsibilities too?', *Cambridge Law Journal*, vol. 65, no. 2, pp. 397–422.

Bregman-Eschet, Y. (2006) 'Genetic Databases and Biobanks: Who Controls Our Genetic Privacy?', *Santa Clara Computer and High Technology Law Journal*, vol. 23, pp. 1–54.

Brewer, R. M. (2006) 'Thinking Critically about Race and Genetics', *Journal of Law, Medicine & Ethics*, vol. 34, no. 3, pp. 513–19.

Bris, S. L., Knoppers, B. M. and Luther, L. (1996) 'International Bioethics, Human Genetics, and Normativity', *Houston Law Review*, vol. 33, pp. 1363–96.

Brock, D. W. (2001) 'Genetics and Confidentiality', *The American Journal of Bioethics*, vol. 1, no. 3, pp. 34–35.

Brodwin, P. (2005) '"Bioethics in Action" and Human Population Genetics Research', *Culture, Medicine and Psychiatry*, vol. 29, pp. 145–78.

Brody, B. A. (1997) 'When Are Placebo-controlled Trials No Longer Appropriate?', *Controlled Clinical Trials*, vol. 18, pp. 602–12.

Brownsword, R. (2003) 'An Interest in Human Dignity as the Basis for Genomic Torts', *Washburn Law Journal*, vol. 42, pp. 413–87.

Brownsword, R. (2004) 'Regulating Human Genetics: New Dilemmas for a New Millennium', *Medical Law Review*, vol. 12, no. 1, pp. 14–39.

Brownsword, R., Cornish, W. R. and Llewelyn, M. (1998) 'Human Genetics and the Law: Regulating a Revolution', *Modern Law Review*, vol. 61, no. 5, pp. 593–97.

Buchanan, A. (1996) 'The Controversy over Retrospective Moral Judgment', *Kennedy Institute of Ethics Journal*, vol. 6, no. 3, pp. 245–50.

Buchanan, A. E. (1991) 'Right to Self-Determination: Analytical and Moral Foundations', *Arizona Journal of International and Comparative Law*, vol. 8, no. 2, pp. 41–50.

Burhansstipanov, L., Bemis, L. T. and Dignan, M. (2002) 'Native American Recommendations for Genetic Research to Be Culturally Respectful', *Jurimetrics*, vol. 42, pp. 149–57.

Busby, H., Hervey, T. and Mohr, A. (2008) 'Ethical EU law? The Influence of the European Group on Ethics in Science and New Technologies', *European Law Review*, vol. 33, no. 6, pp. 803–42.

Byk, C. (1998) 'A Map to a New Treasure Island: The Human Genome and the Concept of Common Heritage', *Journal of Medicine and Philosophy*, vol. 23, no. 3, pp. 234–46.

Camp, J. W., Barfield, R. C., Rodriguez, V., Young, A. J., Fineman, R. and Caniza, M. A. (2009) 'Challenges Faced by Research Ethics Committees in El Salvador: Results from a Focus Group Study', *Developing World Bioethics*, vol. 9, no. 1, pp. 11–17.

Caplan, A. L. (1992) 'When Evil Intrudes', *The Hastings Center Report*, vol. 22, no. 6, pp. 29–32.

Capron, A. M. (1999) 'Is National, Independent Oversight Needed for the Protection of Human Subjects?', *Accountability in Research*, vol. 7, pp. 283–92.

Caulfield, T. and Brownsword, R. (2006) 'Human Dignity: A Guide to Policy Making in the Biotechnology Era?', *Nature Reviews: Genetics*, vol. 7, pp. 72–76.

Caulfield, T. and Harry, S. (2008) 'Popular Representations of Race: The News Coverage of BiDil', *Journal of Law, Medicine & Ethics*, vol. 36, no. 3, pp. 485–90.

Cavalli-Sforza, L. (1996) 'Proposed Model Ethical Protocol for Collecting DNA Samples', *Houston Law Review*, vol. 33, pp. 1433–73.

Cavalli-Sforza, L. (1998) 'The Chinese Human Genome Diversity Project', *The National Academy of Sciences*, vol. 95, pp. 11501–3.

Cavalli-Sforza, L. (2005) 'The Human Genome Diversity Project: Past, Present and Future', *Nature Reviews: Genetics*, vol. 6, pp. 333–40.

Cavalli-Sforza, L., Wilson, A. C., Cantor, C. R., Cook-Deegan, R. M. and King, M. C. (1991) 'Call for a World-wide Survey of Human Genetic Diversity: A Vanishing Opportunity for the Human Genome Project', *Genomics*, vol. 11, pp. 490–91.

Cave, E. (2010) 'Seen But Not Heard? Children in Clinical Trials', *Medical Law Review*, vol. 18, no. 1, pp. 1–27.

Chadwick, R. (1989) 'Playing God', *Cogito*, vol. 3, pp. 186–93.

Chan, V. (2000) 'China: Biotechnology – Regulatory Measures', *International Company and Commercial Law Review*, vol. 11, no. 10, pp. 77–79.

Charo, R. A. (2004) 'Passing on the Right: Conservative Bioethics is Closer Than It Appears', *Journal of Law, Medicine & Ethics*, vol. 32, pp. 307–14.

Charters, C. (2009) 'Indigenous Rights and United Nations Standards: Self-Determination, Culture and Land', *European Intellectual Property Review*, vol. 9, no. 3, pp. 511–17.

Chen, Q. (2010) 'Patent Biotechnology Invention in China', *European Intellectual Property Review*, vol. 32, no. 1, pp. 9–19.

Chen, S. (2001) 'Negotiating a Policy of Prudent Science and Proactive Law in the Brave New World of Genetic Information', *Hastings Law Journal*, vol. 53, pp. 243–63.

Cheng, F., Mary, I. P., Wong, K. K. and Yan, W. W. (1998) 'Critical Care Ethics in Hong Kong: Cross-Cultural Conflicts as East Meets West', *Journal of Medicine and Philosophy*, vol. 23, no. 6, pp. 616–27.

Childress, J. F. (2000) 'Nuremberg's Legacy: Some Ethical Reflections', *Perspectives in Biology and Medicine*, vol. 43, pp. 347–61.

Childress, J. F. and Fletcher, J. C. (1994) 'Respect for Autonomy', *Hastings Centre Report*, vol. 24, no. 3, pp. 33–34.

Cho, M. K. (2006) 'Racial and Ethnic Categories in Biomedical Research: There is no Baby in the Bathwater', *Journal of Law, Medicine & Ethics*, vol. 34, no. 3, pp. 497–99.

Chokshi, D. A., Thera, M. A., Parker, M., Diakite, M., Makani, J. et al, (2007) 'Valid Consent for Genomic Epidemiology in Developing Countries', *PLoS Medicine*, vol. 4, no. 4, e95, pp. 0636–41.

Christakis, N. A. (1988) 'The Ethical Design of an AIDS Vaccine Trial in Africa: The Ethical Design of an AIDS Vaccine Trial in Africa', *The Hastings Center report*, vol. 18, no. 3, pp. 31–37.

Christakis, N. A. and Panner, M. J. (1991) 'Existing International Ethical Guidelines for Human Subjects Research: Some Open Questions', *The Journal of Law, Medicine and Ethics*, vol. 19, no. 3–4, pp. 214–11.

Chu, J. Y., Huang, W., Kuang, Q., Wang, J. M., Xu, J. J., Chu, Z. T., Yang, Z. Q., Lin, K. Q., Li, P., Wu, M., Geng, Z. C., Tan, C. C., Du, R. F. and Jin, L. (1998) 'Genetic Relationship of Populations in China', *The National Academy of Sciences*, vol. 95, pp. 11763–68.

Clayton, E. W. (2002) 'The Complex Relationship of Genetics, Groups, and Health: What It Means for Public Health', *The Journal of Law, Medicine & Ethics*, vol. 30, no. 2, pp. 290–97.

Clayton, E. W. (2005) 'Informed Consent and Biobanks', *The Journal of Law, Medicine & Ethics*, vol. 33, no. 1, pp. 15–21.

Clinton, R. N. (1990) 'Rights of Indigenous Peoples as Collective Group Rights', *Arizona Law Review*, vol. 32, no. 4, pp. 739–48.

Coggon, J. (2007) 'Varied and Principled Understandings of Autonomy in English Law: Justifiable Inconsistency or Blinkered Moralism?', *Health Care Analysis*, vol. 15, no. 3, pp. 235–55.

Cohn, J. N. (2006) 'The Use of Race and Ethnicity in Medicine: Lessons from the African-American Heart Failure Trial', *Journal of Law, Medicine & Ethics*, vol. 34, no. 3, pp. 552–54.

Cole, R. (2005) 'Authentic Democracy: Endowing Citizens with a Human Right in their Genetic Information', *Hofstra Law Review*, vol. 33, pp. 1241–303.

Coleman, C. H. (2005) 'Duties to Subjects in Clinical Research', *Vanderbilt Law Review*, vol. 58, pp. 387–449.

Coleman, C. H. (2009) 'Vulnerability as a Regulatory Category in Human Subject Research', *Journal of Law, Medicine and Ethics*, vol. 37, no. 1, pp. 12–18.

Cooley, D. (2000) 'Good Enough for the Third World', *Journal of Medicine and Philosophy*, vol. 25, no. 4, pp. 427–50.

Cooper, E. B. (1999) 'Testing for Genetic Traits: The Need for a New Legal Doctrine of Informed Consent', *Maryland Law Review*, vol. 85, pp. 346–422.

Costa, R. G. (2007) 'Racial Classification Regarding Semen Donor Selection in Brazil', *Developing World Bioethics*, vol. 7, no. 2, pp. 104–11.

Cox, K. E., Deluhery, A., D'Souza, T. S., Finlayson, R. S., Fritsch, P. S., Grimaldi, L., Goodman, M. A., Hawke, S. L., Joensen, T. J., Kadlec, K. L., Kim, D. C., Larson, G. and Reagh, E. (2002) 'Model Act for Genetic Privacy and Control (MAGPAC) (2002)', *Iowa Law Review*, vol. 88, pp. 121–61.

Curley, D. and Sharples, A. (2002) 'Patenting biotechnology in Europe: the ethical debate moves on', *European Intellectual Property Review*, vol. 24, no. 12, pp. 565–70.

Cyranoski, D. (2005) 'Chinese Clinical Trials: Consenting adults? Not necessarily ...', *Nature*, vol. 435, no. 7039, pp. 138–39.

Daele, W. V. D., Dobert, R. and Seiler, A. (2003) 'Stakeholder dialogue on intellectual property rights in biotechnology: a project of the World Business Council for Sustainable Development', *International Review of Intellectual Property and Competition Law*, vol. 34, no. 8, pp. 932–52.

Dagne, T. W. (2009) 'The Application of Intellectual Property Rights to Biodiversity Resources: A Technique for the South Countries to Maintain Control over the Biodiversity Resources in Their Territories?', *African Journal of International and Comparative Law*, vol. 17, no. 1, pp. 150–65.

Dahre, U. J. (2008) 'The Politics of Human Rights: Indigenous Peoples and the Conflict on Collective Human Rights', *International Journal of Human Rights*, vol. 12, no. 1, pp. 41–52.

De Castro, L. D. (1997) 'Transporting Values by Technology Transfer', *Bioethics*, vol. 11, no. 3–4, pp. 193–205.

De Craemer, W. (1983) 'A Cross-Cultural Perspective on Personhood', *The Milbank Memorial Fund Quarterly Health and Society*, vol. 61, no. 1, pp. 19–34.

DeCamp, M. and Sugarman, J. (2004) 'Ethics in Population-Based Genetic Research', *Accountability in Research*, vol. 11, pp. 1–26.

Deckha, M. (2008) 'The Gendered Politics of Embryonic Stem Cell Research in the USA and Canada: an American Overlap and Canadian Disconnect', *Medical Law Review*, vol. 16, no. 1, pp. 52–84.

Deech, R. (1998) 'Family Law and Genetics', *Modern Law Review*, vol. 61, no. 5, pp. 697–915.

Denny, C. C. and Grady, C. (2007) 'Clinical Research with Economically Disadvantaged Populations', *Journal of Medical Ethics*, vol. 33, no. 7, pp. 382–85.

Devis, D. S. (2002) 'Genetic Research and Communal Narratives', *Jurimetrics*, vol. 42, pp. 199–207.

De Vries, J. Bull, S., Doumbo, O., Ibrahim, M., Mercarau-Puijalon, O. and Parker, M. (2011) 'Ethical Issues in Human Genomics Research in Developing Countries', *BMC Medical Ethics*, vol. 12, no. 5.

Dhai, A. (2005) 'Module Five: Implementation of Ethics Review', *Developing World Bioethics*, vol. 5, no. 1, pp. 73–91.

Diallo, D. A., Doumbo, O. K., Plowe, C. V., Wellems, T. E., Emanuel, E. J. and Hurst, S. A. (2005) 'Community Permission for Medical Research in Developing Countries', *Clinical Infectious Diseases*, vol. 41, no. 2, pp. 255–59.

Dickens, B. M., Gostin, L. and Levine, R. J. (1991) 'Research on Human Populations: National and International Ethical Guidelines', *The Journal of Law, Medicine and Ethics*, vol. 19, no. 3–4, pp. 157–61.

Dickenson, D. (2004) 'Consent, Commodification and Benefit-sharing in Genetic Research', *Developing World Bioethics*, vol. 4, no. 2, pp. 109–24.

Dickert, N. and Sugarman, J. (2005) 'Ethical Goals of Community Consultation in Research', *American Journal of Public Health*, vol. 95, no. 7, pp. 1123–27.

Dinstein, Y. (1976) 'Collective Human Rights of Peoples and Minorities', *International and Comparative Law Quarterly*, vol. 25, no. 1, pp. 102–20.

Diver, C. S. and Cohen, J. M. (2001) 'Genophobia: What is Wrong with Genetic Discrimination?', *University of Pennsylvania Law Review*, vol. 149, pp. 1439–82.

Donchin, A. (2001) 'Understanding Autonomy Relationally: Toward a Reconfiguration of Bioethical Principles', *Journal of Medicine and Philosophy*, vol. 26, no. 4, pp. 365–86.

D'Orazio, P. (2006) 'Half of the Family Tree: A Cal for Access to a Full Genetic History for Children Born by Artificial Insemination', *Journal of Health & Biomedical Law*, vol. 2, pp. 249–76.

Doring, O. (2003) 'China's Struggle for Practical Regulations in Medical Ethics', *Nature Reviews: Genetics*, vol. 4, pp. 233–39.

Dougherty, T. (1998) 'Group Rights to Cultural Survival: Intellectual Property Rights in Native American Cultural Symbols', *Columbia Human Rights Law Review*, vol. 29, pp. 355–400.

Doyle, C. (2009) 'Indigenous Peoples and the Millennium Development Goals – "sacrificial lambs" or Equal Beneficiaries?', *International Journal of Human Rights*, vol. 13, no. 1, pp. 44–71.

Drabiak-Syed, K. (2009) 'State Codification of Federal Regulatory Ambiguities in Biobanking and Genetic Research', *Journal of Legal Medicine*, vol. 30, pp. 299–327.

Drahos, P. (1999) 'Biotechnology patents, markets and morality', *European Intellectual Property Review*, vol. 21, no. 9, pp. 441–49.

Dunne, M. (2002) 'Conference Report: Human Genome – the Research Ethics Dimension', *Medico-Legal Journal of Ireland*, vol. 8, no. 1, pp. 25–26.

Durster, T. (2006) 'Lessons from History: Why Race and Ethnicity Have Played a Major Role in Biomedical Research', *Journal of Law, Medicine & Ethics*, vol. 34, no. 3, pp. 487–96.

Dutfield, G. M. (2004) 'The Innovation Dilemma: Intellectual Property and the Historical Legacy of Cumulative Creativity', *Intellectual Property Quarterly*, vol. 4, pp. 379–421.

Dworkin, R. B. (1993) 'Medical Law and Ethics in the Post-autonomy Age', *Indiana Law Journal*, vol. 68, pp. 727–42.

Ekunwe, E. O. and Kessel, R. (1984) 'Informed Consent in the Developing World', *Hastings Centre Report*, vol. 14, no. 3, pp. 22–24.

Elliott, D. (2001) 'The Genome and the Law: Should Increased Genetic Knowledge Change the Law?', *Harvard Journal of Law and Public Policy*, vol. 25, pp. 61–70.

Ells, C. (2001) 'Shifting the Autonomy Debate to Theory as Ideology', *Journal of Medicine and Philosophy*, vol. 26, no. 4, pp. 417–30.

Emanuel, E. J. (2005) 'Undue Inducement: Nonsense on Stilts?', *The American Journal of Bioethics*, vol. 5, no. 5, pp. 9–13.

Emanuel, E. J. and Grady, C. (2006) 'Four Paradigms of Clinical Research and Research Oversight', *Cambridge Quarterly of Healthcare Ethics*, vol. 16, pp. 82–96.

Engelhardt, H. T. (1980) 'Bioethics in the People's Republic of China', *Hastings Centre Report*, vol. 10, no. 2, pp. 7–10.

Epstein, J. (2009) '"Genetic Surveillance": The Bogeyman Response to Familial DNA Investigations', *University of Illinois Journal of Law, Technology and Policy*, pp. 141–73.

Errico, S. (2007) 'Legislative Comment: The draft UN Declaration on the Rights of Indigenous Peoples: An Overview', *Human Rights Law Review*, vol. 7, no. 4, pp. 741–55.

Errico, S. (2007) 'The Draft UN Declaration on the Rights of Indigenous Peoples: An Overview', *Human Rights Law Review*, vol. 7, no. 4, pp. 741–55.

Evans, B. J. (2006) 'Encouraging Translational Research Through Harmonization of FDA and Common Rule Informed Consent Requirements for Research with Banked Specimens', *Journal of Legal Medicine*, vol. 27, pp. 119–66.

Faden, R. and Faden, A. 1977, 'False Belief and the Refusal of Medical Treatment', *Journal of medical ethics*, vol. 3, no. 3, pp. 133–36.

Fagan, A. (2004) 'Challenging the Bioethical Application of the Autonomy Principle within Multicultural Societies', *Journal of Applied Philosophy*, vol. 21, no. 1, pp. 15–31.

Fan, H. (2007) 'The Missing Link between Self-Determination and Democracy: The Case of East Timor', *Northwestern University Journal of International Human Rights*, vol. 6, no. 1, pp. 176–95.

Fan, R. (1997) 'Self-Determination vs. Family-Determination: Two Incommensurable Principles of Autonomy', *Bioethics*, vol. 11, no. 3–4, pp. 309–22.

Fan, R. (1998) 'Critical Care Ethics in Asia: Global or Local?', *Journal of Medicine and Philosophy*, vol. 23, no. 6, pp. 549–62.

Fan, R. (2006) 'Towards a Confucian Virtue Bioethics: Reframing Chinese Medical Ethics in a Market Economy', *Theoretical Medicine and Bioethics*, vol. 27, no. 6, pp. 541–66.

Farmer, P. (2004) 'Rethinking Medical Ethics: A View from Below', *Developing World Bioethics*, vol. 4, no. 1, pp. 17–41.

Farmer, P. and Campos, N. G. (2004) 'New Malaise: Bioethics and Human Rights in the Global Era', *Journal of Law, Medicine & Ethics*, vol. 32, pp. 243–51.

Ferguson, L. (2008) 'Family, Social Inequalities, and the Persuasive Force of Interpersonal Obligation', *International Journal of Law, Policy and the Family*, vol. 22, no. 1, pp. 61–90.

Fisher, C. B. (1997) 'A Relational Perspective on Ethics-in-Science Decision-making for Research with Vulnerable Populations', *IRB: Ethics and Human Research*, vol. 19, no. 5, pp. 1–4.

Foster, C. E. (2001) 'Articulating Self-determination in the Draft Declaration on the Rights of Indigenous Peoples', *European Journal of International Law*, vol. 12, no. 1, pp. 141–57.

Foster, M. W. (2006) 'Analyzing the Use of Race and Ethnicity in Biomedical Research from a Local Community Perspective', *Journal of Law, Medicine & Ethics*, vol. 34, no. 3, pp. 508–12.

Foster, M. W. and Freeman, W. L. (1998) 'Naming Names in Human Genetic Variation Research', *Genome Research*, vol. 8, no. 755, p. 757.

Foster, M. W. and Sharp, R. R. (2002) 'Race, Ethnicity, and Genomics: Social Classifications as Proxies of Biological Heterogeneity', *Genome Research*, vol. 12, pp. 844–50.

Foster, M. W. and Sharp, R. R. (2004) 'Beyond race: towards a whole genome perspective on human populations and genetic variation', *Nature Reviews: Genetics*, vol. 5, no. 10, pp. 790–96.

Foster, M. W., Bernsten, D. and Carter, T. H. (1998) 'A Model Agreement for Genetic Research in Socially Identifiable Populations', *American Journal of Human Genetics*, vol. 63, pp. 696–702.

Foster, M. W., Eisenbraun, A. J. and Carter and T. H. (1997) 'Communal discourse as a supplement to informed consent for genetic research', *Nature Genetics*, vol. 17, pp. 277–79.

Foster, M. W., Sharp, R. R., Freeman, W. L., Chino, M., Bernsten, D. and Carter, T. H. (1999) 'The Role of Community Review in Evaluating the Risks of Human Genetic Variation Research', *American Journal of Human Genetics*, vol. 64, pp. 1719–27.

Fox, R. C. and Swazey, J. P. (1984) 'Medical Morality is Not Bioethics: Medical Ethics in China and the United States', *Perspectives in Biology and Medicine*, vol. 27, pp. 336–60.

Franklin, R. E. and Goslin, R. G. (1953) 'Molecular Configuration in Sodium Thymonucleate', *Nature*, vol. 171, no. 4356, pp. 740–41.

Frimpong-Mansoh, A. (2008) 'Culture and Voluntary Informed Consent in African Health Care Systems', *Developing World Bioethics*, vol. 8, no. 2, pp. 104–14.

Fu, D. and Tsai, C. (2001) 'How Should Doctors Approach Patients: A Confucian Reflection on Personhood', *Journal of Medical Ethics*, vol. 27, no. 1, pp. 44–50.

Furman, R. L. (1999) 'Genetic Test Results and the Duty to Disclose: Can Medical Researchers Control Liability?', *Seattle University Law Review*, vol. 23, pp. 391–429.

Garrafa, V., Solbakk, J. H., Vidal, S. and Lorenzo, C. (2010) 'Between the Needy and the Greedy: The Quest for a Just and Fair Ethics of Clinical Research', *Journal of Medical Ethics*, vol. 36, pp. 500–4.

Gbadegesin, S. and Wendler, D. (2006) 'Protecting Communities in Health Research from Exploitation', *Bioethics*, vol. 20, no. 5, pp. 248–53.

Gellner, J. L. and Weaver, W. L. (1994) 'A Glossary of Genetic Terms', *Dickinson Journal of Environmental Law and Policy*, vol. 3, pp. 119–29.

Gerstein, M. B., Bruce, C., Rozowsky, J. S., Zheng, D., Du, J., Korbel, J. O., Emanuelsson, O., Zhang, Z. D., Weissman, S. and Snyder, M. (2007) 'What Is a Gene, Post-ENCODE? History and Updated Definition', *Genome Research*, vol. 17, no. 6, pp. 669–81.

Gibbons, S. M. C. (2008) 'Law and the Human Body: Property Rights, Ownership and Control', *Medical Law Review*, pp. 305–13.

Gilbar, R. (2004) 'Medical Confidentiality Within the Family: The Doctor's Duty Reconsidered', *International Journal of Law, Policy and the Family*, vol. 18, no. 2, pp. 195–213.

Gilbar, R. (2007) 'Communicating Genetic Information in the Family: The Familial Relationship as the Forgotten Factor', *Journal of Medical Ethics*, vol. 33, no. 7, pp. 390–93.

Gilbar, R. (2007) 'The Status of the Family in Law and Bioethics: The Genetic Context', *Medical Law Review*, vol. 15, pp. 144–47.

Gillon, R. (1985) 'Autonomy and the Principle of Respect for Autonomy', *British Medical Journal*, vol. 290, pp. 1806–8.

Ginsburg, D. H. (1999) 'Genetics and Privacy', *Texas Review of Law and Politics*, vol. 4, pp. 17–23.

Given, D. V. (1995) 'Forging a Biodiversity Ethic in a Multicultural Context', *Biodiversity and Conservation*, vol. 4, pp. 877–91.

Goldman, O. Q. (1994) 'Need for an Independent International Mechanism to Protect Group Rights: A Case Study of the Kurds', *Tulsa Journal of Comparative and International Law*, vol. 2, pp. 45–89.

Goldner, J. A. (2000) 'Dealing with Conflicts of Interest in Biomedical Research: IRB Oversight as the Next Best Solution to the Abolitionist Approach', *Journal of Law, Medicine and Ethics*, vol. 28, pp. 379–404.

Goldworth, A. (1999) 'Informed Consent in the Genetic Age', *Cambridge Quarterly of Healthcare Ethics*, vol. 8, no. 3, pp. 393–400.

Gordon, M. P. (2009) 'Legal Duty to Disclose Individual Research Findings to Research Subjects', *Food and Drug Law Journal*, vol. 64, pp. 225–60.

Gostin, L. (1991) 'Ethical Principles for the Conduct of Human Subject Research: Population-Based Research and Ethics', *Journal of Law, Medicine and Ethics*, vol. 19, no. 3–4, pp. 191–201.

Gostin, L. O. (1995) 'Genetic Privacy', *Journal of Law, Medicine & Ethics*, vol. 23, pp. 320–30.

Gostin, L. O. (1995) 'Informed Consent, Cultural Sensitivity, and Respect for Persons', *Journal of the American Medical Association*, vol. 274, no. 10, pp. 844–45.

Gostin, L. O. and Hodge, J. G. (1999) 'Genetic Privacy and the Law: An End to Genetics Exceptionalism', *Jurimetrics*, vol. 40, pp. 21–58.

Gostin, L. O. and Laurie, G. T. (2002) 'Personal Privacy and Common Goods: A Framework for Balancing Under the National Health Information Privacy Rule', *Minnesota Law Review*, vol. 86, pp. 1439–79.

Gostin, L. O., Hodge, J. G. and Marks, L. (2002) 'The Nationalization of Health Information Privacy Protections', *Connecticut Insurance Law Journal*, vol. 8, pp. 283–314.

Grady, C. (2009) 'Vulnerability in Research: Individuals with Limited Financial and/or Social Resources', *Journal of Law, Medicine and Ethics*, vol. 37, no. 1, pp. 19–27.

Greely, H. T. (1996) 'The Control of Genetic Research: Involving the "Groups Between"', *Houston Law Review*, vol. 33, pp. 1397–430.

Greely, H. T. (1998) 'Legal, Ethical, and Social Issues in Human Genome Research', *Annual Review of Anthropology*, vol. 27, pp. 473–502.

Greely, H. T. (1999) 'Iceland's Plan for Genomics Research: Facts and Implications', *Jurimetrics*, vol. 40, no. 2, pp. 153–92.

Greely, H. T. (2001) 'Human Genome Diversity: What about the other Human Genome Project?', *Nature Reviews: Genetics*, vol. 2, no. 3, pp. 222–27.

Greely, H. T. (2001) 'Human Genomics Research: New Challenges for Research Ethics', *Perspectives in Biology and Medicine*, vol. 44, no. 2, pp. 221–29.

Greely, H. T. (2001) 'Informed Consent and Other Ethical Issues in Human Population Genetics', *Annual Review of Genetics*, vol. 35, pp. 785–800.

Greely, H. T. (2001) 'The Revolution in Human Genetics: Implications for Human Societies', *South Carolina Law Review*, vol. 52, pp. 377–90.

Greely, H. T. (2005) 'Regulating Human Biological Enhancements: Questionable Justifications and International Complications', *University of Technology, Sydney Law Review*, vol. 7, pp. 87–110.

Green, L. (1991) 'Two Views of Collective Rights', *Canadian Journal of Law and Jurisprudence*, vol. 4, pp. 315–28.

Green, R. M. and Thomas, A. M. (1998) 'DNA: Five Distinguishing Features for Policy Analysis', *Harvard Journal of Law and Technology*, vol. 11, pp. 571–91.

Greenfield, D. (2009) 'Intangible or Embodied Information: The Non-statutory Nature of Human Genetic Material', *Santa Clara Computer and High Technology Law Journal*, vol. 25, pp. 467–538.

Grimm, D. A. (2008) 'Informed Consent for All! No Exceptions', *New Mexico Law Review*, vol. 37, no. Winter, pp. 39–83.

Grodin, M. A. and Annas, G. J. (1996) 'Legacies of Nuremberg: Medical Ethics and Human Rights', *Journal of the American Medical Association*, vol. 276, no. 20, pp. 1682–83.

Gunasekara, G. (2009) 'The "final" Privacy Frontier? Regulating Trans-border Data Flows', *International Journal of Law & Information Technology*, vol. 17, no. 2, pp. 147–79.

Guo, Z. (1995) 'Chinese Confucian Culture and the Medical Ethical Tradition', *Journal of Medical Ethics*, vol. 21, no. 4, pp. 239–46.

Halliday, S. (2004) 'A comparative approach to the regulation of human embryonic stem cell research in Europe', *Medical Law Review*, vol. 12, no. 1, pp. 40–69.

Halliday, S. and Steinberg, D. L. (2004) 'The Regulated Gene: New Legal Dilemmas', *Medical Law Review*, vol. 12, no. 1, pp. 2–13.

Hallowell, N., Foster, C., Eeles, R., Ardern-Jones, A., Murday, V. and Watson, M. (2003) 'Balancing Autonomy and Responsibility: The Ethics of Generating and Disclosing Genetic Information', *Journal of Medical Ethics*, vol. 29, no. 2, pp. 74–79.

Hamilton, C. (2006) 'Biodiversity, Biopiracy and Benefits: What Allegations of Biopiracy Tell Us About Intellectual Property', *Developing World Bioethics*, vol. 6, no. 3, pp. 158–73.

Hamilton, J. A. (2008) 'Revitalizing Difference in the HapMap: Race and Contemporary Human Genetic Variation Research', *Journal of Law, Medicine & Ethics*, vol. 36, no. 3, pp. 471–77.

Hardcastle, R. (2008) 'Law and Human Body: Property Rights, Ownership and Control', *Edinburgh Law Review*, vol. 12, no. 2, pp. 339–40.

Harmon, S. H. E. (2009) 'Semantic, Pedantic or Paradigm Shift? Recruitment, Retention and Property in Modern Population Biobanking', *European Journal of Health Law*, vol. 16, pp. 27–43.

Harris, J. (1999) 'Ethical Genetic Research on Human Subjects', *Jurimetrics*, vol. 40, pp. 77–92.

Harris, J. (2005) 'Scientific research is a moral duty', *Journal of Medical Ethics*, vol. 31, no. 4, pp. 242–48.

Hartman, R. G. (2000) 'Adolescent Autonomy: Clarifying an Ageless Conundrum', *Hastings Law Journal*, vol. 51, pp. 1265–362.

Hartney, M. (1991) 'Some Confusions Concerning Collective Rights', *Canadian Journal of Law and Jurisprudence*, vol. 4, pp. 293–314.

Hayry, M. and Takala, T. (2005) 'Human Dignity, Bioethics, and Human Rights', *Developing World Bioethics*, vol. 5, no. 3, pp. 225–33.

Hellman, D. (2003) 'What Makes Genetic Discrimination Exceptional?', *American Journal of Law and Medicine*, vol. 29, pp. 77–116.

Herring, J. and Chau, P. L. (2007) 'My Body, Your Body, Our Bodies', *Medical Law Review*, vol. 15, no. 1, pp. 34–61.

Heywood, R. (2009) 'Subjectivity in Risk Disclosure: Considering the Position of the Particular Patient', *Professional Negligence*, vol. 25, no. 1, pp. 3–14.

Heywood, R., Macaskill, A. and Williams, K. (2010) 'Informed Consent in Hospital Practice: Health Professionals' Perspectives and Legal Reflections', *Medical Law Review*, vol. 18, no. 2, pp. 152–84.

Hill, P. (2004) 'Ethics and Health Systems Research in "Post"-Conflict Situations', *Developing World Bioethics*, vol. 4, no. 2, pp. 139–53.

Hillsten, S. L. (2008) 'Global Bioethics: Utopia or Reality?', *Developing World Bioethics*, vol. 8, no. 2, pp. 70–81.

Holm, S. (2008) 'Pharamacogenetics, Race and Global Injustice', *Developing World Bioethics*, vol. 8, no. 2, pp. 82–88.

Holtzman, N. A. and Rothstein, M. A. (1992) 'Eugenics and Genetic Discrimination', *American Journal of Human Genetics*, vol. 50, pp. 457–59.

Horng, S. and Grady, C. (2003) 'Misunderstanding in Clinical Research: Distinguishing Therapeutic Misconception, Therapeutic Misestimation and Therapeutic Optimism', *IRB: Ethics and Human Research*, vol. 25, no. 1, pp. 11–16.

Hughes, D. (2008) 'The Missing Voice: A Consideration of Universalism, Cultural Relativism, and the Absence of the Female Perspective', *UCL Jurisprudence Review*, vol. 14, pp. 47–68.

Hurst, S. A. (2008) 'Vulnerability in Research and Health Care: Describing the Elephant in the Room', *Bioethics*, vol. 22, no. 4, pp. 191–202.

Hutton, J. L. and Ashcroft, R. E. (2000) 'Some Popular Versions of Uninformed Consent', *Health Care Analysis*, vol. 8, no. 1, pp. 41–52.

Hyder, A. A. and Wali, S. A. (2006) 'Informed Consent and Collaborative Research: Perspectives from the Developing World', *Developing World Bioethics*, vol. 6, no. 1, pp. 33–40.

Iltis, A. S. (2009) 'Introduction: Vulnerability in Biomedical Research', *Journal of Law, Medicine and Ethics*, vol. 37, no. 1, pp. 6–11.

Information Office of the State Council of the People's Republic of China (2009) 'National Human Rights Action Plan of China (2009–2010)', *Chinese Journal of International Law*, vol. 8, no. 3, pp. 741–77.

Information Office of the State Council of the People's Republic of China (2010) 'China's Ethnic Policy and Common Prosperity and Development of All Ethnic Groups', *Chinese Journal of International Law*, vol. 9, no. 1, pp. 211–59.

International Human Genome Sequencing Consortium (2001) 'Initial Sequencing and Analysis of the Human Genome', *Nature*, vol. 409, no. 6822, pp. 860–921.

International Human Genome Sequencing Consortium (2001) 'The Sequence of the Human Genome', *Science*, vol. 291, no. 1304, p. 1352.

Ip, P. K. (2005) 'Developing Medical Ethics in China's Reform Era', *Developing World Bioethics*, vol. 5, no. 2, pp. 176–87.

Irabor, D. O. and Omonzejele, P. (2009) 'Local Attitudes, Moral Obligation, Customary Obedience and Other Cultural Practices: Their Influence on the Process of Gaining Informed Consent for Surgery in a Tertiary Institution in a Developing Country', *Developing World Bioethics*, vol. 9, no. 1, pp. 34–42.

Jacobs, B., Roffenbender, J., Collmann, J., Cherry, K., Bitsoi, L. L., Bassett, K. and Bassett, C. H. (2010) 'Bridging the Divide between Genomic Science and Indigenous Peoples', *The Journal of Law, Medicine & Ethics*, vol. 38, no. 3, pp. 684–96.

Janger, E. J. (2005) 'Genetic Information, Privacy and Insolvency', *The Journal of Law, Medicine & Ethics*, vol. 33, no. 1, pp. 79–88.

Jegede, A. S. (2009) 'Culture and Genetic Screening in Africa', *Developing World Bioethics*, vol. 9, no. 3, pp. 128–37.

Joffe, S., Cook, E. F., Clearly, P. D., Clark, J. W. and Weeks, J. (2001) 'Quality of Informed Consent in Cancer Clinical Trials: a Cross-sectional Survey', *Lancet*, vol. 358, no. 23, pp. 1772–77.

Joh, E. E. (2006) 'Reclaiming "Abandoned" DNA: The Fourth Amendment and Genetic Privacy', *Northwestern University Law Review*, vol. 100, pp. 857–84.

Johnston, C. (2004) 'Does the UK Biobank Have a Legal Obligation to Feedback Individual Findings to Participants?', *Medical Law Review*, vol. 12, pp. 238–67.

Johnston, J. and Thomas, M. (2003) 'Summary: The Science of Genealogy by Genetics', *Developing World Bioethics*, vol. 3, no. 2, pp. 103–8.

Jones, M. A. (1999) 'Informed Consent and Other Fairy Stories', *Medical Law Review*, vol. 7, no. 2, pp. 103–34.

Jones, P. (1999) 'Human Rights, Group Rights and Peoples' Rights', *Human Rights Quarterly*, vol. 21, no. 1, pp. 80–107.

Jorde, L. B., Watkins, W. S. and Bamshad. M. J. (2001) 'Population Genomics: A Bridge from Evolutionary History to Genetic Medicine', *Human Molecular Genetics*, vol. 2001, no. 10, pp. 2199–207.

Juengst, E. T. (1998) 'Groups as Gatekeepers to Genomic Research: Conceptually Confusing, Morally Hazardous, and Practically Useless', *Kennedy Institute of Ethics Journal*, vol. 8, no. 2, pp. 183–200.

Juengst, E. T. (2004) 'Face Facts: Why Human Genetics Will Always Provoke Bioethics', *Journal of Law, Medicine & Ethics*, vol. 32, pp. 267–75.

Jungreis, R. (2007) 'Fearing the Fear Itself: The Proposed Genetic Information Nondiscrimination Act of 2005 and Public Fears about Genetic Information', *Journal of Law and Policy*, vol. 15, pp. 221–47.

Karnell, G. W. G. (1995) 'Protection of Results of Genetic Research by Copyright or Design Rights?', *European Intellectual Property Review*, vol. 17, no. 8, pp. 355–58.

Kass, N., Hyder, A. A., Ajuwon, A., Appiah-Poku, J., Barsdorf, N., Elsayed, D. E., Mokhachane, M., Mupenda, B., Ndebele, P., Ndossi, G., Sikateyo, B., Tangwa, G. and Tindana, P. (2007) 'The Structure and Function of Research Ethics Committees In Africa: A Case Study', *PLoS Medicine*, vol. 4, no. 1, pp. 26 31.

Kass, N. E., Matowicz, M. R., Hull, S. C., Faden, R. R., Plantinga, L., Gostin, L. O. and Slutsman, J. (2003) 'The Use of Medical Records in Research: What Do Patients Want', *Journal of Law, Medicine & Ethics*, vol. 31, pp. 429–33.

Kass, N. E., Sugarman, J., Faden, R. and Schoch-Spana, M. (1996) 'Trust: The Fragile Foundation of Contemporary Biomedical Research', *The Hastings Center Report*, vol. 26, pp. 25–29.

Katz, J. (1993) 'Human Experimentation and Human Rights', *Saint Louis University Law Journal*, vol. 38, pp. 7–54.

Katz, J. (1996) 'The Nuremberg Code and the Nuremberg Trial: A Reappraisal', *Journal of the American Medical Association*, vol. 276, no. 20, pp. 1662–66.

Kaye, C. L., Laxova, R., Livingston, J. E., Lloyd-Puryear, M. A., Mann, M., McCabe, E. R. B. and Therrell, B. L. (2001) 'Integrating Genetic Services into Public Health: Guidance for State and Territorial Programs from the National Newborn Screening and Genetics Resource Center (NNSGRC)', *Community Genetics*, vol. 4, pp. 175–96.

Keane, D. (2010) 'Survival of the Fairest? Evolution and the Geneticization of Rights', *Oxford Journal of Legal Studies*, vol. 30, no. 3, pp. 467–94.

Keller, J. (1997) 'Autonomy, Relationality, and Feminist Ethics', *Hypatia*, vol. 12, no. 2, pp. 152–64.

Kennedy, G., Doyle, S. and Lui, B. (2010) 'Data Protection in the Asia-Pacific Region', *Computer Law & Security Review*, vol. 25, no. 1, pp. 59–68.

Kent, A. (2003) 'Consent and Confidentiality in Genetics: Whose Information Is It Anyway?', *Journal of Medical Ethics*, vol. 29, no. 1, pp. 16–18.

Kim, C. (1987) 'The Modern Chinese Legal System', *Tulane Law Review*, vol. 61, no. 6, pp. 1413–52.

Kimmelman, J. (2005) 'Medical Research, Risk, and Bystanders', *IRB: Ethics and Human Research*, vol. 27, no. 4, pp. 1–6.

Kimmelman, J. (2007) 'Missing the Forest: Further Thoughts on the Ethics of Bystander Risk in Medical Research', *Cambridge Quarterly of Healthcare Ethics*, vol. 16, pp. 483–90.

Kinderlerer, J. and Longley, D. (1998) 'Human Genetics: The New Panacea?', *Modern Law Review*, vol. 61, no. 5, pp. 603–20.

King, N. M. P. (2000) 'Defining and Describing Benefit Appropriately in Clinical Trials', *Journal of Law, Medicine and Ethics*, vol. 28, pp. 332–43.

Kipnis, K. (2003) 'Seven Vulnerabilities in the Pediatric Research Subject', *Theoretical Medicine and Bioethics*, vol. 24, no. 2, pp. 107–20.

Kirkland, R. (2008) '"Enhancing Life?" Perspectives from Traditional Chinese Value-Systems', *Journal of Law, Medicine & Ethics*, vol. 36, no. 1, pp. 26–40.

Knoppers, B. M. (2005) 'Biobanking: International Norms', *The Journal of Law, Medicine & Ethics*, vol. 33, no. 1, pp. 7–14.

Knoppers, B. M. and Chadwick, R. (2005) 'Human Genetic Research: Emerging Trends in Ethics', *Nature Reviews: Genetics*, no. 6, pp. 75–79.

Knoppers, B. M., Hirtle, M. and Glass, C. (1999) 'Genetic Technologies: Commercialization of Genetic Research and Public Policy', *Science*, vol. 286, no. 5448, pp. 2277–78.

Knoppers, B. M., Hirtle, M. and Lormeau, S. (1996) 'Ethical Issues in International Collaborative Research on the Human Genome: The HGP and the HGDP', *Genomics*, vol. 34, pp. 272–82.

Knoppers, B. M., Hirtle, M., Lormeau, S., Laberge, C. M. and Laflamme, M. (2009) 'Control of DNA Samples and Information', *Genomics*, vol. 50, pp. 385–401.

Kobrin, J. A. (1983) 'Confidentiality of Genetic Information', *UCLA Law Review*, vol. 30, pp. 1283–315.

Kohlmeier, G. (2007) 'The Risky Business of Lifestyle Genetic Testing: Protecting Against Harmful Disclosure of Genetic Information', *UCLA Journal of Law & Technology*.

Kong, W. M. (2004) 'The Regulation of Gene Therapy Research In Competent Adult Patients, Today And Tomorrow: Implications of EU Directive 2001/20/EC', *Medical Law Review*, vol. 12, p. 164.

Kopelman, L. M. (2005) 'The Incompatibility of the United Nations' Goals and Conventionalist Ethical Relaticism', *Developing World Bioethics*, vol. 5, no. 3, pp. 234–43.

Koski, G. (2000) 'Risks, Benefits, and Conflicts of Interest in Human Research: Ethical Evolution in the Changing World of Science', *The Journal of Law, Medicine & Ethics*, vol. 28, pp. 330–31.

Kottow, M. H. (2003) 'The Vulnerable and the Susceptible', *Bioethics*, vol. 17, no. 5–6, pp. 460–71.

Krajewska, A. (2009) 'Conceptual Quandaries about Genetic Data – A Comparative Perspective', *European Journal of Health Law*, vol. 16, pp. 7–26.

Kuo, W. H. (2008) 'Understanding Race at the Frontier of Pharmaceutical Regulation: An Analysis of the Racial Difference Debate at the ICH', *Journal of Law, Medicine & Ethics*, vol. 36, no. 3, pp. 498–505.

LaFleur, W. R. (2008) 'Enhancement and Desire: Japanese Qualms About Where Biotechnology is Taking Us', *Journal of Law, Medicine & Ethics*, vol. 36, no. 1, pp. 65–72.

Landman, W. and Schuklenk, U. (2005) 'UNESCO "Declares" Universals on Bioethics and Human Rights – Many Unexpected Universal Truths Unearthed by UN Body', *Developing World Bioethics*, vol. 5, no. 3, p. iii–vi.

Latha, S. S. (2009) 'Biopiracy and Protection of Traditional Medicine in India', *European Intellectual Property Review*, vol. 31, no. 9, pp. 465–77.

Laughton, A. H. (2007) 'Somewhere to Run, Somewhere to Hide? International Regulation of Human Subject Experimentation', *Duke Journal of Comparative and International Law*, vol. 18, no. 1, pp. 181–212.

Laurie, G. (2004) 'Patenting stem cells of human origin', *European Intellectual Property Review*, vol. 26, no. 2, pp. 59–66.

Laurie, G. T. (1999) 'Obligations Arising From Genetic Information – Negligence and the Protection of Familial Interests', *Child and Family Law Quarterly*, vol. 11, no. 2, pp. 97–108.

Laurie, G. T. (2000) 'Protecting and Promoting Privacy in an Uncertain World: Further Defences of Ignorance and the Right Not to Know', *European Journal of Health Law*, vol. 7, pp. 185–91.

Laurie, G. T. (2001) 'Challenging Medical-Legal Norms: The Role of Autonomy, Confidentiality, and Privacy in Protecting Individual and Familial Group Rights in Genetic Information', *Journal of Legal Medicine*, vol. 22, pp. 1–54.

Lavery, J. V., Harrington, L. C. and Scott, T. W. (2008) 'Ethical, Social, and Cultural Considerations for Site Selection for Research with Genetically Modified Mosquitoes', *The American Society of Tropical Medicine and Hygiene*, vol. 79, no. 3, pp. 312–18.

Lawton, A. (1997) 'Regulating Genetic Destiny: A Comparative Study of Legal Constraints in Europe and the United States', *Emory International Law Review*, vol. 11, pp. 365–418.

Leavitt, F. J. (2006) 'Is Any Research Population Not Vulnerable?', *Cambridge Quarterly of Healthcare Ethics*, vol. 15, no. 1, pp. 81–88.

Lee, S. S., Mountain, J. and Koenig, B. A. (2001) 'The Meanings of "Race" in the New Genomics: Implications for Health Disparities Research', *Yale Journal of Health Policy, Law, and Ethics*, vol. 17, no. 44, pp. 33–75.

Lemmens, T. and Freedman, B. (2000) 'Ethics Review for Sale? Conflict of Interest and Commercial Research Review Boards', *Milbank Quarterly Review*, vol. 78, pp. 547–84.

Lemmens, T. and Miller, P. B. (2003) 'The Human Subjects Trade: Ethical and Legal Issues Surrounding Recruitment Incentives', *Journal of Law, Medicine & Ethics*, vol. 31, pp. 398–418.

Levine, C., Faden, R., Grady, C., Hammerschmidt, D., Eckenwiler, L. and Sugarman, J. (2004) 'The Limitations of "Vulnerability" as a Protection for Human Research Participants', *The American Journal of Bioethics*, vol. 4, no. 3, pp. 44–49.

Levine, R. J. (1988) 'Uncertainty in Clinical Research', *Law, Medicine and Health Care*, vol. 16, pp. 174–82.

Levine, R. J. (1991) 'Informed Consent: Some Challenges to the Universal Validity of the Western Model', *The Journal of Law, Medicine and Ethics*, vol. 19, no. 3–4, pp. 207–13.

Levine, R. J. (1999) 'The Need to Revise the Declaration of Helsinki', *The New England Journal of Medicine*, vol. 341, no. 7, pp. 531–34.

Lewinski, S. V. (2009) 'Indigenous Heritage and Intellectual Property', *European Intellectual Property Review*, vol. 31, no. 2, pp. 111–12.

Li, E. (2008) 'Bioethics in China', *Bioethics*, vol. 22, no. 8, pp. 448–54.

Liddell, K. (2004) 'Genetic Privacy: a Challenge to Medico-Legal Norms', *Edinburgh Law Review*, vol. 8, no. 3, pp. 424–25.

Liddell, K. and Hall, A. (2005) 'Beyond Bristol and Alder Hey: the future regulation of human tissue', *Medical Law Review*, vol. 13, no. 2, pp. 170–223.

Liddell, K., Bion, J., Chamberlain, D., Druml, C., Kompanje, E., Lemaire, F., Menon, D., Vrhovac, B. and Wiedermann, C. J. (2006) 'Medical Research Involving Incapacitated Adults: Implications of the EU Clinical Trials Directive 2001/20/EC', *Medical Law Review*, vol. 14, no. 3, pp. 367–417.

Lillquist, E. and Sullivan, C. A. (2006) 'Legal Regulation of the Use of Race in Medical Research', *Journal of Law, Medicine & Ethics*, vol. 34, no. 3, pp. 535–51.

Lis, J. M. and Murray, M. G. (2008) 'The Ins And Outs of Independent IRBs', *Journal of Health & Life Sciences Law*, vol. 2, pp. 73–122.

List, J. M. (2005) 'Histories of Mistrust and Protectionism: Disadvantaged Minority Groups and Human-Subject Research Policies', *American Journal of Bioethics*, vol. 5, no. 1, pp. 53–56.

Llewelyn, M. (1997) 'The Legal Protection of Biotechnological Inventions: An Alternative Approach', *European Intellectual Property Review*, vol. 19, no. 3, pp. 115–27.

Lock, M. (1994) 'Interrogating the Human Diversity Genome Project', *Social Science & Medicine*, vol. 39, no. 5, pp. 603–6.

Lombardo, P. A. (1996) 'Genetic Confidentiality: What's the Big Secret?', *University of Chicago Law School Roundtable*, vol. 3, pp. 589–614.

London, L., Orner, P. J. and Myer, L. (2008) '"Even if You're Positive, You Still Have Rights Because You Are A Person": Human Rights and the Reproductive Choice of HIV-Positive Persons', *Developing World Bioethics*, vol. 8, no. 1, pp. 11–22.

Lott, J. P. (2005) 'Module Three: Vulnerable/Special Participant Populations', *Developing World Bioethics*, vol. 5, no. 1, pp. 30–54.

Lustig, A. (2008) 'Enhancement Technologies and the Person: Christian Perspectives', *Journal of Law, Medicine & Ethics*, vol. 36, no. 1, pp. 42–50.

Lynoe, N., Sandlund, M., Jacobsson, L., Nordberg, G. and Jin, T. (2004) 'Informed Consent in China: Quality of Information Provided to Participants in a Research Project', *Scandinavian Journal of Public Health*, vol. 32, no. 6, pp. 472–75.

Mackenzie, C. and McDowell, C. (2007) 'Beyond "Do No Harm": the Challenge of Constructing Ethical Relationships in Refugee Research', *Journal of Refugee Studies*, vol. 20, no. 2, pp. 299–319.

Mackenzie, R. (2005) 'Reprogenetics and Pharmacogenetics: In Whose Best Interests?', *Medicine and Law*, vol. 24, pp. 343–54.

Macklin, R. (1998) 'A Defence of Fundamental Universal Principles: A Response to Robert Baker', *Kennedy Institute of Ethics Journal*, vol. 8, no. 4, pp. 403–22.

Macklin, R. (1999) 'International Research: Ethical Imperialism or Ethical Pluralism?', *Accountability in Research*, vol. 7, pp. 59–83.

Macklin, R. (2001) 'After Helsinki: Unresolved Issues in International Research', *Kennedy Institute of Ethics Journal*, vol. 11, pp. 17–36.

Macklin, R. (2003) 'Bioethics, Vulnerability, and Protection', *Bioethics*, vol. 17, nos 5–6, pp. 472–86.

Macklin, R. (2003) 'Dignity is a Useless Concept', *British Medical Journal*, vol. 327, pp. 1419–20.

Macklin, R. (2005) 'Yet Another Guideline? The UNESCO Draft Declaration', *Developing World Bioethics*, vol. 5, no. 3, pp. 244–50.

Macklin, R. and Sherwin, S. (1975), 'Experimenting on Human Subjects: Philosophical Perspectives', *Case Western Reserve Law Review*, vol. 25, pp. 434–71.

Maclean, A. (2000) 'Now You See It, Now You Don't: Consent and the Legal Protection of Autonomy', *Journal of Applied Philosophy*, vol. 17, no. 3, pp. 277–88.

Macpherson, C. C. (2004) 'Research Sponsors Duties to Developing World Host Nations: The Ongoing WMA Discussion of Possible Revisions to the 2000 Declaration of Helsinki (Paragraph 30)', *Developing World Bioethics*, vol. 4, no. 2, pp. 173–75.

Madden, D. (2004) 'Ethical and Legal Issues in Psychiatric Genetics Research', *Medico-Legal Journal of Ireland*, vol. 10, no. 1, pp. 38–47.

Madden, D. (2004) 'Legal Status of Archived Human Tissue', *Medico-Legal Journal of Ireland*, vol. 10, no. 2, pp. 76–83.

Malinowski, M. J. (2005) 'Technology Transfer in BioBanking: Credits, Debits, and Population Health Futures', *The Journal of Law, Medicine & Ethics*, vol. 33, no. 1, pp. 54–69.

Malinowski, M. J. (2009) 'Dealing with the Realities of Race and Ethnicity: A Bioethics-Centered Argument in Favor of Race-Based Genetics Research', *Houston Law Review*, vol. 45, pp. 1415–73.

Mandel, G. N. (2007) 'History Lessons for a General Theory of Law and Technology', *Minnesota Journal of Law, Science & Technology*, vol. 8, pp. 551–70.

Maniko, J. A. (2001) 'Who Should Know? The Disclosure Debate Over Genetic Information', *Seton Hall Legislative Journal*, vol. 26, pp. 151–80.

Manson, N. C. (2006) 'What is Genetic Information, and why is it Significant? A Contextual, Contrastive, Approach', *Journal of Applied Philosophy*, vol. 23, no. 1, pp. 1–16.

Margalit, A. and Moshe, H. (1994) 'Liberalism and the Right to Culture', *Social Research*, vol. 61, no. 3, pp. 491–510.

Markett, M. J. (1996) 'Genetic Diaries: An Analysis of Privacy Protection in DNA Data Banks', *Suffolk University Law Review*, vol. 30, pp. 185–226.

Markl, H. (2002) 'Who Owns the Human Genome? What Can Ownership Mean With Respect to Genes?', *International Review of Intellectual Property and Competition Law*, vol. 33, pp. 1–5.

Marshall, J. (2008) 'A Right to Personal Autonomy at the European Court of Human Rights', *European Human Rights Law Review*, vol. 3, pp. 337–56.

Masiyakurima, P. (2009) 'Biodiversity and the Law: Intellectual Property, Biotechnology and Traditional Knowledge', *Environmental Law Review*, vol. 11, no. 2, p. 146.

Mastroianni, A. C. (1999) 'National, Independent Oversight Reinforcing the Safety Net for Human Subjects Research', *Accountability in Research*, vol. 7, pp. 303–9.

Matthew, D. B. (2008) 'Race, Religion, and Informed Consent – Lessons from Social Science', *Journal of Law, Medicine & Ethics*, vol. 36, no. 1, pp. 150–73.

Mautner, M. (2008) 'From "Honor" to "Dignity": How Should a Liberal State Treat Non-liberal Cultural Groups?', *Theoretical Inquiries in Law*, vol. 9, no. 2, pp. 609–42.

Mazumdar, A. (2007) 'Information, copyright and the future', *European Intellectual Property Review*, vol. 29, no. 5, pp. 180–86.

McDonald, M. (1991) 'Should Communities Have Rights? Reflections on Liberal Individualism', *Canadian Journal of Law and Jurisprudence*, vol. 4, no. 217, p. 237.

McGregor, J. L. (2005) '"Undue Inducement" as Coercive Offers', *The American Journal of Bioethics*, vol. 5, no. 5, pp. 24–25.

McGregor, J. L. (2007) 'Population Genomics and Research Ethics with Socially Identifiable Groups', *Journal of Law, Medicine and Ethics*, vol. 35, pp. 356–70.

McHale, J. V. (2004) 'Regulating genetic databases: some legal and ethical issues', *Medical Law Review*, vol. 12, no. 1, pp. 70–96.

McLean, S. A. M. (1998) 'Interventions in the Human Genome', *Modern Law Review*, vol. 61, no. 5, pp. 681–96.

McLean, S. A. M. (2004) 'Regulating Research and Experimentation: A View from the UK', *Journal of Law, Medicine and Ethics*, vol. 32, no. 4, pp. 604–12.

McLochlin, D. L. (2001) 'Whose Genetic Information is it Anyway? A Legal Analysis of the Effects that Human Genome will have on Privacy Rights and Genetic Discrimination', *John Marshall Journal of Computer and Information Law*, vol. 19, no. 609, p. 646.

McNeill, P. (1997) 'Paying People to Participate in Research: Why not?', *Bioethics*, vol. 11, no. 5, pp. 390–96.

Mehlman, M. J. and Berg, J. W. (2008) 'Human Subjects Protections in Biomedical Enhancement Research: Assessing Risk and Benefit and Obtaining Informed Consent', *Journal of Law, Medicine & Ethics*, vol. 36, no. 3, pp. 546–59.

Meier, B. M. (2007) 'Advancing Health Rights in a Globalized World: Responding to Globalization through a Collective Human Right to Public Health', *Journal of Law, Medicine and Ethics*, vol. 35, no. 4, pp. 545–55.

Mello, M. M. and Wolf, L. E. (2010) 'The Havasupai Indian Tribe Case – Lessons for Research Involving Stored Biologic Samples', *The New England Journal of Medicine*, vol. 363, no. 3, pp. 204–7.

Merz, J. F., McGee, G. E. and Sankar, P. (2004) '"Iceland Inc."?: On the ethics of commercial population genomics', *Social Science and Medicine*, vol. 58, no. 6, pp. 1201–9.

Meslin, E. M., Sutherland, H. J., Lavery, J. V. and Till, J. E. (1995) 'Principlism and the Ethical Appraisal of Clinical Trials', *Bioethics*, vol. 9, no. 5, pp. 399–418.

Michels, R. (1999) 'Are Research Ethics Bad for Our Mental Health?', *The New England Journal of Medicine*, vol. 340, pp. 1427–30.

Milford, C., Wassenaar, D. R. and Slack, C. M. (2006) 'Resources and Needs of Research Ethics Committees in Africa: Preparations for HIV Vaccine Trials', *IRB: Ethics and Human Research*, vol. 28, no. 2, pp. 1–9.

Miller, F. G. (2008) 'Research on Medical Records without Informed Consent', *Journal of Law, Medicine & Ethics*, vol. 36, no. 3, pp. 560–66.

Miller, F. H. (2002) 'Phase II of the Genetics Revolution: Sophisticated Issues for Home and Abroad', *American Journal of Law and Medicine*, vol. 28, pp. 145–50.

Mitchell, G. R. and Happe, K. (2001) 'Defining the Subject of Consent in DNA Research', *Journal of Medical Humanities*, vol. 22, no. 1, pp. 41–53.

Mitchell, G. R. and Happe, K. (2001) 'Informed Consent after the Human Genome Project', *Rhetoric & Public Affairs*, vol. 4, no. 3, pp. 375–406.

Mookherjee, M. (2008) 'Autonomy, Force and Cultural Plurality', *Res Publica*, vol. 14, no. 3, pp. 147–68.

Moreno, J. D. (2001) 'Goodbye to All That: the End of Moderate Protectionism in Human Subjects Research', *The Hastings Center Report*, vol. 31, pp. 9–17.

Moreno, J. D. (2004) 'Bioethics and the National Security State', *Journal of Law, Medicine & Ethics*, vol. 32, pp. 198–208.

Morris, A. (2005) 'Gillick, 20 Years on: Arrested Development or Growing Pains?', *Professional Negligence*, vol. 21, no. 3, pp. 158–75.

Morse, A. (1999) 'Searching for the Holy Grail: the Human Genome Project and its Implications', *Journal of Law and Health*, vol. 13, pp. 219–56.

Moufang, R. (1994) 'Patenting of Human Genes, Cells and Parts of the Body? The Ethical Dimensions of Patent Law', *International Review of Intellectual Property and Competition Law*, vol. 25, no. 4, pp. 487–515.

Moulton, B. W. (2006) 'DNA Fingerprinting and Civil Liberties', *Journal of Law, Medicine and Ethics*, vol. 34, pp. 147–48.

Moustakas, J. (1989) 'Group Rights in Cultural Property: Justifying Strict Inalienability', *Cornell Law Review*, vol. 74, no. 6, pp. 1179–227.

Natowicz, M. R., Alper, J. K. and Alper, J. S. (1992) 'Genetic Discrimination and the Law', *American Journal of Human Genetics*, vol. 50, pp. 465–75.

Nelkin, D. (2002) 'A Brief History of the Political Work of Genetics', *Jurimetrics*, vol. 42, pp. 121–32.

Newcity, M. (2009) 'Protecting the Traditional Knowledge and Cultural Expressions of Russia's "Numerically small" Indigenous Peoples: What has been Done, What Remains to be Done', *Texas Wesleyan Law Review*, vol. 15, pp. 357–414.

Newton, S. K. and Appiah-Poku, J. (2007) 'Opinions of Researchers Based in the UK on Recruiting Subjects from Developing Countries into Randomized Controlled Trials', *Developing World Bioethics*, vol. 7, no. 3, pp. 149–56.

Newton, S. K. and Appiah-Poku, J. (2007) 'The Perspectives of Researchers on Obtaining Informed Consent in Developing Countries', *Developing World Bioethics*, vol. 7, no. 1, pp. 19–24.

Nie, J. B. (2005) 'Cultural Values Embodying Universal Norms: A Critique of a Popular Assumption about Cultures and Human Rights', *Developing World Bioethics*, vol. 5, no. 3, pp. 251–57.

Noah, B. A. (2003) 'The Participation of Underrepresented Minorities in Clinical Research', *American Journal of Law and Medicine*, vol. 29, no. 2–3, pp. 221–45.

Normile, D. (2004) 'Consortium Hopes to Map Human History in Asia', *Science*, vol. 306, no. 5702, p. 1667.

Obasogie, O. K. (2008) 'Beyond Best Practices: Strict Scrutiny as a Regulatory Model for Race-Specific Medicines', *Journal of Law, Medicine & Ethics*, vol. 36, no. 3, pp. 491–97.

Odell-West, A. (2009) 'The Absence of Informed Consent to Commercial Exploitation for Inventions Developed from Human Biological Material: A Bar to Patentability?', *Intellectual Property Quarterly*, vol. 3, pp. 373–90.

O'Neill, O. (2003) 'Some Limits of Informed Consent', *Journal of Medical Ethics*, vol. 29, no. 1, pp. 4–7.

Onyemelukwe, C. (2008) 'Research Involving Humans in African Countries: A Case for Domestic Legal Frameworks', *African Journal of International and Comparative Law*, vol. 16, no. 2, pp. 152–77.

Opderbeck, D. W. (2004) 'The Penguin's Genome, or Coase and Open Source Biotechnology', *Harvard Journal of Law and Technology*, vol. 18, pp. 167–227.

Ossorio, P. A. (2007) 'The Human Genome as Common Heritage: Common Sense or Legal Nonsense?', *Journal of Law, Medicine & Ethics*, vol. 35, no. 3, pp. 425–39.

Packer, S. (2006) 'Medical Ethical Considerations in Collaborative Research', *Hofstra Law Review*, vol. 35, pp. 771–91.

Parker, D. B. and Barrett, R. J. (2003) 'Collective danger and individual risk: cultural perspectives on the hazards of medical research', *Internal Medicine Journal*, vol. 33, no. 9–10, pp. 463–62.

Participants of the 2001 Conference on Ethical Aspects of Research in account of exploitation in Developing Countries (2004) 'Moral standards for research in developing countries: from "reasonable availability" to "fair benefits"', *Hastings Centre Report*, vol. 34, no. 3, pp. 17–28.

Payne, P. W. (2008) 'For Asians Only? The Perils of Ancestry-Based Drug Prescribing', *Journal of Law, Medicine & Ethics*, vol. 36, no. 3, pp. 585–88.

Pearson, H. (2006) 'What is a Gene?', *Nature*, vol. 441, pp. 399–401.

Pentassuglia, G. (2001) 'The EU and the protection of minorities: the case of Eastern Europe', *European Journal of International Law*, vol. 12, no. 1, pp. 3–38.

Perrey, C., Wassenaar, D., Gilchrist, S. and Ivanoff, B. (2009) 'Ethical Issues in Medical Research in the Developing World: A Report on a Meeting Organised by Foundation Merieux', *Developing World Bioethics*, vol. 9, no. 2, pp. 88–96.

Phillips, D. F. (1996) 'Institutional Review Boards Under Stress: Will They Explode or Change?', *Journal of the American Medical Association*, vol. 276, no. 20, pp. 1623–26.

Porras, D. A. (2006) 'The "Common Heritage" of Outer Space: Equal Benefits for Most of Mankind', *California Western International Law Journal*, vol. 37, no. 1, pp. 143–76.

Poste, G. (1999) 'Privacy and Confidentiality in the Age of Genetic Engineering', *Texas Review of Law & Politics*, vol. 4, pp. 25–32.

Pottage, A. (1998) 'The Inscription of Life in Law: Genes, Patents, and Bio-politics', *Modern Law Review*, vol. 61, no. 5, pp. 740–65.

Prettyman, G. R. (2007) 'Ethical Reforms in Biotechnology Research Regulations', *Virginia Journal of Social Policy and the Law*, vol. 15, pp. 51–109.

Racine, E. (2003) 'Discourse Ethics as an Ethics of Responsibility: Comparison and Evaluation of citizen Involvement in Population Genomics', *Journal of Law, Medicine & Ethics*, vol. 31, pp. 390–97.

Rao, R. (2007) 'Genes and Spleens: Property, Contract, or Privacy Rights in the Human Body?', *Journal of Law, Medicine and Ethics*, vol. 35, no. 3, pp. 371–82.

Rawlinson, M. C. and Donchin, A. (2005) 'The Quest for Universality: Reflections on the Universal Draft Declaration on Bioethics and Human Rights', *Developing World Bioethics*, vol. 5, no. 3, pp. 258–66.

Reardon, J. (2001) 'The Human Genome Diversity Project: A Case Study in Coproduction', *Social Studies of Science*, vol. 31, no. 3, pp. 357–88.

Redmayne, M. (1998) 'The DNA Database: Civil Liberty and Evidentiary Issues', *Criminal Law Review*, no. 7, pp. 437–54.

Reilly, P. R. (1998) 'Rethinking Risks to Human Subjects in Genetic Research', *American Journal of Human Genetics*, vol. 63, pp. 682–85.

Rennie, S. (2006) 'Is it Ethical to Study What Ought Not to Happen?', *Developing World Bioethics*, vol. 6, no. 2, pp. 71–77.

Resnik, D. B. (1999) 'Privatized Biomedical Research, Public Fears, and the Hazards of Government Regulation: Lessons from Stem Cell Research', *Health Care Analysis*, vol. 7, pp. 273–87.

Resnik, D. B. (2004) 'The Distribution of Biomedical Research Resources and International Justice', *Developing World Bioethics*, vol. 4, no. 1, pp. 42–57.

Resnik, D. B. and Sharp, R. R. (2006) 'Protecting Third Parties in Human Subjects Research', *IRB: Ethics and Human Research*, vol. 28, no. 4, pp. 1–7.

Reverby, S. M. (2008) '"Special Treatment": BiDil, Tuskegee, and the Logic of Race', *Journal of Law, Medicine & Ethics*, vol. 36, no. 3, pp. 478–84.

Richards, M. (2001) 'How Distinctive is Genetic Information?', *Studies in History and Philosophy of Science Part C: Biological and Biomedical Sciences*, vol. 32, no. 4, pp. 663–87.

Rid, A. and Wendler, D. (2010) 'Risk-benefit Assessment in Medical Research: Critical Review and Open Questions', *Law, Probability & Risk*, vol. 9, no. 3–4, pp. 151–77.

Rimmer, M. (2003) 'Beyond Blue Gene: intellectual property and bioinformatics', *International Review of Intellectual Property and Competition Law*, vol. 34, no. 1, pp. 31–49.

Ringelheim, J. (2010) 'Minority Rights in a Time of Multiculturalism – The Evolving Scope of the Framework Convention on the Protection of National Minorities', *Human Rights Law Review*, vol. 10, no. 1, pp. 99–128.

Rivera, R., Borasky, D., Rice, R. and Carayon, F. (2005) 'Many Worlds, One Ethic: Design and Development of A Global Research Ethics Training Curriculum', *Developing World Bioethics*, vol. 5, no. 2, pp. 169–75.

Rivera-Loez, E. (2002) 'Ethics and Genetics in Latin America', *Developing World Bioethics*, vol. 2, no. 1, pp. 11 20.

Roberts, D. E. (1995) 'The Genetic Tie', *The University of Chicago Law Review*, vol. 62, no. 1, pp. 209–73.

Roberts, D. E. (2006) 'Legal Constraints on the Use of Race in Biomedical Research: Toward a Social Justice Framework', *Journal of Law, Medicine & Ethics*, vol. 34, no. 3, pp. 526–34.

Roberts, D. E. (2008) 'Is Race-Based Medicine Good for Us?: African American Approaches to Race, Biomedicine, and Equality', *Journal of Law, Medicine & Ethics*, vol. 36, no. 3, pp. 537–45.

Roosevelt III, K. (1998) 'The Newest Property: Reproductive Technologies and the Concept of Parenthood', *Santa Clara Law Review*, vol. 39, pp. 79–140.

Ross, R. F. (2001) 'Genetic Exceptionalism vs. Paradigm Shift: Lessons from HIV', *Journal of Law, Medicine & Ethics*, vol. 29, pp. 141–46.

Rothenberg, K. H. (1997) 'Breast Cancer, the Genetic "Quick Fix" and the Jewish Community', *Health Matrix: Journal of Law-Medicine*, vol. 7, pp. 97–124.

Rothstein, M. A. (1999) 'Why Treating Genetic Information Separately is a Bad Idea', *Texas Review of Law and Politics*, vol. 4, pp. 33–37.

Rothstein, M. A. (2005) 'Expanding the Ethical Analysis of Biobanks', *The Journal of Law, Medicine & Ethics*, vol. 33, no. 1, pp. 89–101.

Rothstein, M. A. (2007) 'Genetic Exceptionalism and Legislative Pragmatism', *Journal of Law, Medicine & Ethics*, vol. 35, pp. 59–65.

Rown, L. B. (2009) 'You Don't Own Me: Recommendations to Protect Human Contributors of Biological Material after Washington University v. Catalona: Student Notes and Comments', *Chicago-Kent Law Review*, vol. 84, pp. 227–70.

Rule, J. T. and Shamoo, A. E. (1997) 'Ethical Issues in Research Relationships between Universities and Industry', *Case Western Reserve Law Review*, vol. 5, pp. 239–49.

Ruof, M. C. (2004) 'Vulnerability, Vulnerable Populations, and Policy', *Kennedy Institute of Ethics Journal*, vol. 14, no. 4, pp. 411–25.

Sade, R. M. (2008) 'Religions and Cultures of East and West: Perspectives on Bioethics', *Journal of Law, Medicine & Ethics*, vol. 36, no. 1, pp. 7–9.

Sanders, C. H. (1998) 'Genetic Secret: Protecting Privacy and Confidentiality in the Genetic Era', *Harvard Journal of Law and Technology*, vol. 11, pp. 865–70.

Sanders, D. (1991) 'Collective Rights', *Human Rights Quarterly*, vol. 13, no. 3, pp. 368–86.

Sankar, P., Cho, M. K. and Mountain, J. (2007) 'Race and Ethnicity in Genetic Research', *American Journal of Medical Genetics*, vol. 143, pp. 961–70.

Sarma, D. (2008) '"Hindu" Bioethics?', *Journal of Law, Medicine & Ethics*, vol. 36, no. 1, pp. 51–58.

Saver, R. S. (2006) 'Medical Research and Intangible Harm', *University of Cincinnati Law Review*, vol. 74, pp. 941–1012.

Schneider, B. and Schuklenk, U. (2005) 'Module Six: Special Issues', *Developing World Bioethics*, vol. 5, no. 1, pp. 92–108.

Schroeder, D. and Lasen-Diaz, C. (2006) 'Sharing the Benefits of Genetic Resources: From Biodiversity to Human Genetics', *Developing World Bioethics*, vol. 6, no. 3, pp. 135–43.

Schuklenk, U. (2005) 'Module One: Introduction to Research Ethics', *Developing World Bioethics*, vol. 5, no. 1, pp. 1–13.

Schuklenk, U. and Kleinsmidt, A. (2006) 'North-south Benefit Sharing Arrangements in Bioprospecting and Genetic Research: A Critical Ethical and Legal Analysis', *Developing World Bioethics*, vol. 6, no. 3, pp. 122–34.

Schwartz, P. M. (1997) 'Economics of Personal Health Care Information', *Texas Law Review*, vol. 76, pp. 1–75.

Scott, L. D. (2003) 'Research-Related Injury Problems and Solutions', *Journal of Law, Medicine & Ethics*, vol. 31, pp. 419–28.

Secker, B. (1999) 'The Appearance of Kant's Deontology in Contemporary Kantianism: Concepts of Patient Autonomy in Bioethics', *Journal of Medicine and Philosophy*, vol. 24, no. 1, pp. 43–66.

Selgelid, M. J. (2005) 'Module Four: Standards of Care and Clinical Trials', *Developing World Bioethics*, vol. 5, no. 1, pp. 55–72.

Selgelid, M. J. (2005) 'Universal Norms and Conflicting Values', *Developing World Bioethics*, vol. 5, no. 3, pp. 267–73.

Senn, S. (2002) 'Ethical Considerations Concerning Treatment Allocation in Drug Development Trials', *Statistical Methods in Medical Research*, vol. 11, no. 5, pp. 403–11.

Sharp, R. R. and Foster, M. W. (2000) 'Genetic Research and Culturally Specific Risks: One Size Does Not Fit All', *Trends in Genetics*, vol. 16, no. 2, pp. 93–95.

Sharp, R. R. and Foster, M. W. (2000) 'Involving Study Populations in the Review of Genetic Research', *Journal of Law, Medicine & Ethics*, vol. 28, pp. 41–51.

Sharp, R. R. and Foster, M. W. (2002) 'An Analysis of Research Guidelines on the Collection and Use of Human Biological Materials from American Indian and Alaskan Native Communities', *Jurimetrics*, vol. 42, no. 165, p. 186.

Sharp, R. R. and Foster, M. W. (2002) 'Community Involvement in the Ethical Review of Genetic Research: Lessons from American Indian and Alaska Native Populations', *Environmental Health Perspectives*, vol. 110, pp. 145–48.

Sharp, R. R., Foster, M. W. and Mulvihill, J. J. (2001) 'Pharmacogenetics, race, and ethnicity: social identities and individualized medical care', *Therapeutic Drug Monitoring*, vol. 23, no. 232, p. 238.

Sheikh, A. (2006) 'Are Racial and Ethnic Minorities Less Willing to Participate in Health Research?', *PLoS Medicine*, vol. 3, no. 2, pp. 0166–67.

Sheikh, A. A. (2008) 'Issues of Capacity and Consent', *Medico-Legal Journal of Ireland*, vol. 14, no. 2, pp. 30–33.

Shultz, M. M. (1985) 'From Informed Consent to Patient Choice: A New Protected Interest', *The Yale Law Review*, vol. 95, no. 2, pp. 219–99.

Silver, A. and Stein, M. A. (2003) 'Human Rights and Genetic Discrimination: Protecting Genomics' Promise For Public Health', *Journal of Law, Medicine and Ethics*, vol. 31, pp. 377–89.

Silver, L. M. (1999) 'Meaning of Genes and "Genetic Rights"', *Jurimetrics*, vol. 40, pp. 9–20.

Skegg, P. G. D. (1999) 'English Medical Law and "Informed Consent": An Antipodean Assessment and Alternative', *Medical Law Review*, vol. 7, no. 2, pp. 135–65.

Skene, L. (1998) 'Patients' Rights or Family Responsibilities? Two Approaches to Genetic Testing', *Medical Law Review*, vol. 6, no. 1, pp. 1–41.

Sleeboom-Faulkner, M. (2005) 'The Harvard Case of Xu Xiping: Exploitation of the People, Scientific Advance, or Genetic Theft?', *New Genetics and Society*, vol. 24, no. 1, pp. 57–78.

Sleeboom-Faulkner, M. (2006) 'How to Define a Population: Cultural Politics and Population Genetics in the People's Republic of China and the Republic of China', *BioSocieties*, vol. 1, pp. 399–419.

Smith, C. B., Battin, M. P., Jacobson, J. A., Francis, L. P., Botkin, J. R., Asplund, E. P., Domek, G. J. and Hawkins, B. (2004) 'Are There Characteristics of Infectious Diseases That Raise Special Ethical Issues?', *Developing World Bioethics*, vol. 4, no. 1, pp. 1–16.

Smith, G. P. and Burns, T. J. (1994) 'Genetic Determinism or Genetic Discrimination?', *Journal of Contemporary Health Law and Policy*, vol. 11, pp. 23–61.

Smith, M. J. (2001) 'Population-based Genetic Studies: Informed Consent and Confidentiality', *Santa Clara Computer and High Technology Law Journal*, vol. 18, pp. 57–93.

Sommer, T. (2007) 'The scope of gene patent protection and the TRIPS agreement – an exclusively nondiscriminatory approach', *International Review of Intellectual Property and Competition Law*, vol. 38, pp. 30–51.

Spaak, T. (2006) 'Genetic Discrimination', *Minnesota Journal of Law, Science & Technology*, vol. 7, pp. 639–55.

Sprunger, S. A. and Julian-Arnold, G. (1996) 'Promoting and Managing Genome Innovations', *Risk: Health, Safety and Environment*, vol. 7, pp. 197–200.

Sreenivasan, G. (2003) 'Does Informed Consent to Research Require Comprehension?', *Lancet*, vol. 362, no. 13, pp. 2016–18.

Starfield, B. (2004) 'Promoting Equity in Health Through Research and Understanding', *Developing World Bioethics*, vol. 4, no. 1, pp. 76–95.

Stenton, G. (2004) 'Biopiracy within the Pharmaceutical Industry: A Stark Illustration of How Abusive, Manipulative and Perverse the Patenting Process can be Towards Countries of the South', *European Intellectual Property Review*, vol. 26, no. 1, pp. 17–26.

Stirrat, G. M. and Gill, R. (2005) 'Autonomy in Medical Ethics after O'Neill', *Journal of Medical Ethics*, vol. 31, no. 3, pp. 127–30.

Stone, T. H. (2003) 'The Invisible Vulnerable: The Economically and Educationally Disadvantaged Subjects of Clinical Research', *Journal of Law, Medicine & Ethics*, vol. 31, no. 1, pp. 149–54.

Straus, J. (1995) 'Patenting Human Genes in Europe – Past Developments and Prospects for the Future', *International Review of Intellectual Property and Competition Law*, vol. 26, no. 6, pp. 920–50.

Stuhlinger, V., Ortwengel, G., Thoeni, M. and Taudinger, R. (2009) 'Biomedical Research and Human Research Subject Protection: Is There Need for Action in Germany and Austria?', *European Journal of Health Law*, vol. 16, pp. 45–68.

Sunder, M. (2000) 'Intellectual Property and Identity Politics: Playing with Fire', *Journal of Gender, Race and Justice*, vol. 4, no. 1, pp. 69–98.

Sunder, M. (2001) 'Cultural Dissent', *Stanford Law Review*, vol. 54, no. 3, pp. 495–67.

Suter, S. M. (2001) 'The Allure and Peril of Genetics Exceptionalism: Do We Need Special Genetics Legislation?', *Washington University Law Quarterly*, vol. 79, pp. 669–748.

Tallbear, K. (2007) 'Narratives of Race and Indigeneity in the Genographic Project', *Journal of Law, Medicine & Ethics*, vol. 35, no. 3, pp. 412–24.

Tangwa, G. B. (2004) 'Between Universalism and Relativism: A Conceptual Exploration of Problems in Formulating and Applying International Biomedical Ethical Guidelines', *Journal of Medical Ethics*, vol. 30, pp. 63–67.

Tangwa, G. B. (2004) 'Bioethics, Biotechnology and Culture: A Voice from the Margins', *Developing World Bioethics*, vol. 4, no. 2, pp. 125–38.

Tauer, J. E. (2001) 'International Protection of Genetic Information: The Progression of the Human Genome Project and the Current Framework of Human Rights Doctrines', *Denver Journal of International Law and Policy*, vol. 29, pp. 209–37.

Taylor, A. L. (1999) 'Globalization and Biotechnology: UNESCO and International Strategy to Advance Human Rights and Public Health', *American Journal of Law and Medicine*, vol. 25, pp. 479–541.

Taylor, J. S. (2004) 'Autonomy and Informed Consent: A Much Misunderstood Relationship', *The Journal of Value Inquiry*, vol. 38, no. 3, pp. 383–91.

The Chimpanzee Sequencing and Analysis Consortium (2005) 'Initial Sequence of the Chimpanzee Genome and Comparison with the Human Genome', *Nature*, vol. 437, no. 7055, pp. 69–87.

Thornberry, P. (1989) 'Self-determination, Minorities, Human Rights: A Review of International Instruments', *International & Comparative Law Quarterly*, vol. 38, no. 4, pp. 867–99.

Tindana et al (2012) 'Seeking Consent to Genetic and Genomic Research in a Rural Ghanaian Setting: A Qualitative Study of the MalariaGEN Experience', *BMC Medical Ethics*, vol. 13, no. 15.

Tindana, P. O., Kass, N. and Akweongo, P. (2006) 'The Informed Consent Process in a Rural African Setting: A Case Study of the Kassena-Nankana District of Northern Ghana', *IRB: Ethics and Human Research*, vol. 28, no. 3, pp. 1–6.

Tobias, J. S. (2001) 'Research Governance, Consent and Evidence-Based Medicine', *Medico-Legal Journal*, vol. 69, pp. 40–68.

Tolchin, B. (2008) 'Human Rights and the Requirement for International Medical Aid', *Developing World Bioethics*, vol. 8, no. 2, pp. 151–58.

Tomasson, M. (2009) 'Legal, Ethical, and Conceptual Bottlenecks to the Development of Useful Genomic Test', *Annals of Health Law*, vol. 18, pp. 231–60.

Tomossy, G. F. and Weisstub, D. N. (1997) 'The Reform of Adult Guardianship Laws: The Case of Non-Therapeutic Experimentation', *International Journal of Law and Psychiatry*, vol. 20, no. 1, pp. 113–39.

Tovino, S. A. (2007) 'Functional Neuroimaging Information: A Case for Neuro Exceptionalism?', *Florida State University Law Review*, vol. 34, pp. 415–89.

Tristram Engelhardt, H. (1998) 'Critical Care: Why There Is No Global Bioethics', *Journal of Medicine and Philosophy*, vol. 23, no. 6, pp. 643–51.

Tsai, D. F.-C. (2005) 'The Bioethical Principles and Confucius' Moral Philosophy', *Journal of Medical Ethics*, vol. 31, no. 3, pp. 159–63.

Tsosie, R. (2007) 'Cultural Challenges to Biotechnology: Native American Genetic Resources and the Concept of Cultural Harm', *Journal of Law, Medicine & Ethics*, vol. 35, no. 3, pp. 396–411.

Tsosie, R. and McGregor, J. L. (2007) 'Genome Justice: Genetics and Group Rights', *Journal of Law, Medicine & Ethics*, vol. 35, no. 3, pp. 352–55.

Tuner, C. (2009) 'The Burden of Knowledge', *Georgia Law Review*, vol. 43, pp. 297–365.

Tutton, R., Smart, A., Martin, P. A., Ashcroft, R. and Ellison, G. T. H. (2008) 'Genotyping the Future: Scientists' Expectations about Race/Ethnicity after BiDil', *Journal of Law, Medicine & Ethics*, vol. 36, no. 3, pp. 464–70.

Underkuffler, L. S. (2007) 'Human Genetics Studies: The Case for Group Rights', *Journal of Law, Medicine and Ethics*, vol. 35, pp. 383–95.

Valerio Barrad, C. M. (1993) 'Genetic Information and Property Theory', *Northwestern University Law Review*, vol. 87, pp. 1037–86.

Van Ness, P. H. (2001) 'The Concept of Risk in Biomedical Research Involving Human Subjects', *Bioethics*, vol. 15, no. 4, pp. 364–70.

Varelius, J. (2008) 'On the Prospects of Collective Informed Consent', *Journal of Applied Philosophy*, vol. 25, no. 1, pp. 35–44.

Vargas-Parada, L., Kawa, S., Salazar, A., Mazon, J. J. and Flisser, A. (2006) 'Informed Consent in Clinical Research at a General Hospital in Mexico: Opinions of the Investigators', *Developing World Bioethics*, vol. 6, no. 1, pp. 41–51.

Vastag, B. (2000) 'Helsinki Discord? A Controversial Declaration', *Journal of the American Medical Association*, vol. 284, no. 23, pp. 2983–85.

Veerapen, R. J. (2007) 'Informed Consent: Physician Inexperience is a Material Risk for Patients', *Journal of Law, Medicine & Ethics*, vol. 35, no. 3, pp. 478–85.

Wachbroit, R. (1993) 'Rethinking Medical Confidentiality: The Impact of Genetics', *Suffolk University Law Review*, vol. 27, pp. 1391–410.

Walker, R. L. (2008) 'Medical Ethics Needs a New View of Autonomy', *Journal of Medicine and Philosophy*, vol. 33, no. 6, pp. 594–608.

Wang, R. T. and Henderson, G. E. (2008) 'Medical Research Ethics in China', *The Lancet*, vol. 372, no. 9653, pp. 1867–68.

Warren, S. D. and Brandeis, L. D. 1890, 'The Right of Privacy', *Harvard Law Review*, vol. 4, no. 5, pp. 193–220.

Warren-Jones, A. (2004) 'Patenting DNA: A Lot of Controversy over a Little Intangibility', *Medical Law Review*, vol. 12, no. 1, pp. 97–124.

Warren-Jones, A. (2006) 'Identifying European moral consensus: why are the patent courts reticent to accept empirical evidence in resolving biotechnological cases?', *European Intellectual Property Review*, vol. 28, no. 1, pp. 26–37.

Watson, J. D. and Crick, F. H. C. (1953) 'Genetic Implications of the Structure of Deoxyribonucleic Acid', *Nature*, vol. 171, no. 4361, pp. 964–67.

Watson, J. D. and Crick, F. H. C. (1953) 'Molecular Structure of Nucleic Acids – A Structure of Deoxyribose Nucleic Acid', *Nature*, vol. 171, no. 4356, pp. 737–38.

Weeden, J. L. (2006) 'Genetic Liberty, Genetic Property: Protecting Genetic Information', *Ave Maria Law Review*, vol. 4, pp. 611–64.

Weijer, C. (1999) 'Protecting Communities in Research: Philosophical and Pragmatic Challenges', *Cambridge Quarterly of Healthcare Ethics*, vol. 8, pp. 501–13.

Weijer, C. (2000) 'The Ethical Analysis of Risk', *Journal of Law, Medicine and Ethics*, vol. 28, pp. 344–61.

Weijer, C. and Anderson, J. A. (2002) 'A Critical Appraisal of Protections for Aboriginal Communities in Biomedical Research', *Jurimetrics*, vol. 42, pp. 187–98.

Weijer, C., Goldsan, G. and Emanuel, E. J. (1999) 'Protecting Communities in Research: Current Guidelines and Limits of Extrapolation', *Nature Genetics*, vol. 23, pp. 275–80.

Weisstub, D. N. (1996) 'Roles and Fictions in Clinical Research Ethics', *Health Law Journal*, vol. 4, pp. 259–82.

Wendler, D. (2002) 'What Research with Stored Samples Teaches Us About Research with Human Subjects', *Bioethics*, vol. 16, no. 1, pp. 33–54.

White, B. C. and Zimbelman, J. (1998) 'Abandoning Informed Consent: An Idea Whose Time Has Not Yet Come', *Journal of Medicine and Philosophy*, vol. 23, no. 5, pp. 477–99.

Widdows, H. (2009) 'Between the Individual and the Community: The Impact of Genetics on Ethical Models', *New Genetics and Society*, vol. 28, no. 2, pp. 173–88.

Widdows, H. (2011) 'Localized Past, Globalized Future: Towards an Effective Bioethical Framework Using Examples from Population Genetics and Medical Tourism', *Bioethics*, vol. 25, no. 2, pp. 83–91.

Wilkins, M. H. F., Strokes, A. R. and Wilson, H. R. 1953, 'Molecular Structure of Deoxypentose Nucleic Acids', *Nature*, vol. 171, no. 4356, pp. 738–40.

Wilkinson, R. (2010) 'The Governance of Genetic Information: Who Decides? (Publication Review)', *Medical Law Review*, vol. 18, no. 2, pp. 267–73.

Wilks, I. (1997) 'The Debate over Risk-related Standards of Competence', *Bioethics*, vol. 11, no. 5, pp. 413–26.

Williams, J. R. (2005) 'UNESCO's Proposed Declaration in Bioethics and Human Rights – A Bland Compromise', *Developing World Bioethics*, vol. 5, no. 3, pp. 210–15.

Williams-Jones, B. (2002) 'History of a Gene Patent: Tracing the Development and Application of Commercial BRCA Testing', *Health Law Journal*, vol. 10, pp. 123–46.

Williamson, T. M. (2001) 'Research, Informed Consent, and the Limits of Disclosure', *Bioethics*, vol. 15, no. 4, pp. 341–63.

Winickoff, D. E. (2007) 'Partnership in U.K. Biobank: A Third Way for Genomic Property?', *Journal of Law, Medicine & Ethics*, vol. 35, no. 3, pp. 440–56.

Winker, M. A. (2006) 'Race and Ethnicity in Medical Research: Requirements Meet Reality', *Journal of Law, Medicine & Ethics*, vol. 34, no. 3, pp. 520–25.

Wittenberg, L., Pitcher, E., DeLisi, D. C., Gollin, M. and McGoodwin, W. (1998) 'Probing the Human Genome: Who Owns Genetic Information?', *Boston University Journal of Science & Technology Law*, vol. 4, pp. 108–53.

Wolf, S. M. (1995) 'Beyond "Genetic Discrimination": Toward the Broader Harm of Geneticism', *Journal of Law, Medicine & Ethics*, vol. 23, pp. 345–53.

Wolf, S. M. (2004) 'Law and Bioethics from Values to Violence', *Journal of Law, Medicine & Ethics*, vol. 32, pp. 293–306.

Wolf, S. M. (2006) 'Debating the Use of Racial and Ethnic Categories in Research', *Journal of Law, Medicine & Ethics*, vol. 34, no. 3, pp. 483–86.

Wolf, S. M., Kahn, J. P. and Wagner, J. E. (2003) 'Using Preimplantation Genetic Diagnosis to Create a Stem Cell Donor: Issues, Guidelines and Limits', *Journal of Law, Medicine & Ethics*, vol. 31, pp. 327–39.

Wolf, S. M., Lawrenz, F. P., Nelson, C. A. and et al (2008) 'Managing Incidental Findings in Human Subjects Research Analysis and Recommendations', *Journal of Law, Medicine & Ethics*, vol. 36, no. 2, pp. 219–48.

Wong, N. D., Sun, M., Zhou, H. Y. and Black, H. R. (1991) 'A Comparison of Chinese Traditional and Western Medical Approaches for the Treatment of Mild Hypertension', *Yale Journal of Biology and Medicine*, vol. 64, pp. 79–87.

Woodward, B. (1999) 'Challenges to Human Subject Protections in US Medical Research', *Journal of the American Medical Association*, vol. 282, no. 20, pp. 1947–52.

Wriggins, J. (1997) 'Genetics, IQ, Determinism, and Torts: the Example of Discovery in Lead Exposure Litigation', *Boston University Law Review*, vol. 77, pp. 1025–88.

Xu, X. and Schork, N. J. (1997) 'Linking Genes and Environmental Exposure: Why China Presents Special Opportunities', *Cancer Causes & Control*, vol. 8, no. 3, pp. 518–23.

Xu, X., Yang, J., Chen, C., Wang, B., Jin, Y., Fang, Z., Wang, X. and Weiss, S. T. (1999) 'Familial Aggregation of Pulmonary Function in a Rural Chinese Community', *American Journal of Respiratory and Critical Care Medicine*, vol. 160, no. 6, pp. 1928–33.

Yarborough, M. and Sharp, R. R. (2002) 'Restoring and Preserving Trust in Biomedical Research', *Academic Medicine*, vol. 77, pp. 8–14.

Yelpaala, K. (2001) 'Owning the Secret of Life: Biotechnology and Property Rights Revisited', *McGeorge Law Review*, vol. 32, pp. 112–219.

Zeng, W. and Resnik, D. (2009) 'Research Integrity in China: Problems and Prospects', *Developing World Bioethics* vol. 10, no. 3, pp. 164–171.

Zhang, Q. (2009) 'The Chinese Regulatory Licensing Regime for Pharmaceutical Products: A Law and Economics Analysis', *Michigan Telecommunications and Technology Law Review*, vol. 15, no. 2, pp. 417–52.

Zhou, Q. (2006) 'The Legal Status of Human Gene and Genetic Information [Lun Renlei Jiyin ji Jiyinxinxi de Falvdiwei]', *Science-Technology and Law* (in Chinese), vol. 63, pp. 113–17.

Zion, D., Gillan, L. and Loff, B. (2000) 'The Declaration of Helsinki, CIOMS and the ethics of research on vulnerable populations', *Nature Medicine*, vol. 6, no. 6, pp. 615–17.

Zoloth, L. (2008) 'Go and Tend the Earth: A Jewish View on an Enhanced World', *Journal of Law, Medicine & Ethics*, vol. 36, no. 1, pp. 10–25.

Zwick, M. E. (2002) 'The Central Role of Variation in Human Genetics', *Jurimetrics*, vol. 42, pp. 133–39.

Newspapers and other sources

Gillespie, A. (2000) *Maori, Biodiversity and International Law http://lianz.waikato. ac.nz/PAPERS/al_gulespie/biodiversity.pdf,* Last accessed 12th september 2013.

Gold, E. R. and Caulfield, T. A. (2003) *Human Genetic Inventions, Patenting and Human Rights*, Health Law Institute of University of Alberta.

Hunt-Grubbe, C. 'The elementary DNA of Dr Watson', *The Times* (14 October 2007).

Mahnaimi, U. and Colvin, M. 'Israel Planning "Ethnic" Bomb as Saddam Caves In', *The Sunday Times* (15 November 1998).

Nomper, A. (2005) *Open Consent – A New Form of Informed Consent for Population Genetic Databases*, University of Tartu.

Pomfret, J. and Nelson, D. 'In Rural China, a Genetic Mother Lode, *The Washington Post* (20 December 2000).

Tansey, J. and Burgess, M. M. (2004) *The Foundations, Applications and Ethical Dimensions of Biobanks*, Centre for Applied Ethics of University of British Columbia.

Xiong, L. and Wang, Y. (2001) 'Lingren shengyi de guoji jiyin hezuo yanjiu xiangmu [The Suspicious International Collaborate Genetic Research Project]' (in Chinese) *Outlook Weekly* (26 March 2001).

Xue, D. and Lin, Z. (2001) 'A Focus Topic of Bioethics' (in Chinese), *Guangming Daily* (16 April 2001).

Yang, H. (2002) 'For the Sake of Our National Security: Carefully Preserve Our Genetic Code' (in Chinese), *China Production Daily* (12 April 2002).

Yang, H. (2000) 'We Will Start to Research the Characteristics of the National/ ethnic Disease Gene' (in Chinese), *Beijing Youth* (28 October 2000).

Zitner, A. (2002) 'Harvard Gene Study in China Is Questioned', *The Los Angeles Times* A-15 (30 March 2002).

Index